Live Victoriously!
Don English

Enlightenment

Of

EVIL

Murder,

Abuse,

Transcendence

A personal story
by
Don English

*In memory of my parents, Donald and Elizabeth English,
and my dear friend Kaaren Cheney, who all taught me courage*

Courage always stirs a response

Daisaku Ikeda

Enlightenment

Of

EVIL

When my mother passed away, I decided I wanted to write a book that would tell the story of how she and I miraculously veered off the *road to hell* and survived a life filled with abuse, alcohol addiction, arrest and conviction. The road to hell was paved by my older psychopathic brother with his evil-minded ways. Before my brother murdered a man, before he was sentenced to life in prison, before his girlfriend accidentally died by falling out of his moving car, before he was incarcerated for mugging old ladies, before he stole our father's car at twelve years of age ... before all of this, he was my big brother, someone I trusted. Even though he was a person who threatened to kill my father, raped me, buried me alive, and beat the hell out of my mother and me. And still, I wanted a big brother; I wanted him to love me. How crazy is *that*?

That is all in the past. Today things are as they should be. My brother is locked away for life and I finally have the answers I have sought my entire life. Answers to why he did the things he did to me. Why my parents were oblivious to his pernicious deeds, and why it took so long to free myself from his manipulative evilness. This memoir is my story, the journey, and the answers. It will shock, surprise, illuminate and keep the "fact checkers" checking for days. But in the end, all will know—it is absolutely true. All the unbelievable coincidences and events really did happen.

www.enlightenmentofevil.com

Published by **Proof It Gets Better Publishing**
610 Pamlar Avenue, San Jose, California 95128
Copyright ©2011 by Don English

ISBN: 978-0-615-49300-8

Cover Design and Interior Design by
Heidi Heath Garwood, www.heathdesign.com

Table Of Contents

Acknowledgments

My loving partner, Jim: Thank you for your love and patience. This book would have not been written without your endless support.

Daisaku Ikeda, Buddhist philosopher, peacebuilder, educator and my spiritual mentor: Your wise words continue to support and motivate my efforts to believe in myself and to work for peace and the happiness of all. And to your wife Kaneko whose inspiring words I have come to cherish: *"You will definitely see all your prayers and efforts dignify your existence."* She is right, as right can be.

Sheila Ellison, my writing coach and editor: Thanks for your immeasurable confidence in me and immeasurable help. Your initial question after reading my first writings was: "What was it that caused you to survive?" The long answer: *Enlightenment of Evil, a personal story*.

My dearest friend Phyllis Turner Lawrence: You have taught me over and over the deepest meaning of the word "friendship." And as my line editor, you are dazzling.

Maureen Cervelli: Your endless compassionate effort to serve others has encouraged me in the darkest of times. You have been the light for me, and for so many others.

My Village of Angels who have shown up at just the right time. You know who you are. I am so, so fortunate to have each of you in my life.

Claudia Marshall, the angel coordinator: Who has graciously introduced me to the angels who have helped my book take *flight*.

Heidi Heath Garwood, my fabulous book designer who jumped on board before I even had a ship to sail. And to her niece Amanda Dill, one of the important fact checkers who worked to make sure that the ship would even float.

Brooke Ellison, editor: Your great questions and edits contributed so much.

Brenda Feldman: My amazing publicist who I know truly believes in me.

To friends of Bill W's and my Soka Gakkai family all over the world.

Introduction

People kept telling me I had a story worth writing. But with only an eighth-grade education, I thought this would be an impossible feat. So instead of writing, I told stories, while I cut and styled the hair of several of my special clients who had been involved in my life for many years. These clients encouraged me to write down some of the stories I shared with them. In the beginning, my response to suggestions to document my life was, "Sure—I'll think about it." And then I would immediately say to myself, *Yeah, that's just what the world needs ... another memoir. And really, life happens to all of us, doesn't it?*

My answer to their question became a canned one: "*I'll think about it.*"

The conversation that finally convinced me to begin writing was with a movie producer client. And like the others who insisted I write my story, she confirmed I had an unbelievable tale. She was very sincere so I answered her question as sincerely as she asked it.

"I hope you'll do more than think about it," she insisted, turning her head so I could not take another snip from her hair. "I mean ... from what you've told me," she continued reaching out her hand to cup the top of mine, "you and your mother have endured quite a lot."

I stepped back so my hand slipped away. "You know what, Elizabeth (appreciating the coincidence that her name was the same as my mother's), I have thought about what my life would sound like in a book and I can't help but think," I paused, shifting my weight to the other leg, "who would want to read a book about that kind of pain?"

"You know, Don ... if you encourage only one person with your victories ... well, isn't that what life is all about?"

That is my hope with the story I am about to tell you—that you will not only be engrossed, but also encouraged. The following is true, unbelievable in its synchronicity perhaps, but true nonetheless.

CHAPTER ONE

The Call 1981, Los Altos, California

I had been successfully hiding from my brother for ten years when I found out he murdered someone.

The phone rang just as I was about to walk out the door of my hair salon. I was the only one left and it had been a long day, so I decided to let the answering machine get it.

"Hello," a deep male voice echoed across the empty room. Something about his tone—somber and stiff—kept me from walking out. "I usually don't like leaving a message," the man continued, "but this is Jerry Sanders from the Humboldt County Public Defender's office in Eureka." He paused, just as if he knew I was standing there deciding whether or not to pick up.

I set my keys and checkbook down on our antique mahogany reception desk so quickly that I almost knocked over the glass bowl arranged with long-stemmed Agapanthus. I barely caught it with one hand as I reached for the phone with the other.

"Hello?" I answered.

"Can I speak to Mr. English, please?"

"Speaking," I said, carefully sliding the glass vase back from the edge.

"Do you have a minute?"

"Sure," I said, my mind playing out the different scenarios of why a lawyer from Eureka might be calling me.

"Unfortunately, Mr. English, I have some bad news."

I waited. My heart beat faster but my hand remained steady, resting on the cool smooth edge of the vase.

"Your brother has been charged with murder."

"Oh my God," I whispered automatically.

"I'm sorry about this," the lawyer continued, sounding genuinely concerned, "but I need to know if your brother has any family connections here in Eureka. He's in the county jail and so far refuses to answer any questions."

"No ... none I can think of," I answered, pretty sure there wasn't.

My throat constricted hearing Michael had finally done it, done something terrible, finally committed murder; it sent a wave of horror over me. I sunk into the receptionist's chair and began drawing X's and circles along the top of the salon's appointment book.

"Here's what I know so far," the lawyer went on. "Your brother moved to Eureka and hooked up with a woman who was making a living as a prostitute to pay for their drugs. Michael did admit to police they were both addicts."

No mistake that this was my brother.

"Mr. English, is there something you can think of ... anything at all ... about why he might have been in Eureka? It would be immensely helpful. Your brother is in a very serious situation. The nature of this specific murder—I don't want to panic you unnecessarily, but I'm fairly confident that, if he is convicted, he's very likely to get the death penalty."

"The death penalty?" I tried to recall when I last saw my brother Michael. "I haven't even seen him since I was 16. He and his wife brought their daughter, Michaela, over to our Mom's apartment. That was about nine years ago I think."

"I'm at my wit's end. You and your mother are all the family he has, and I have no other leads." I had nothing to say. We were his only family, but I didn't know anything about his life for the past several years, and that was a choice I very purposefully had made.

After a period of silence, Mr. Sanders let out an exasperated sigh. "OK, I'm going to tell you *why* I have such little hope for your brother. I'm probably over-stepping my boundaries, but you need to know how severe this is, and why I need your help."

The frantic pacing of his speech seemed to punctuate his desperation.

"Michael and his girlfriend, Mona, were high on speed and heroin most of the week," he said.

"This happened last week?"

"Yes. Allegedly, Mona returned from servicing an older man and they initiated the planning. She'd told Michael about a large safe in one of the back bedrooms."

The man had been in his early seventies, and was described as highly respected in the community. Fairly well off and he obviously sported an active libido.

"They must have thought it would be easy to break in, get him to open the safe, and then skip town with the stolen goods."

The lawyer was pretty sure this part of Michael's story was true.

"The rest is speculative, to say the least, because of all the drugs they were taking. Michael has little memory of what happened next."

How convenient; he was still a master of lies and excuses.

"The first time they broke in, the man was a lot stronger than Michael expected. They struggled. Michael said he punched him in the face a few times, but the man kept fighting. He was screaming so loudly that Mona and Michael decided to leave, afraid the neighbors might call the police."

I could hear someone on the other end interrupt him. He paused for a moment before returning.

"Michael said they left mad as hell because they didn't get the money. They were desperate for a fix at this point. It was Mona's idea to go back the following night to try again."

I wanted to interject that this was Michael's mode of operation—he never took the blame for anything.

"She was strung out pretty bad ... that was his account of why she was so determined to go back," Mr. Sanders added.

"What's happened to her?"

"She's been arrested and is being held in the county jail."

He immediately changed the subject and explained that since this was such a high profile case there was a gag order. "Everything I tell you is in the strictest confidence, Mr. English. Do you understand?"

"Yes, I understand," I responded, though I had no clue what a gag order was exactly. "Are you saying that nobody knows about this yet?"

"Because of the bizarre nature of the murder, it is absolutely imperative that the press does not get a hold of any of the information. The publicity might irrevocably taint a jury pool."

He paused for a quick moment and then asked, "Would you be willing to come to Eureka and testify as a character witness on your brother's behalf?"

"What?" I was so shocked at the thought of speaking *for* Michael that I reacted with disbelief.

"I think it would really help Michael for the jury to see he has his family's support."

"You don't understand," I shot back immediately. "Anything I would say about my brother would put him in the electric chair faster."

"I don't think so, Don." He paused for longer moment. "Let me tell you about the murder. There wouldn't be anything you could say that would hurt him. It's hard to explain, but I can't tell you unless I know you will— well, if not agree now to help him, at least consider it. I'm grasping at straws here." His voice rose a few octaves. "Your brother doesn't seem to want to help himself. He's despondent and hardly talking. I don't want to sound hopeless, but his situation is very bleak. What they did to this man puts them both on death row."

I looked down at the day's opened appointment book where I'd been etching deep circles and X's in black ink. The side of my hand was totally smudged and most of the day's appointments were unreadable. I reached for one of the receptionist's Kleenex tucked off to the side of the desk, and tried to wipe off the edge of my hand. It only made it worse.

I turned and caught my reflection in the mirror opposite me. The whole right side of my face was black with ink. I must have been running my hand through my hair in a constant loop of nervous habit the whole time the lawyer had been speaking.

I shook my head, disgusted with what I'd done. I told him I would have to hear the details of the murder before I could make a decision. I didn't even know why I was giving him that much— maybe curiosity. Maybe a small part of me felt some sort of genetic obligation and pity. I am still not sure.

I listened to the beginning of Mr. Sanders' account of the murder. "As I said, they decided to go back the next evening," he began. "Even though Michael and Mona claimed they were surprised the man was home and not in the hospital, what they did was still considered premeditated murder."

My heart pounded louder and louder with each horrible description of what the police and crime scene investigators had found that night. I looked back into the mirror using the tissue to wipe away the ink, making it more smeared than before.

"All that I am about to say is based on the reports from the scene, which I have in front of me. Michael has refused to speak to the authorities, to me, to anyone."

"I understand."

"After sustaining the initial beating from Mona and Michael the first night, the man returned from the hospital with his broken jaw wired shut. However, it appears that he was still strong enough to put up a second fight."

I wished I was listening to a horror scene being read from a fictional screenplay instead of a real scene from my brother's life. I took a deep breath and tried to prepare myself to listen to how my demonic brother tortured and killed a man, making the last moments of his life a living nightmare.

"Detectives and crime scene investigators suspect the man was tortured because he wouldn't open the safe. Trails of blood allowed the investigators to conclude it was indeed a gruesome murder."

I closed my eyes and resisted the impulse to throw up.

"Don? Are you still there?"

"Yes," I finally whispered.

"I'm sorry," he apologized. "This has to be hard for you to hear."

"No, that … that's alright." I cleared my throat and waited a moment before asking, "How did the man eventually die?"

"The actual cause of death was suffocation. It was either your brother or Mona. One of them held a pillow over his face and smothered him to death. Both claim they can't remember."

"They smothered him to death?" I couldn't help but remember all the times Michael put a pillow over *my* face and held it there until I thought I was taking my last breath. His gloating ten-year-old face flashed before me, laughing. I had been only four then, and now he'd killed a man the same way.

"That's why the prosecuting attorney is going for the death penalty for both of them, even though it was just one murder. There's no way to prove which one killed him."

"Remember," the lawyer seemed to suddenly remember himself, "this is all confidential, Don."

"Sure," I muttered. *As if there was anyone I wanted to know about it.*

"Michael's case will probably produce sensational headlines. As far as I know, two people have never received the death penalty for one murder."

"I thought there was a gag order. Won't that keep it out of the papers?"

"The gag order is on the details; we can't keep the fact that a murder occurred out of the papers."

"I see."

"When I went over the CSI report," Sanders lowered his voice to a whisper, "I was surprised to read how what they did with the body was noted as being '*humanly impossible*.'"

I suddenly recalled how, when I was little, Michael had unequivocally convinced me that he possessed "magical powers." To my surprise, I had actually forgotten that. But now, from what his lawyer was implying, it sounded like Michael and Mona had performed some unbelievable, almost *magical* act.

I was so preoccupied with my thoughts it took me a minute to refocus in on what the defense attorney was saying.

"They shoved the body under a bed and proceeded to move pieces of furniture from other parts of the house and pile them on top of the bed. They stacked up enough furniture to touch the top of the ceiling."

"O-o-o-h," I mumbled, shaking my head.

"The real baffling part is how the two of them could have gotten all that furniture into the room and then gotten themselves out. The room was so full the firemen had to saw through the walls to get inside."

Sanders paused again; I could tell this wasn't easy for him.

I gathered all the resolve I had left and forced my voice to be firm and steady, "Mr. Sanders, my mother and I have been hiding from Michael for the last several years and have no intention of letting him know anything about us, especially not where we live. The last time he found us, he beat my mother and took her money. He threatened, after ripping the phone from the wall, that if I called the police, he'd come back and make me wish I never had."

"I understand, but . . . "

"No," I interrupted. "I don't think you do. As soon as he left our apartment I did go to a pay phone and called the police. After they picked him up— while they were walking Michael into the police station—he escaped. They said he just vanished! I'm telling you, Mr. Sanders, my brother is like Houdini."

Although I was still somewhat in shock, my voice grew stronger and I became increasingly emphatic. "No! I will not give him another chance to come after us again. I will *not*," saying it as much to him as I was to myself.

After I hung up with the lawyer I knew I needed to call my mother right away. I got out of the chair and paced around the room, trying to put everything the lawyer had said into perspective. *But there was no perspective when it came to my brother.* I sat back down and dialed my mother's number. I knew she'd be home, so I would have to tell her right then. No dress rehearsals could prepare anyone for this kind of news. I contemplated the horror I was about to reveal to her as the phone rang a third time.

"Hello," she pleasantly answered, without a clue about how her life was about to change.

"I hope you're sitting down, Mom."

The Question   1958, Arlington, Virginia

When you die, and if you've been good, you will go to heaven.
    So they tell me.
And when you die, if you've been bad, you will go to hell.
    So they tell me.

But where do you go if you were born in hell?

I could hear my mother upstairs running the water for our afternoon bath. Every little boy knows if his mother loves him, and I *knew* my mother loved me. At four years old, taking a bath with my loving mother was one of life's great pleasures.

"What does it mean to die?" I asked, feeling her soapy hands lather deep in the crevices of my shoulder blades. I scooted my tiny fleshy bottom back against her thighs and giggled at the squeaky sound of it rubbing against the white enameled metal. "Mommy?" I asked again, thinking she hadn't heard me.

Her soapy hands dipped down into the water. She closed her fingers and cupped her palms. They became like ladles, pouring water to rinse the suds off from around my neck. She nestled her chin against my face and answered my question like she was telling me a bedtime story, "So you want to know where you go when you die?"

Her soft lips rested against my ear and for some reason I kept quiet. I wanted to tell her, *No, that was not my question. I want to know what "to die" means!* But I felt hypnotized and continued to listen.

Michael, my older brother by six years, had inspired my question. When we were alone, he would often say to me, "I want you to die." Then he'd pinch at my skin, like a crab with claws. When he grew tired of pinching me, he would stick pencils and small twigs up my rectum. He never said anything while he was inserting whichever object was handy. Pain would pierce my body, but my mind was still free to believe that he was just mad at me for something I had done wrong. The wounds to my rectum were never as bad as the savage pinching and the way he nastily repeated those words, "I want you to die, I want you to die."

Mother's lips left my ear but she continued on, "When you die and if you've been good, you will go to a place called heaven. Heaven is far, far above the clouds and that is where all the beautiful angels live. They dance and play and have fun all day long," she whispered, in an almost sing-song voice.

I turned my head slightly and looked up at her, "I bet those angels aren't as pretty as you, Mommy."

She looked down at me and warmly smiled and then softly kissed the top of my head, leaving a trace of her pink lipstick against what people called my towhead. Then her voice turned serious, as she warned me, "But when you die, if you have been bad, then you will go deep, deep down into the ground and the only people down there are bad people."

She paused. My body stiffened, "But Mommy, aren't there any angels down there to play with?"

"Yes, honey, there are angels in hell. I mean, in the ground."

"What do the bad angels do all day?"

She started to lightly pick at my skin—playfully, almost like a tickle— and explained, "The bad angels spend all day pinching bad little boys, and make them wish they had never been bad." And then she tickled me some more. When the heat from my urine hit her thighs, she screeched, "Donnie! What did you do?"

Mother stood up and hoisted me out of the tub; I was dripping in water and urine. In one fell swoop, she sternly plopped me on the floor, hastily grabbed her towel, and harshly accused me: "Donnie, did you pee in the bath?"

I only remember rapidly shaking my head side-to-side and not being able to comprehend anything she was saying. I could hear her repeating the word "lie" over and over, but all I could think of was Michael and the pinching crabs.

There was a loud crash from the adjoining room as Michael cleaned our bedroom, banging the vacuum into the wall, intending to disturb our bath. I jumped, shocked by the sound, my heart pounding, my face getting hot.

"Do you understand what you did?" I heard Mom ask angrily.

My mind and my heart had both finally begun to slow down. "Yes," I sadly nodded. Looking up at her, I stepped in between her legs and wrapped my arms around them, hugging her. "I'm sorry, Mommy." I knew that whatever it was that I had done was very shameful, maybe even *bad*, and something I would never forget. It was our last bath together.

In the days that followed, whenever Michael would start to pinch me, I thought about the bad angels Mom talked about. Afraid to ask her more about them, I would sit and talk with my stuffed bunny rabbit to see if he could tell me what it meant to die, but he didn't know either. So I was left confused, and afraid.

Soon after my last bath with Mom, an upcoming event pushed my thoughts away from Michael's sadistic ways. We were moving to California! My father was an Army Sergeant stationed in Washington DC, and his promotion to Master Sergeant came with a transfer to Fort Ord, an army base on the Monterey Peninsula. He was teaching me how to tie my shoes when he told me the exciting news.

"There! Now you try it," he said, encouraging me to wrap the loops twice. His patient melodic voice always made me feel I could do anything. "Perfect!" he commended me as I tightened the two loops together. "Now stand up and turn around."

I immediately followed his directions, wondering what kind of game we were going to play.

"Look what I have!" he said, telling me to turn back around. He was holding a stuffed Donald Duck. He reached behind the large pillow on the Danish sofa and pulled out yet another toy. This time I could tell right away—it was Mickey Mouse!

"Daddy, let me hold 'em, let me hold 'em!" I begged, tugging at his pant leg.

"OK! But first they have a question for you," he teased. Holding my new friends up in the air and speaking in a duck voice, Dad asked, "Do you remember where Mickey and I live?" Already reaching up on my tiptoes to grab them, I paused and thought for a moment.

"Disneyland!" I shouted. "Disneyland! Disneyland!"

"That's right," he said, laughing and kneeling down to place the toys in my arms.

I immediately squeezed them and kissed the sides of their faces.

As soon as I calmed down, Daddy explained, "We have appointments to visit not just Donald and Mickey, but all the Disney characters!"

"Even Goofy?" I asked, hoping he would be there too.

"All of them, Donnie. Every single one."

The only person I knew I was going to miss by moving to California was our babysitter, Sarah Anne. Her bright blue eyes and thick black eyelashes were mesmerizing; the lashes touched her eyebrows each time her eyes opened wide. Orange-sized breasts made it hard for anyone to believe she was only thirteen. I loved to watch her brush her long golden blonde hair with the tortoise shell miniature hairbrush she always kept handy. Once she had finished her last stroke, she'd swing all her hair around to one side and pet it like a kitty's fluffy tail. The scent of coconut would fill the air. She was so sweet and she looked just like the Christmas Angel Dad put on the top of our tree each December.

Sarah Anne took a real liking to Michael even though he was three years younger. Already, at only ten years old, Michael's charming personality had a mysterious effect on people. His almost-perfect, Adonis-like body and face, combined with his thick chocolate brown hair and eyes that matched, made him an extraordinarily good-looking boy. His eyes were piercing, but at the same time, oddly vacant. And when he wanted to, he could turn the warm brown of his eyes into unblinking pitch black.

One of the evenings Sarah Anne was babysitting us, I was playing with my toy cars behind the living room sofa. I heard Michael and Sarah Anne talking together as they came into the room. They couldn't see me, so I decided to stay quiet and play hide and seek. They were giggling as they came over to the sofa and sat down next to each other. I knew Sarah Anne had just brushed her hair because a swath of her sweet-smelling golden mane swept over the back of the sofa.

Sarah Anne started to talk in a soft whisper, "Michael, are you sure Donnie is upstairs?"

Wow, I thought to myself, *I get to hear a secret!*

"I have a big surprise for you," Sarah Anne went on.

She talked so softly that I had to strain to hear her. "Michael," she said in a dulcet tone, "after we get through French kissing, I'm going to do to you what I was telling you about earlier."

Michael didn't respond. I heard the smacking of lips, so I figured they were kissing.

When is this "French thing" going to happen? I wondered impatiently. I was struggling to stay still when I heard Sarah Anne ask, one more time, if he was sure I was upstairs.

"Yes! I'm sure!" Michael whispered with irritation.

"OK," she went on, "are you ready for me to do what I said I would, down there?"

Michael did not answer, but I heard him stand up and undo his belt.

The sounds of unzipping and shuffling followed—they seemed to be rearranging themselves in preparation for what was about to happen. Sarah Anne whispered, "Don't be nervous." There was a small moment of silence. Then, inexplicably, sounds of slurping filled the room.

What was going on? I wanted to just jump up and investigate, but fear of my brother allowed my self-control to win out. Michael half-giggled, telling Sarah Anne that it tickled, but she didn't respond. Instead, the sounds of slurping continued. My leg started to cramp and I slowly stretched it out. My shoe banged against the end table. The sound echoed throughout the room. The commotion that followed sounded like a swarm of bees had been let loose. They both jumped up and Sarah Anne yelled, "Shit!" I tried to get out of the line of fire, crawling rapidly towards the door.

I got halfway across the room before Michael bellowed out, "Come back here!" I stopped, turned around to face them, and immediately started to cry.

"Oh, Donnie, it's OK," Sarah Anne sang across the room. "You didn't do anything wrong." She rushed over to me and bent down, letting her hair sweep over my eyes.

"What?" Michael shouted, stepping towards us.

I looked up at Sarah Anne's face through the golden strands and saw her give Michael a firm wink.

"Oh. Yeah. Yeah, you didn't do anything wrong, Donnie," Michael repeated in a monotone voice, angrily picking up on her cue. "Why don't you go up to your room and play for awhile?"

I took a few long, cautious steps until I was out of the room. As soon as I got halfway up our stairs, I heard Michael call my name.

"Donnie!" he snarled from the bottom stair.

I turned and held tight to the banister to steady myself.

"I don't have to tell you again about not coming out of your room, do I?" he growled through his teeth.

"No," I shakily replied, and ran to my room and closed the door. I held onto the door handle with both hands. I knew I was going to pay.

It was only a matter of time.

CHAPTER THREE

Mr. Movie Star   1958, Anaheim, California

Dad was a "real catch," people would say. But it took me awhile to understand who wanted to catch him and why. I was playing in the hallway with my toy cars the day before we were to leave for Disneyland when I overheard my mother in the living room.

Mom was telling her best friend about how cruel two other women had been the night before, when she and my dad were saying goodbye to their friends at the military club. This club was the cornerstone of their social life, in part due to Dad's amazing operatic voice. "You know he's always the life of the party, and last night," my mother explained, "he was onstage singing "Red Roses for a Blue Lady," making the women swoon, as usual. After he got back to his seat, I got up and went to the restroom."

Mom's voice cracked then, and it was clear she was on the verge of tears. I crawled on all fours across the hardwood floor, peeked into the living room, and saw Mom sitting on the sofa, holding a box of Kleenex in her lap. She continued, "These two 'Southern belle' types, who were guests at *our* table, came into the restroom. They didn't know I was in one of the stalls when they started talking about Don."

I sat huddled quietly against the wall, out of sight.

"The first one said, 'Why, I could just sit and listen to that gorgeous man sing all day long. He has the most romantic voice and I'm just sure he's going to be discovered someday! And then we all can say, 'Well, we knew him when.'"

Mom's fake Southern accent trailed off and her voice began to quiver, "You won't believe what they said next! They actually started to talk about *me*. When the one 'Southern belle' finally stopped raving about Don, she asked her friend if she'd met his 'little wife.' And as if calling me a 'little wife' wasn't bad enough, the other one blurted back, 'Oh, you mean that sad, sad looking woman holding his hand? Why it's a shame such a good-looking man is married to a woman whose looks are so beneath his. I bet

I could wiggle right up to him and bat my eyelashes and steal him away if I wanted to.'"

Her friend placed her hands on top of my mother's and commiserated, "Awful, they are just awful bitches!"

Mom sniffled and blew her nose. "I couldn't sit there and listen any longer. So I got up, flushed the toilet, and then flung the bathroom stall door open and stood there, letting them get a good look at me! They looked like they'd just seen a ghost. I smoothed the front of my dress and made my way over to the sink. The only sounds were my high heels clicking across the tile floor. When I got to the sink, I turned on the faucet and looked into the mirror, acknowledging both of them with a forced smile. I don't know where I got the courage, but after I stood there for a moment puckering my lips together and examining my lipstick, I turned around and clasped the counter behind me and let them have it!"

Mom's friend, who had been consoling her quietly up to then, suddenly cheered, "Oh my God, Betty! You didn't! I can't believe you actually spoke to them! What did you say?"

"Well, when I turned around, I just stood there looking them up and down in their skintight brocade dresses. What I said to them was, 'So, you think I'm a sad little wife? And that my gorgeous husband was out of his mind to marry someone whose looks were so beneath his?' They both stood stock still, so to shock them into some kind of reaction, I added, 'Isn't that what you *said*?'"

By now her friend was chortling, her head swiveling to follow my mom's movements as she acted out every gesture. My mom was gaining steam, realizing what guts she had shown.

"And with that, I took a paper towel, wiped my hands a few times, and squeezed it into a ball.

"I spun back around on my high heels and faced them. 'So you both will be leaving the club tonight with your dull, average-looking husbands, who'll probably be so drunk they won't even be able to drive. And I—the sad, sad little wife—will be going home with ... how did you put it? *That gorgeous man with the most romantic voice*? So you go right ahead ... bat away those false eyelashes of yours. I guarantee, it'll never work!'"

My mom and her friend were holding hands now, almost convulsing with laughter. Mom had to gasp for a breath to go on.

"I tossed the paper ball at them and opened the bathroom door. Just as the door was about to close, I looked over my shoulder and said, 'Oh! Just one more thing … you can both kiss my ass!' And I slammed the door shut. I gripped the door knob, took one hell of a deep breath and immediately headed for the bar."

"That's where I would have gone!" her friend chirped.

"I ordered a screwdriver in the tallest glass they had. After I finished that one, I ordered another one, and the next thing I remember, it was morning and I was nursing the worst hangover. I'm still feeling the effects!"

I dropped the plastic truck I had been holding. It clattered to the floor and Mom called out, "Who's there?" I didn't answer, but when I heard, "Go play outside," I knew she had figured out it was me.

By late morning, my mother's tears had dried and we were on our way to California! My parents' faces glowed as I watched them from the back seat of the red and white 1958 Chevrolet Biscayne that Dad had purchased especially for the trip. Everything was going well—until our third day. Michael kept getting carsick so we stopped at several unscheduled tourist attractions to break up the drive.

When we got to the Grand Canyon, Michael opened the car door as soon as we stopped. Jumping out like he had been trapped for days, he immediately dashed towards the edge of the cliff.

"Get back here!" Mom hollered. She jumped out to chase him, still screaming, "Michael Ray English! You get back here! Do you hear me?"

Dad and I got out at the same time. "Daddy, can I try and take a picture?" I asked, hoping the answer would be yes. I felt the heat from the dirt creep over my ankles and was glad Mom had had us wear our summer shorts. The rising hot air from the bottom of the canyon created a wavy mirage-like film that floated across the view.

Dad rubbed his hand over the white bristles of my crewcut and told me maybe another time, and we walked to where Mom and Michael were standing.

17

"Betty!" he called, holding up the camera as he backed up a few steps, "Stay right there. That's a great shot!"

I ran towards Mom and Michael, in their picture pose, but darted right past them so I could look over the edge of the brilliantly orange- and red-hued canyon. The swirl of colors spread out as far as I could see. It made me think of my latest escape to my own worlds of wonder with my beloved crayons and coloring books. I was amazed and thrilled. *I can actually see "Raw Umber," "Copper," and "Brick Red" right here, in real life! There really are Wonders of the World ...*

"Get back here, Donnie!" Mom screamed, jolting me out of my reverie. I reluctantly came back from the edge to stand in the picture.

"Back up a little," Dad ordered.

"Don, are you *crazy*?"

"Just take two steps back!" He sounded frustrated at Mom's frightened reaction.

"Look, boys, your father is trying to get rid of us. If we move any further to the edge, we'll be gone for sure!"

"For God's sake, Betty, you're a good five feet away." He fidgeted with the camera.

"Come on, boys," she said wrapping her arms around us like Mother Goose. She herded us two steps closer to my dad instead of in the direction he asked.

"Take the picture!" Mom yelled, huddling with us.

He lifted the camera up, snapped the picture and swore under his breath. We walked back to the car, joyless. I was thinking: *This is it? Ten minutes and one photograph? There's so much to see ...*

"What were you thinking, Don?" I heard Mom huff at Dad.

"You're always over-dramatizing things ... over-reacting, like I would actually do something to put my own kids in danger! It's like you have to have a say in everything I do. I'm getting tired of it!"

"Go to hell!" Mom shouted.

Michael and I jumped in the backseat of the car and watched their back and forth bickering through the front windshield. They argued for a while longer before returning to the front seat.

We drove on in complete silence. After about an hour, Dad turned on the radio and I relaxed a little, listening to him whistle and sing along whenever a song came on that he liked. Mom ignored him and talked with Michael for most of the time. I began to notice how when Mom and Dad would argue, Michael would always take Mom's side. Dad once said that Michael was good at "buttering people up."

I liked when we did things together as a family because Michael was on his best behavior, treating me like his "dear little brother," until my parents stepped away long enough for him to punch or pinch me. So if I kept close to my parents, I knew I would be safe.

I did not understand why a small thing like standing too close to the edge was causing my mom to be so mad. But I was happy that her attention to Michael was keeping him from squeezing my knee.

After a while, I squirmed and Dad asked if I needed to use the bathroom. Then Michael laughed and made a joke about how I "drank too much juice and couldn't hold it like a man," which I thought was pretty unfair, but neither parent stepped up to defend me.

I thought my parents' standoff would be over when we stopped for food. But it wasn't. Mom stayed angry with Dad for most of the trip.

They finally started talking to one another many hours later when we drove into Orange County in Southern California, looking for a motel.

"Well, here we are!" Dad announced, as we passed the sign welcoming us to the Magic Kingdom of Disneyland.

"How about that motel? It looks interesting?" Mom said, speaking directly to Dad for the first time since we left the Grand Canyon. She pointed to a green neon sign reading "Vacancy."

It was just getting dark and Dad replied, "Looks good, but I see other ones down the road. We can come back if we don't find a better one ... if that's OK with you, honey?"

I watched Mom smile and nod her head.

Good, I thought, *they are finally making up.*

19

Dad rolled down his window and flipped his cigarette out. Red and blue lights immediately flashed brightly behind us. The next thing I knew, a police car had pulled up behind us and directed him to pull over.

"Shit!" Mom and Dad said at the same time.

"What happened?" Michael asked, scooting up towards the front seat, while looking behind at the approaching policeman.

"It'll be alright," Dad reassured us. "I have a feeling my cigarette butt landed on that policeman's windshield."

Dad opened his door and got out. The officer bent down and looked at us through the window, tipping his hat.

"Is Daddy going to jail?" I was remembering what the Doggy Policemen did in cartoons.

"No, honey, he's not going to jail." Mom's tone was tense.

Through the side window I watched Dad laughing with the policeman. "Are Daddy and the policeman going to be friends now?"

"I wouldn't doubt it, honey. Your father is a real charmer."

Dad shook hands with the policeman. And as he returned to our car and opened the door, he hollered back, "You're alright, Jack!" I was surprised to hear my father use the officer's given name.

"Whew, that was a close one," Dad announced, sliding back into his seat. "Having people think I'm a movie star sure helps."

"Who were you mistaken for this time?" Mom had witnessed this mistaken identity phenomenon before.

"That's the funny thing about it—no one seems to know exactly who I look like!"

"Well, movie star or not, you could talk your way out of a paper bag. You definitely have the gift of gab."

Dad chuckled and started the car. As he turned the car around, he told her that we were going to go back to the motel she had originally pointed out.

Mom cooed, as she scooched across the seat and kissed him on the cheek, "I love you, Mr. Movie Star."

The name of the motel was "The Sands." "Like the desert," Dad mentioned as we drove into the parking lot that was landscaped with large cacti and a few palm trees lit up with multi-colored lights.

By the time we got settled in our room my excitement was building like a boiling volcano. I ran around and bounced up and down on each bed. Michael, trying to do a somersault over me, fell on the floor. Mom shouted for us to calm down and then handed us our PJ's from the suitcase she was busy unpacking. It wasn't long before I collapsed on the bed and fell asleep holding Mickey in one arm and Donald in the other.

CHAPTER FOUR

Our Debut   1958, Anaheim, California

The early morning sun blazing through the motel's large window woke us all at the same time. Mom got our breakfast out of the ice chest she'd packed and carried all the way from what I still thought of as "home"—Virginia—and then laid out the outfits she'd put together before we left. She was always very particular about how we looked and, after all, this would be the English family *debut* at the world-famous Disneyland!

I sat on the unmade bed, all dressed and ready to go, watching Dad tighten his black shiny belt while he admired himself in the closet mirror. He turned sideways and Mom, passing by, slapped his butt, or what little there was of it. "No ass at all," she said, laughing. She always made fun of Dad's flat bottom.

His tall, almost 6'1" body was strongly built. It showcased the midnight blue pleated slacks and the crisp white short sleeve shirt that he beautifully tucked flat around his slim waist. His aqua blue eyes looked like pieces of ice, and the way he slicked back his taupe brown hair made it easy to see why people swore they had seen him in the movies. When he would smile at you, you would feel warm all over; you knew he must be someone important.

The outfit Mom picked out was perfect, in a Minnie Mouse sort of way. It was a crimson red halter top dress with white polka-dots. It fit real snug and blurred to pink when she made a fast twirl. She was on the petite side—only about 5'1"—but her proportions were the popular "36-24-36." It was too bad that her fine facial features were overshadowed by her large nose. People commonly mistook her for Italian or, worse in those days, Jewish. The brown of her hair was as dark as black coffee and she wore it cut short, with soft waves flipping up, kissing the top of her cheeks. Her brown eyes appeared more golden at times, except when she'd wear her signature apple red lipstick— then they would deepen into a brownish maroon.

We arrived at the tall majestic iron-gated entrance, and the ticket man asked Dad what movie he'd seen him in. Dad removed his sunglasses, "So you don't know?" He asked him to guess. Michael and I chuckled as the man squinted intently at our father's face.

"What's the holdup?" the people behind us grumbled. "It's OK," the attendant said, giving up on the guessing game. He stamped our hands and directed us to go on through.

Michael read the tall street sign in front of us: "Main Street."

Bang! Bang! Sounds echoed off the cobblestone street where two robbers dressed like cowboys came running out of what looked like a bank. I ran to my father and hid behind his legs. "What are they doing? What's happening?" I asked excitedly, but somehow still knowing it was make-believe.

Mom laughed and stepped away, wandering over to a hat stand in front of a store filled with different colored hats. She grabbed a large white floppy straw hat and put it on, calling for us to look.

"What do you think?" she sang out, waving as she pulled down the wide brim, and bowing in a deep curtsy.

"Come on, Mom," Michael yelled with a whine, placing his hands on his hips, slumping into a look of frustration, "Let's find the Matterhorn! I think it's this way."

Mom put the hat back and playfully sauntered over to us. "OK, Michael, but first we're going to go see the River Boat." She pointed to the stack of street signs on a tall pole and said, "Look, 'Mark Twain River Boat' that way."

"Let's go! Maybe Mickey and Donald will be there!" I exclaimed.

Michael grumbled as Dad put his arm around his shoulder and encouraged him to have patience. He slid out from under Dad's arm, sulking as he wandered ahead of us. As usual, he was upset that our parents were doing what I wanted first. As soon as he knew Mom and Dad couldn't see him, he tripped me, hissing, "Mickey and Donald are stupid and they smell like rotten eggs!"

He pouted the entire time we toured the River Boat ride. When Mom told him we had to see one more thing before we would get to the

Matterhorn, I thought he was going to explode. I was sure there would be retribution later, but I bravely ignored his piercing stares and red puffed cheeks. Instead of letting him ruin Fantasyland for me, I squealed with excitement as we approached the "Mad Tea Party" and I pointed to the spinning tea cups.

"Mom, look! There are the big teacups you told me about."

"Yes, honey. Aren't they pretty? I told you they were just like the teacups in our painting."

Ever since Mom knew about our trip to Disneyland, she would refer to the large painting Dad bought when he was stationed in Munich, Germany, where I was born. The canvas displayed an old-fashioned table set for a formal tea party. The heavy oil painting spotlighted a pink-tinted glass pitcher full of red roses with a few petals dispersed artistically around the pastel-colored china. "Just waiting for Alice and the Mad Hatter to appear in our painting," Mom would tell me when she read from Alice in Wonderland. She was so taken with the artwork that while we were still in Germany, she found a china tea set that was an exact replica of the one in the painting. Together, the oil painting and the tea set were her pride and joy.

I could not believe my eyes when I saw the gigantic cups and saucers spinning and darting back and forth, narrowly missing each other. The colors of the cups were like in the painting—pink, green, blue, yellow, and even an orange like the color of a Creamsicle bar.

"Can we ride on them, Mommy?" I begged, as I pulled on her hand, attempting to drag her along with me.

"What a stupid ride!" Michael moaned loud enough for Dad to hear him.

"Michael," Dad said, in an effort to calm the troubled waters. "This is for your little brother. It will be fun … you can ride with him and show him how big boys spin the cups."

"Oh boy!" I cried, "Michael, will you ride with me? Will you?" Even though my brother terrified me, I was excited that we might ride the teacups together. *If I can just show him how brave I am as we spin and twirl, he'll stop wishing I was dead.*

He stood and thought about it, and said he would, but only if Mom and Dad agreed to take him to ride the Matterhorn right afterwards.

I stood alongside Michael on the long line, watching our parents off to the side. Dad lit a cigarette and kept talking with Mom without looking over.

"This is a stupid ride!" Michael jeered.

"No it's not."

"It's a sissy ride ... no wonder you want to go on it."

"Come on!" I said when the attendant unlatched the rope. I headed directly to the orange teacup. "I like this one. Let's get on this one!"

The smooth seat was cool and I slid back and forth until Michael stepped in.

"Mommy, look!" I hollered, waving, trying to get her attention.

I heard the motor start up and fumes from gasoline were all around us. As the cup started darting from side to side, Michael began turning the wheel.

"Wheee! Wheee!" I laughed and waved to our parents. "Look! Look!" But they still weren't looking. When I turned back, the ride began to speed up and Michael made our cup spin even faster, and began laughing.

"Stop! Stop! We're going too fast!" I screamed, terrified the other cups were going to crash into us. I slumped down in my seat, and the pull of gravity forced me to slide into Michael.

"Get off me!" he yelled.

"Stop! Stop!" I kept screaming. The odor from the gas got stronger, causing me to heave, but nothing came out. I closed my eyes and felt my body go limp with fear and exhaustion. Michael's laughter roared until the ride finally came to an end. Stepping away from the cups, I felt woozy and wasn't able to speak.

"What's wrong, little brother, didn't you like the monster teacups? You want to ride 'em again?"

I had never been so frightened. Once again Michael had found a way to be in control, to intentionally make me miserable, even on the ride I had thought would be my favorite. When we found our way back to Mom and Dad, I could see their lips moving, asking me if I had a good time, but my voice was nowhere to be found.

"Oh, he had a great time!" Michael smiled, slapping me on the back. "OK, let's find the Matterhorn!"

I didn't regain my wits until we were about to leave Disneyland. The rest of the day is still a blur. I remember I saw Mickey and Donald standing at the gate as we were about to walk out. "Goodbye, Mickey! Goodbye, Donald!" I called out from my father's side.

I remember standing by my father, feeling safe and loved. I leaned into the side of his leg and looked up and wrapped my arms around him. "I love you Daddy, I do! I do! I do!"

He looked down and rubbed the top of my head, "I love you too, son."

And then, together, we gave one last wave goodbye to the Magic Kingdom.

CHAPTER FIVE

Just The Beginning 1958, Monterey, California

Our parents found a house to rent in Marina, a town just north of the Fort Ord army base. There was no forewarning that our new house would be out in the country. When we turned down the long, winding gravel driveway, all I could see were golden hills dotted with heritage oak trees and bundles of tumbleweeds that scattered across the unpaved road.

Finally, about a mile down, a dark green, flat roof came into view. We stopped at the end of the driveway and looked at the house with a porch wrapped halfway around it. Mom sighed and said something I couldn't hear. We all stared into the wide-open space in silence, stunned for a moment.

"What do you think about being in the country?" She tried to sound cheerful as she glanced at Michael and me in the back seat.

Michael spoke up first and very dramatically. "Where are the neighbors? I don't see any neighbors! I can't believe this!"

Mom turned back around, pulling down the visor to look into the clip-on mirror. Without looking back at us, she stammered her response. "I-I told you we would be out in the country, didn't I? We'll have fun, you just—"

"Who will I play with?" Michael interrupted, slapping the window so hard I jumped. "There's not even a place for me to ride my bike."

Dad turned around and said calmly, "We only have to live here for about three months until a house becomes available on base. Three months, then we'll be moving."

His clear blue eyes faded to gray as a shadow swept across his face. "Do you think you can handle it until then?"

Sensing our father's discomfort, Michael and I looked at each other, looked back at Dad, and then we each nodded reluctantly.

When Mom saw an agreement had been made, she got out. I pushed the top of her seat forward and squeezed through, stepping out onto

ENLIGHTENMENT OF EVIL   29

gravel. Immediately a large, rust-colored lizard ran over my sandal! I screamed at the top of my lungs and jumped back into the car, just as Michael was getting out. He pushed by me with a "You sissy!" and chased the lizard from under the car.

I looked out the car window and searched the gravel to make sure the coast was clear before I got out again and followed Mom and Dad up the porch stairs. I took a deep breath and caught the lingering scent from a skunk that smelled like it was far off in the distance. As they opened the front door, I noticed a porch swing off to the side.

"Dad, can I sit on this?"

"Sure," he replied, as they walked into the house.

I inspected the tattered cushion for any creatures, took a seat, and pushed away from the floor to get a good swing. I swung back and forth and watched Michael kicking through the bushes, still hunting for the runaway lizard. The crackling twigs were the only noise I could hear, along with the occasional chirping of some kind of bird.

So this is "the country," I mused, with my eyes still fixed on Michael. He skipped out of the bushes and reached down to scoop up a handful of gravel, throwing the rocks out one at a time into the arid field that surrounded us. The air was warm and the breeze felt good against my skin. I swung a few more times and then jumped off. I stepped inside the front door to see our first house in California, but before I could get a good look, I heard a loud yelp from outside the door.

"I got 'em! I got 'em!" Michael hollered.

I froze for a moment and listened, but there was only dead silence. I walked through the living room and saw Mom and Dad step out to the backyard. Michael called out my name, drawing out each word.

"Don-nie, I have … something for … you. Where … are … you?" He was using the phony sing-song voice I was learning to loathe.

I headed out the back door to catch up with Mom and Dad, not wanting to imagine the horrible things Michael had done to the lizard.

Dad had to report the very next day for his new job in charge of military families moving in and out of the base housing. Mom would have to start looking for a job, preferably also on base. But we never worried about my mother getting a job because of what Dad called her "can-do attitude." She put 100 percent into whatever she did—whether it was her career, her children, or being a wife. She could pack and unpack with such organization, we could move out of one house and settle into another within three days.

Sure enough, Mom had unpacked and organized everything in our new house by Sunday afternoon. At Sunday dinner Mom and Dad informed Michael that he had shown enough maturity on the road trip and at Disneyland to be trusted to babysit me.

He accepted this new responsibility with a forced grin. My brother already had learned not to let people know what he was really thinking. By always acting so "good" when adult eyes were upon him, and now—never showing that he wanted nothing to do with babysitting me—he was able to fool Mom and Dad into believing he would actually take care of me for the entire summer. I had my doubts.

After we finished dinner I noticed Michael sneak out to the backyard. Careful to keep my distance, I went to my bedroom and watched him through the window. He walked around the huge yard that to me resembled a fenced graveyard. Most of the wood spikes from a decrepit fence were broken and lay nestled on the ground. Overgrown weeds forcefully emerged from between the broken slats. An old rickety tool shed sat far in the back and leaned cockeyed against the only section of fence that was still standing. I kept watching Michael and wondered what he found so interesting out there.

I heard Mom call me to come take a bath. It wasn't until later, after I turned six, that Michael and I no longer had to take baths together in order to save money. So when I got into the tub, she called for Michael to join me. Michael appeared distracted. Normally he would tease me and pinch at me, but this time he left me alone. I wondered if he was mad that he was going to have to watch me. I thought about asking him, but the already lukewarm water had become cold, so we both washed quickly and got out.

After our bath I went right to bed, but I lay awake, still wondering what was in the backyard that had piqued Michael's interest. A chill swept over me. I reached down to the end of my bed and pulled my fuzzy blue blanket up over my nose, breathing hard into the blue satin trim. The warm air covered my face and soon I drifted off to sleep.

When I awoke the next morning, Michael was especially quiet. Today was his first day as my official babysitter—Mom went with Dad to the base to look for work—and I could tell he was not in a good mood. To make matters worse, our parents were not increasing his allowance. Michael would suffer with new responsibilities, but without any gain. That meant someone had to pay.

Michael passed by me in the hall and went into the kitchen to fix our breakfast. He placed two bowls of cereal and a pitcher of orange juice on the blue and white checked vinyl tablecloth. We both sat down to eat. The crunching of our cereal and the low hum of the refrigerator standing across from us were the only sounds in the house. This silence seemed somehow threatening and made me queasy; I couldn't even finish my cereal. I took my dishes to the sink and rinsed them off.

I went on with my morning routine, which was to first change out of my PJ's. I tiptoed down the hall and went into my room, closing the door quietly behind me. Just as I started to pull my pants up, the bedroom door blasted open with such startling force that I fell to the floor.

"What do you think *you're* doing?" Michael towered over me, glaring. "Did you ask if you could leave the table? I am your babysitter now and you will only do what I tell you, when I tell you!"

I lay on the floor and looked up at his face. His right upper lip curled up like a wild dog's snarl. I had never seen Michael act like *this* before. At first I thought it might be a game. When he stripped his belt from his pants, brought the two ends together, and slapped the belt against one of his palms, I knew it was not a game.

"Take your pants off," he commanded.

Since they were wrapped around my ankles anyway, I rolled over and slipped them over my feet.

He raised his belt and slapped it hard across the bed, loudly ordering, "You will do what I tell you, do you understand?"

I started to cry. "What did I do, Michael? I don't understand!"

"Stop crying right now or you will feel this belt across your butt."

32

I turned over on my knees and started to crawl under the bed to escape. Before I got halfway under, I felt Michael's hand grab the waistband of my underwear and pull me back against the wall.

"Help!" I cried. "Help! ... Help!" I kept screaming, tasting the salty tears running into my mouth.

Michael stood up and slapped the belt hard against the bed again.

"You can scream as loud as you want, little brother. Did you forget we are out in the country all by ourselves and there's no one around to hear you? Now stop crying, or I will give you something to cry about!"

Somehow I gained control of my sobbing. He ordered me to get up and follow him around the house while he did his morning chores.

"Can't I put my clothes on?"

With a withering look, he replied, "You should be happy I let you keep your underwear on!"

Michael knew I was painfully modest and used that pain to control me. Between them, Dad and Mom didn't have one modest bone in their bodies, which I could never understand. Dad would stand completely naked, almost proud, and shave his face with us coming and going out of the bathroom. Mom acted the same way, never covering herself up when Michael or I would come into her room. Maybe because Mom had very little privacy growing up poor with two brothers and Dad spent so many years in the military, it didn't bother them to be naked around people. But for me, I felt embarrassed. As an adult I would suffer nightmares from the mere thought of being seen naked.

Several times that morning I tried to slip back into my room to get my clothes, but Michael always caught me. After my third failed attempt, he became angry and told me to follow him. He opened the kitchen door that led to the garage, reached up, and pulled the string from the hanging light bulb. A dim glow shone over the empty boxes stacked against the wall. I trembled as a hanging spider web drifted across my neck. It was still clinging to me after Michael ordered me to stop and stand still.

"Don't you move from that spot." He glanced down at my bare feet, glowing white against the dingy cement floor. "I'm going outside, and when I come back, you better not have moved even *one inch* from that spot."

He raised his hand and shook his forefinger at me, casting a long moving shadow across the garage wall. "If you move," he said, deepening his voice, "you will pay! *Do you understand?*" I stood silent with fear, unable to speak. "Do you understand?" he demanded again, his eyes turning a fearsome coal-black under the dim light.

I lifted my chin slowly and then nodded my head for what seemed like a hundred jerky times.

"Good," he said and walked over to the corner of the garage. He picked up an empty canning jar that lay on its side and unscrewed the lid, testing it to see if it would open. He turned his head slowly, back to me, deep in thought for a moment, and then he walked towards the back door. The sleeve of his dark blue shirt caught the top of the broom handle that leaned against a small square window. It dragged across the glass and fell to the floor with a sharp snapping sound. He kicked it aside, leaving a puff of dust which flickered up through the narrow beams of sunlight shining through the streak-filled window.

All I could see through the dusty pane was the silhouette of Michael's dark blue shirt moving briskly through the backyard and stopping at the old shed. My curiosity won over my fear—I stepped closer to the window, making a fist to wipe the glass.

Michael was standing by the shed using a crowbar to pry open its mangled door. Finally successful, he went inside, just for a few moments. When he emerged, he was staring into the glass jar he'd brought from the garage. I panicked when I saw him starting to walk back. As quick as I could, I retraced my footsteps to the original spot. The door flew open and shining light streamed across my telltale footprints. Before taking another step, Michael looked down, his stare frozen on the tiny trail.

"You moved," he grunted, and put the glass jar up to my face. "Look at my new friends," he smirked, staring into the glass.

"No!" I screamed. "Get them away, get them away!"

The glass jar was filled with earwigs. Dozens of tiny brown and black waxed shells dripped down from the lid, each armed with little wire pincers, crawling frantically over each other. I was terrified and fell backwards into a stack of empty boxes; they came tumbling down on top of me.

"Get up, Donnie," my brother said harshly, while looking to see if I was actually hurt, not wanting to get into trouble with our parents.

Realizing I was OK, I pushed myself up from the boxes and stood rubbing my back where the cardboard corners had jabbed into my ribs.

"I have a deal for you," Michael said, after acknowledging I was fine and then placing the jar behind his back. "I will not let these pincer bugs out if you follow all of my instructions. You do exactly what I tell you and they stay in the jar."

CHAPTER SIX

The Deal 1958, Monterey, California

When I stepped out of the garage the afternoon sun blinded me. I hobbled along the trail of dirt and pebbles that led us to the old broken-down shed. We stopped. Michael kicked aside the old crowbar that lay in the path and turned around to give me an eerie grin.

"Remember the deal?" he admonished me, putting the jar of bugs right in front of my face.

"Take your underwear off." He maintained the grin.

I moaned and squished up my face like I was squeezing out a wet sponge.

"No" I said in a long whine. "No, please, no."

"Did you say no?" Michael began to slowly unscrew the rusty lid, which made a gritty sound with each turn.

My eyes stayed fixed on the jar.

I saw a bug crawl out. "OK!" I cried. I pulled my underwear down and stepped out, leaving the two white cotton circles abandoned, lying limp in the dirt.

"Good," Michael said, almost with a low growl. Then he grabbed the side of the old battered shed door and pulled it open. The rusted metal hinges let out long moaning squeals as he pushed the heavy door back all the way.

"Go in," he said, stepping away from the large dark opening. I froze and stared into the dark.

"Go in!" Michael sharply ordered me, while lifting the lid off the jar and allowing a few more bugs to escape. I jumped away from the bugs and darted into the shed, stepping on a nail. I fell, rolling headfirst across the dirt floor. I grabbed my foot, pressing into the pain as I wailed for help; Michael just slammed the door.

My screams became cries, but soon the realization hit that nobody was there to help me. I sat quietly, breathing in the smell of the wet earth. A warm liquid oozed from my foot and covered my hands like a sheer glove, turning cool with the dampness. I reached up to my face to wipe away what I thought was a spider web, but instead I felt the waxy shelled bodies of earwigs. They started to crawl down my face. One fell onto my shoulder and soon they were everywhere, pinching and rolling across my skin. I panicked as my imagination ran wild with thoughts of what else might be with me in the dark.

The smells, the fear, and the penetrating dampness weighed down on me until my mind was filled with silence. I fell into a deep sleep, dreaming I was in another place, and in another body, and I was safe. This was the first of many times that I remember leaving my body to escape the pain my brother inflicted upon me.

I awoke to the sound of the shed door squeaking open, letting light wash over my blood-streaked body. As I lifted my head, I could see the ominous silhouette of that same navy blue shirt in the doorway.

Michael let out a loud gasp when he saw me. "Shit! Shit! Shit! Where did all this blood come from?"

When he saw the trail of blood that led to the rusty nail, he rushed into the shed and instructed me to put my arms around his neck. I did what he said. He lifted me up and then carried me back to the house. As soon as we got into the kitchen, he pulled out a chair from the table and helped me sit down. He picked up my foot and examined it closely, mumbling something about how it was a good thing that it had clotted on its own.

"You're going to be alright, Donnie," he said, still looking at my foot. "I'm gonna draw you a bath and help you get cleaned up."

I heard him muttering to himself out in the kitchen, scrambling through cabinets, knocking things to the ground. "Fuck, where are the Band-Aids? … Jesus, he better be OK, or I'm screwed!"

When I got into the bathtub, the water turned pink and then gray as the blood and dirt dissolved from my body. Michael used an old, pale yellow washcloth to gently wash away the dirt and caked blood from my foot. Then he began telling me the story we were going to tell Mom and Dad when they got home.

"We were just playing outside and you ran into the shed and stepped on a nail and then I helped you get back in the house and I cleaned your foot, and that's what happened," Michael rapidly directed me, rubbing my foot a little harder with the washcloth.

"And that's what *happened*, right?" I felt his hand press in deeper.

"Donnie, are you listening to me?" he demanded, his voice rising with frustration. Then he repeated the story all over again.

It was hard for me to concentrate because all I could think about was jumping into my father's arms and burying my nose in his smooth pressed khaki shirt, inhaling the scent of his morning splash of Old Spice cologne. I wanted him to come home. I wanted my Daddy.

Michael squeezed my arm and raised his voice, bringing me out of my daze and demanding that I repeat the story.

"Uh … uh … I was playing out in the back, and … I, I stepped on a nail. And then you washed it off." I repeated, trembling and doing my best to remember. But even as I recited the story, I planned to tell Mom and Dad what really happened.

Michael squeezed my arm even harder and told me to repeat the story over again.

"From the beginning," he insisted, raising his voice when mine began to quiver.

"We only have an hour until they get home, so you better remember!"

He stood up slowly and lifted me out of the tub and then handed me a towel, putting his arm around my waist to help me walk back to the bedroom.

He sat me down on the edge of the bed and went to the dresser and got me a pair of underwear. He knelt down, stretched the waistband wide, and told me to step in. I placed my hand on his shoulder and stood up, balancing myself as I stared down into the two white circles. I stepped in and he pulled them up, letting the elastic band snap tight around my waist.

Still squatting in front of me, he warned, "I hope you're not thinking about adding anything to the story we're going to tell Mom and Dad."

Michael got up, poked his forefinger under my chin and pressed hard, forcing my head backwards and causing me to fall onto the bed. My eyes looked up at the ceiling and I grabbed the fuzzy part of the bedspread with both hands and held on tight so that I wouldn't fall off.

"You *better* remember the story exactly like I told you," he said, gritting his teeth.

"If you tell on me, you will be sorry, I mean it! You will be sorry!" And then he shoved me off the bed and charged out of the room, grumbling malevolently about how much he hated me.

As I lay on the floor rubbing my chin, I heard the door slam. I was convinced that once I told Mom and Dad everything, they would teach my mean brother a lesson. But for right now, I had to wait. I hobbled out to the living room and sat on the sofa by the big window that looked out onto the driveway. I could see Michael sitting quietly on the porch swing, staring out into the distance.

We both waited.

I watched the clouds pass by, and as the wind started to blow, long shadows began to form against the golden slopes. A jackrabbit bounded from behind one of the tumbleweeds and disappeared into the dried bushes that matched the color of his fur. I kept looking to see if his pointed ears would pop up again. I wondered if Michael had seen him too.

Suddenly Michael stood up and I could hear tires grinding through the gravel. The car stopped and Dad got out as Michael held the car door open. Mom walked around the car and listened to what he was telling Dad.

They all anxiously came up the porch stairs at the same time, but Dad came through the front door first. When I saw him, I lost control and started to cry. Dad came to me and held my face in his hands and told me everything was going to be OK. He bent down and inspected my foot, shaking his head. "Damn it, what happened here?" He glared at Michael.

"He went outside barefoot, even though I told him not to, and stepped on a nail," Michael lied, pretending he felt badly for me.

Mom dashed into my room and got my favorite blue blanket and handed it to Dad. He wrapped it around me, and as he picked me up in his strong arms and carried me out to the car, he explained that I needed to go to the doctor so he could give me a very important shot.

We all piled into the car and sped away to the hospital. I heard my parents say that the rust on the nail could cause my jaws to lock up, but the shot would stop that from happening. *Jaws lock up?* I thought, *that sounds really painful! If the shot can stop that, I won't even cry when the doctor gives it to me.* And I didn't.

Afterwards Dad said he was proud of me, and gave me a big hug. Michael kept reiterating how it was my fault: "He shouldn't have gone out barefoot. I made breakfast for us and I was just trying to clean up the dishes when Donnie snuck outside. He knew better."

After we finished dinner that night, I decided to tell the truth about what Michael really had done to me. I wasn't sure the shot from the doctor had worked, because when I went to tell the story, my jaws did seem to freeze up, but once I got a few words out, they seemed to work just fine.

"Daddy …," I said, interrupting him after he praised Michael for taking such good care of me.

He sat back in his chair, looking at me attentively. "Yes, son?"

"The reason I stepped on the nail was because Michael made me take off my clothes and locked me in the shed … the bugs were …"

"What!" Dad shouted, spinning around to glower at Michael. "Did you do that to your brother?"

The angry, defiant look on Michael's face told my father what he wanted to know. He got up from the table and yelled with a fury I had never heard before, "Michael, you need to be taught a lesson!"

Dad grabbed Michael, hauled him into the living room, and pulled him over his knees and spanked him over and over. I stood beside Mom and watched.

Michael never made one sound and never shed one tear. All he did was pucker his lips hard against his teeth and scowl at the wall. When Dad was through, he told him to go to his room and Michael furiously stomped off. When he got to the hallway, he looked back at me with eyes blacker than I had ever seen … and then he grinned.

I hobbled over to Dad and climbed up into his lap, burying my face into his chest. I reached up and rubbed my hand over the stubbles on his chin and stuck my nose deep into his shirt and breathed in his scent.

"I love you, Daddy," I whispered, happy he had taught Michael a lesson.

CHAPTER SEVEN

The Wrath of Michael   1959, Monterey, California

I awoke the next morning hearing the sounds of Mom and Dad's muffled voices as they got ready to go to the base, Dad for work, and Mom to continue her job-hunt. A cold draft brushed across my face, so I pulled my baby blanket up over my nose and panted in short breaths to send the mask of cold air away. The bandage on my foot had slipped off during the night and ended up inside my pajama bottoms. When I reached in and found the bloody gauze, the events from the day before flooded my mind. A chill shuddered throughout my body.

"Keys!" I could hear my father swearing, "Where in the hell are those damn keys? I put them right ..."

Mom replied with a familiar and assured answer, "I've found them, honey."

Their voices became muffled again and then I heard the front door close. The silence returned.

"G-r-r-r!" Michael roared, leaping into my bedroom and landing on his haunches at the end of my bed.

"So you thought by telling on me you could stop me from doing what I want! You were wrong!" He waved his arms wildly. "And now you're going to pay. Did you see how when Dad spanked me last night I didn't even cry? That's because I have powers. Powers that help me get whatever I want!"

I sat trembling against my headboard with my baby blanket pulled up to my face, unable to utter a word.

"Get up!" he screamed.

I crawled out of bed in slow motion, consumed with fear. Once my feet hit the floor, Michael chased me into our parents' bedroom and ordered me to start making their bed. Dad had recently taught me how to make a bed the military way, stressing how the blankets had to be tucked in so tight a dime would bounce right off of them.

As soon as I got the top sheet tucked in, Michael picked me up and threw me onto the bed. He grabbed one of the bed pillows and covered my face, holding it there, making it impossible to breathe. The scent of my mother's perfume, White Shoulders, penetrated my senses as I breathed in her memory. Michael finally released the pillow and air began to fill up my lungs once again.

"What's your problem, Donnie? Can't you breathe?"

I rolled off the bed and landed on a pile of blankets that were lying on the floor. He dragged me back onto the bed and began to tickle me relentlessly until I was unable to catch my breath. Smothering, then tickling—this became our morning ritual—whenever I was left alone with him. When I gave up and collapsed, he stood beside the bed, his eyes pitch-black with fury.

"I can use my special powers whenever I want. I'm like the Big Bad Wolf," he growled, as he breathed in a belly full of air and then blew it out, spitting in my face. "If you ever tell on me again, I will take Dad away from you. *I will kill him.* You will never, ever see your father again."

The next weekend we took an excursion to Fisherman's Wharf in Monterey to celebrate Mom getting hired as a secretary in a civil service position, right in the same building as Dad's office. They slipped into one of the tourist shops that sold shells and t-shirts. They told us to wait outside. Once they disappeared through the doorway, Michael grabbed my hand and led me around the corner to a secluded spot where pigeons were eating grain someone had scattered about.

"Watch," he said, letting go of my hand to reach into his jacket pocket. He brought out a good-sized rock and threw it, hitting a silver and black pigeon directly on the head.

I screamed as the poor bird toppled to its side.

"Bull's eye!" he chuckled, as the rest of the pigeons took off, escaping in a gust of air.

I screamed so loud that Michael slapped his hand over my mouth and, in a guttural whisper, hissed "Shut up! If you don't shut up, I *will* use my powers to kill Dad … just like I did with that stinking pigeon."

"Michael? Donnie?" Dad was calling from around the corner.

Michael looked back and pressed his hand even harder over my mouth. He viciously snarled, "Do you *understand?*"

I gulped and nodded desperately. After he let go, he reached for my hand, leading me and singing with a happy voice, "Daddy, we're over here."

By the beginning of August, Michael had tired of our morning ritual and began plotting his next move. Of course, when he told me he had planned something new and fun, I went along happily, hoping it would not involve tickling and smothering.

The first day of his "new plan," he took me out to one of the fields about four blocks away from our house, and then we hiked up to the top of a hill. The weather was cool and breezy, normal for that time of year on the coastline of the Monterey Bay.

The next time we climbed up the hill, it was during an unseasonal heat wave. Michael made me carry a big shovel that was too heavy for me to lift, so I had to drag it along in the dirt. He had found stored in the garage one of Dad's folded Army canvas tents and carried it over one shoulder, as we traipsed up the hill. He told me we were going to make a bomb shelter, "just like Dad did when he was in Korea." This was one of the times Michael treated me nicely and made me feel like he really did want to be a good brother to me. "It's going to be our very own, Donnie. You'll like it … just wait and see." Just the day before, he had shown me how to whittle a duck from a bar of Ivory soap with the Swiss army knife Dad had given him for his birthday. I pondered, *Maybe I am getting old enough for him to see we could have fun together*.

Once we got to our site, he spent all of his time digging out a large hole. When it reached about four feet deep, he lined it with the dark green canvas tent. As I watched him jump in the hole and spread out the canvas, he told me we needed to go back home and pick up one more thing. My shirt was drenched with sweat from the heat. On our way back home, I was thirsty and barely able to walk; Michael held up the canteen and turned it over to show me it was empty.

The dry earth was hot and dust rose up from the matted trail that we had flattened by the many hikes we'd made, trudging back and forth, as we dug our bomb shelter. Once we arrived home, I followed him along the side of the house and into the backyard. We ended up behind the old shed where there was a large piece of plywood that leaned lopsided against the crumbling rotted wall.

"This is the perfect size," he stated. "Grab the back end, so we can get it up the hill." As soon as we got halfway up the hill, he realized he'd forgotten to fill the canteen and sent me back down to refill it. When I returned, Michael was standing at the edge of the hole with the plywood leaning up against his legs. He grabbed the canteen from me and took a big swallow. Wiping his mouth, he pointed down into the hole, and, to my tremendous shock, he told me to climb in.

"What?" I blurted out, peering into the canvas-lined cavity.

At first, he tried to convince me that this was an honor. "This is our bomb shelter, Donnie, and now you get to be the first to try it out."

"No!" I turned to run, hollering, "I'm not going in there! I'm not!"

"Go ahead and run!" Michael yelled. "I guess you don't want to see our father again, do you?"

I stopped, my shoulders raised up to my ears, and grudgingly turned back around.

"I thought you'd change your mind," he sneered. "Now come back and get down there!"

My tears started flowing as I looked towards the bottom of the hole. The heat of the sun had warmed the canvas, sending up a strong musty smell that became more fetid as I approached the large opening.

"Please, Michael, don't make me go down there!" I bawled. "Please, don't make me!"

He dropped the board with obvious frustration and grabbed the front of my shirt, bellowing, "Shut up! *Shut up, you little baby!* Stop crying, right now!"

My cries had transformed into convulsions, making it hard for me to catch my breath. That must have scared him, because he suddenly calmed down and let go of my shirt.

"OK, OK, Donnie," he said, "You have to stop crying, do you understand?" He put his hand on my shoulder as if he cared and said in a soft tone, "You only have to go in there for a little while—I promise."

His threat was like a non-stop broken record in my head, leading me to only one conclusion: *I can't lose my father; I would be lost* ... I took another look down into the gaping hole.

"If I go in there," I stuttered, still staring into the pit, "you won't take Daddy away from me? You promise?"

"You just get in there and you'll see Daddy tonight."

I sat down on the edge and dangled my feet over the side.

"Go on," Michael pressed. "You want to see him tonight, don't you?"

The coarse material scraped my elbows like a rug burn as I slid down along the side of the stiff canvas and fell to the bottom.

Slap! Michael dropped across the hole the big piece of plywood he'd made me help lug up the hill. He slid the wood into place, leaving a small triangular opening up at the corner for air. For a moment I froze, only able to focus on the rays of light shining on the crumbling earth that trickled down from the shovels of dirt Michael was heaving over the top of the plywood.

The sound of the pounding dirt scared me into action. I rushed over to the opening and cupped my hands around my mouth, and yelled up through the hole, "Michael! Michael! Let me out! Let me out!"

The next time I screamed, he walked over to the air opening and kicked in some loose dirt clogs, which then came pouring down into my mouth.

"Please don't leave me!" I cried, spitting out the dirt. "Please don't leave me! Michael, *please* don't leave me!" I pleaded, over and over.

I finally gave up, completely spent. I fell back across the stiffness of the army tent. A strong chemical smell emanated from the canvas as the air became thicker and warmer. In the dark, I stretched out my legs to touch one side, my back tight against the other. I stood up and pushed as hard as I could, but the dirt-covered plywood was too heavy to move. My throat started to burn and my head began to throb as I tried to focus on the one ray of light that shone down like a miniature flashlight beam, piercing a hole in the plywood. But my eyes stung so much I *had* to close them.

"He has to come back," I whimpered repeatedly, as I rocked back and forth in this catacomb with only enough room to fold up in a fetal position.

Tears poured out, soaking into a lumpy part of the coarse canvas, and softening it into a wet pillow. I laid my face across it, desperately wishing for Michael to come back. I finally gave up on even wishing; out of exhaustion, I fell asleep.

My big brother did come back much later, lifted the heavy board and reached in so I could grab his wrists. He pulled me out of my grave, acting like he had done me a favor by not leaving me there to die. I stumbled behind him down the hill, my legs cramped from spending the entire day wrapped in a tight little ball.

Whenever he was left to babysit me over the next weeks, Michael would take me up to the field and force me into the grave—I had no doubt about his threat to kill my father. I had come to firmly believe he really had special powers, just as he claimed.

The utter fear of death that has followed me throughout my life began with Michael's sick game of burying me alive.

Each time, once I'd hear the shoveling of the dirt stop, I knew I was trapped. Terror would envelop me again and I would disappear deep into the tunnels of my mind. Whenever I entered this dreamlike state, I believed everything I imagined was really happening. This was the way I survived. I'd leave that poor little boy buried in the grave and create another Donnie in my mind that had the power to travel anywhere he wanted. I discovered that I, too, had different—but still special—powers. My imagination became my reality. There was no pain or fear where I went, only love and fun. In this dream state I would always be with my Daddy.

We would go to his office and take strolls around the army base, and have lunch in the Mess Hall. If I wanted doughnuts for lunch, I could have them.

Sometimes we would leave his work and go to the beach and build sandcastles in the cool white sand. Huge crashing waves would echo in the distance, and every once in awhile, a gigantic wave would sneak up behind us and flood through our sandy structures, the fluffy white sea foam pouring over the make-believe moats. When the water drifted back out to sea, the skeletons of our castles looked like melted ice cream cones. We'd jump up, and with our pants all wet, we would run laughing against the sea breeze, our shirts billowing like kites surfing in the wind. As we ran down the beach, Dad would stop and pick me up and set me on his shoulders. I'd sit straight up, stretch my arms out wide, singing out to the lavender sculptured sand dunes, "I'm a seagull! I'm a seagull!"

And soon a golden orange mist would rise up against the setting sun and we would say farewell to the gorgeous day as we walked hand in hand back into my mind.

In that state, the hours went by like minutes.

Eventually Michael would return. Scaring me to death as he stomped across the plywood, he brayed: "It's time to come out now, Donnie ... it's time to come o-u-t!"

My fright from his pounding feet quickly turned into feelings of joy; I would laugh and cheer when I heard him return.

"You're back ... you're back," I'd shriek up through the small opening. And then I'd back away quickly, afraid that dirt might come down on me once again.

"I knew you'd come back," I whispered to myself. "I knew you would ..." And then Michael would reach down into the grave and carefully help me climb out. Each day, I would collapse in his arms before we walked back home. Relief replaced the fear—the plywood hadn't collapsed—I wasn't buried alive—and my father would live.

Yes, my father would live ... *as long as I never told.*

Our walks back home after Michael would set me free were not filled with conversation. He would walk briskly ahead of me, kicking rocks with a happy stride; sometimes I'd hear him hum tunes from popular songs. I am sure his good mood came from having me buried away, so he could spend the day with the friends he'd met down at the little convenience store he rode his bike to whenever Mom would run out of milk. His hard work of digging the grave was nothing compared to the freedom that having me confined and out of his way all day allowed him. Babysitting had its rewards.

After entering the house I would wash the dirt off my body, dash straight to the living room, and take my usual position, kneeling against the back cushion of the couch, my eyes fixed on the driveway.

Each night, when I saw Dad get out of the car, my heart danced because I knew *today* I had saved him from Michael's special powers. I spent time in that hole so that my Daddy would be safe. My eyes danced from the top of his head all the way down to his shoes, drinking him in like I was a thirsty beast. When he came through the door, I leapt into his arms and pressed my lips hard against his neck. I loved inhaling the salty sea air from our imaginary day at the beach, the scent mixing perfectly with the morning's splash of Old Spice.

Tomorrow would come too soon.

CHAPTER EIGHT

Believe It ... or Not   1981, Los Altos, California

The moment I got off the phone with my mother, I called Diane MacAlister. She was a friend and a client for over six years who also happened to be an attorney. I was feeling as trapped as I actually had been when Michael shoved me into that hole in the ground, unable to breathe. With Mr. Sanders' plea for us to testify echoing in my head, I felt like Michael was again stomping on the plywood, shocking me from the peace of my dream world. But this time, it was not a child's escape dream world he was interrupting; I was a grown man and the owner of the most exclusive hair salon on the Peninsula. He was pounding his way back into my life—about to destroy it all.

I sat with the phone in my hand. I stared at Diane's name printed neatly in our client phone book.

I shouldn't tell her, I lamented to myself. But there was no one else I could trust, and I was worried about the bad press. Would the media come to my salon? All the time, effort and hard work spent building my celebrity hairstylist status could be crushed with one newspaper article. Once again, a sensational headline about the murder Michael and Mona committed flashed across my mind's screen. I imagined the worst.

That image propelled me to pick up the phone and dial her number.

"Hello, Diane. Something's happening and I need to talk to you, do you have time to meet?" She had never heard such urgency in my voice.

"I'm just leaving work, I'll come now," she replied, her voice heavy with concern.

I sat with my shoulders slumped, staring at my reflection. How soon would it be before Michael's toxic behavior re-entered my world? I looked out the reception room's large picture window, anticipating Diane's car driving up; once again I was the six-year-old child waiting for my father to arrive home. The dark-tinted window allowed me to see out without anyone else seeing in. I watched Diane approach and did my usual knee-jerk survey of how well she had styled her hair—a common hairstylist thing. It's what we all do. After all, it is the stylists' work of art. I never had to worry about Diane though; she was always what I'd call "perfection," from head to toe. And this evening was no different. She was wearing a deep cranberry St. John knit suit that complemented her rich, root beer brown hair color, a shade I had formulated especially for her. I opened the door and greeted her with a hug. I leaned against the door frame, not sure whether to blurt it out or to ease into the story. I began reviewing my notes.

"What happened?" Diane asked, looking at me nervously.

I decided to blurt it out. "My brother's been charged with murder."

"Let's sit down."

I turned and led her back into the reception room. I guided her to a seat on the maroon velvet antique sofa that sat diagonally across from the salon's reception desk. Repeating what Mr. Sanders had told me caused my shirt to dampen slightly with perspiration. I lifted the silk material away from my chest a few times and then rested my clenched fists in my lap. I was still stunned by the phone call and relayed the information like I was reading from a manuscript written about someone else's life. When I got to the part that the murder had taken place in Eureka and it was almost certain the prosecuting attorney would file for the death penalty, she interrupted.

"The murder happened in Eureka, right?"

"Yes."

"Well, we have a major coincidence here, Don."

She pulled airline tickets from her small leather clutch bag.

"You see, I have a friend who I went to law school with, and he and I have been going back and forth to find a time we could get together and catch up on old times." Diane paused, looking up from the tickets she held in her hands. Her almond-shaped emerald green eyes danced past me and then back again, as she revealed that her law school chum was the chief prosecuting attorney in Eureka and that she was leaving for there in the morning for the long-planned visit. Shocked, I stared at her, my mouth open to say something, but too aghast to speak; surely a director from a movie set would appear any second to yell "Cut!"

We sat with our eyes locked, digesting all that had just transpired.

"Have you thought about Mr. Sanders' question about why Michael might have been in Eureka?" Diane asked. "If he can find some other connection, he might leave you alone."

"I don't think so—I have a friend there. You remember Debra—the stylist who opened Dorian Grey with me? She lives there."

Diane nodded. "Did Michael know her?"

"No, and I've only been to Eureka with Debra once. It was about a year and a half ago, right after we opened the salon. She asked me to drive with her to go see her family because she hadn't been home for almost two years. We got into an argument just before we got there."

Somehow this memory was helping me to relax. Diane must have noticed that the look of dread had drained from my face because she encouraged me to continue talking.

"What were you arguing about?"

"We were driving in her convertible. I had to shout so she could hear me as we drove through these winding roads about twenty miles from Eureka. *'I bet the scenery here is quite beautiful!'* I kept shouting, trying not to open my mouth too wide because there were bug carcasses plastered against her windshield. I took that as a warning that I should scream through my teeth."

Diane laughed as my fists began to unclench, and I started to more comfortably gesture, acting out the scene.

"Debra pretended not to hear me. *'It's probably breathtaking,'* I screamed louder, *'but all I can see is a hurricane of evergreen branches mixed with flashes of sunlight!'*"

I exhaled more deeply; my chest seemed less constricted as we went on. "Debra started yelling back that her father was the head of highway regulations for that area, and according to him, the posted speed limit was 10 miles under what the roads could actually handle."

"Oh great!" Diane laughed.

"Right?" I said. "So I turned my head towards her for a moment and then instantly turned back when I saw she was taking her eyes off the road to yell at me. She continued yelling her defense, 'My sports car is made for these kinds of roads! It's built low to the ground! Fiat X19s can go 65 around curves, Don.'"

Diane's eyes smiled as she listened attentively, nodding her head.

I laughed at the memory and enjoyed the temporary respite from my brother's harrowing tale. "Of course, the speed limit was 55."

"I'll be driving those roads tomorrow from the airport," Diane interjected with a chuckle and a smile.

"Can I get you anything to drink?" I asked.

"Oh thank you, Don. I'm fine, actually. So, my trip should be very interesting," she said a little more sternly, getting back to the virtually unbelievable coincidence we had discovered. "I'll let you know what he says. He may not say anything, since your brother's case is under that gag order, but I will squeeze as much information out of him as I can."

"That would be great. And thanks, Diane, I really appreciate your help."

We both stood up and I gave her a hug goodbye.

I knew I needed to address my fear about the national attention the murder might receive, so I got the phone number for the Eureka newspaper. I called to see if they would give me any information about the murder, but there was no answer. I imagined lurid front page headlines, with Michael's full name and picture giving away my shame. I was both certain and scared that soon journalists would be at my door, wanting to know about "the accused's" only brother. On my way home, I stopped off at a local bookstore to see if by chance they carried any Eureka newspaper, but they didn't.

I walked out of the store, praying that news of the murder might get out-positioned by a more important story. Remembering the bitter certainty in Mr. Sanders' voice about the gruesome series of events, the odds that there would be little publicity were not very good. I figured it would only be a matter of time.

Searching for a distraction, I stopped off at one of the chain department stores down the street from my salon to see if they had the pair of jeans I'd seen at their Hayward store the day before, where I'd bought a mauve windbreaker.

That's what I'll do, I said to myself, driving into the store's parking lot. *I'll go try on those jeans.*

It turned out that they didn't have the new style jeans. But as I left the store, a heavy-set young man and a similarly-sized woman, who identified themselves only as "Security," stopped me and asked where I had bought the jacket I was wearing. At first I thought it was a strange question, but then I realized I was wearing the windbreaker I had bought the day before. Answering their question, it suddenly hit me, *They think I am stealing it! How strange,* I thought … *here I was worried about how Michael was ruining my reputation with his horrific crime, and now I was the one under suspicion.*

"Oh," I said casually, glancing down at my jacket. "I bought it yesterday at your Hayward store."

"No, you didn't," the woman security guard exclaimed. "I saw you steal it! You weren't wearing it when you came in."

Stunned by her accusation, I was sure I must be dreaming. The awful timing, with what was happening in Eureka and now was happening to me—considering that my reason for going shopping was to *forget* about the crime—was so unsettling.

Fighting to stay calm, I pulled out of my wallet the credit card that I used to pay for the jacket and said she could run the card and see for a fact that I had bought the item the day before. She let out a big "Hmmph!" as she walked towards the store's office, muttering to her male counterpart that she did see me steal the jacket. When we got to the sales desk, I handed the clerk my credit card, asking her to check and see that I had indeed purchased the jacket yesterday.

"I'm sorry," the clerk said, "the recorded sales take a week to show up."

"See how smart he is?" The security guard loudly interjected. "He knew that. I'm telling you he's lying. I saw him steal that jacket!"

"You know what?" I shouted back at her, afraid I was going to snap. "You need to keep your mouth shut. I have a business right up the street and there might be someone here who knows me!"

This is all I need today, I thought, *as I defended myself. Not only am I going to be known for having a brother who is a sociopathic murderer, I'm going to jail as a presumed shoplifter.*

"Good!" she responded, putting her hands on her broad chubby hips. "They should know you're a thief. Why don't you give it up? You know you took the jacket!"

"I want to see the manager! And someone needs to put a muzzle on her mouth!" I called out, pointing directly at my accuser.

"Hey!" The male security guard walked over and bumped his puffed chest right into mine. "Don't talk to my wife that way!"

Oh great! A husband and wife security team! No one will believe this, I lamented to myself and then loudly proclaimed, "I don't care *who* she is, she needs to keep her mouth shut."

Luckily, the manager showed up right at that moment, and seemed to know all about the alleged theft.

"What's your name?" inquired the manager, a young woman who looked about my age. In hopes of turning this ugly situation around, I answered politely and handed her my charge card.

"Please go into the system and check—I bought the jacket yesterday."

"I'm sorry, Mr. English, but it takes a week to show up."

"Great …" I exhaled, struggling to maintain my composure. I caught myself wishing that someone, anyone, would come through the door and rescue me. But knowing that wasn't going to happen, I took a deep breath and gave it one last shot, trying not to imagine the combined headlines. Determined that both English brothers were *not* going to be under arrest on the same day, I turned my back to the security couple and peered into the manager's eyes.

"I have an idea. This jacket is a new item, right?"

She shrugged her shoulders with uncertainty.

"I'm telling you," the guard's voice screeched from behind me, "These are all lies! I saw him take that jacket."

I was surprised the manager didn't say anything when she heard the loud accusation being hollered through the store. She did put her hand up, though, nodding at me to continue.

"OK," I said, with some degree of indignation still in my voice. "Since the jacket is a new style, you can check your inventory. If all your jackets are here, it will prove that mine could not be from this store."

The manager said something to the clerk standing beside her and they left us, heading to the back of the store. I stood at the desk, keeping my back turned so I would not have to look at my accusers. Surprisingly, the manager and sales clerk returned right away.

"Mr. English, that was a good idea," said the manager through a forced smile. "You were right. They are all there." She glanced over at the security guards after she made the pronouncement.

"You were acting suspicious," Mrs. Security Guard huffed again.

I ignored her comment.

"Don't I even get an apology?" I looked around expecting the host from the TV show *Candid Camera* to appear and tell me this was all a hoax.

The manager spoke with hesitation, as if she still was not convinced I wasn't a thief: "Sure, I guess."

"Forget it!" I said, raising my voice. "Am I free to go?"

The sales clerks, the manager, and Mr. and Mrs. Security Guard just stood there, glaring at me.

"This is insane," I yelled, shaking my head with disbelief as I turned and walked out of the store.

Some distraction ... I complained to myself all the way back to my car.

CHAPTER NINE

My Present

1981, Los Altos, California—1960, Marina, California

Two days later, when Diane finally called to report on her findings, I was at the salon; the ordeal with the jacket was the last thing on my mind.

"Don," she started out rather dramatically, after our greetings. "I'm not sure how to tell you this." After a long pause, the drama continued in her voice. "From what my friend Carl told me, your brother most likely *will* get the death penalty."

"So he talked to you about it?"

"Yes, and because there are aspects about the case that have already been made public, he was able to share quite a bit. I never told him I knew you, so he was feeling pretty free to talk about the case. He said what your brother did was unthinkably gruesome and he really has no doubts that he is definitely guilty."

"So do you think Michael's case will make the national news?" I suddenly blurted out, not able to hold back about what I feared most.

"I know you don't want to hear this," Diane said, her voice waning, "but my friend is counting on it … the more attention the better. And as he said, for what Michael did, he deserves whatever he gets."

"I have to agree with that," I said, feeling a growing terror that my reputation would be ruined by his horrendous crime. My salon staff, my clients, my friends—none of whom even knew I *had* a brother—were all now going to read about him in the newspaper. I had worked extremely hard for many years to deal with the abuses I had suffered at my brother's hands; I just wanted him to disappear from my life. In that moment, I didn't care if Michael got sentenced to death; in fact, on some level, I was hoping for it, just to have the terror of him out of my life once and for all.

"Don, there are details you don't know, unimaginable things."

"Things I don't know?"

"Several of the man's toes and fingers had been cut off and there was a trail of blood leading to the safe, so they believe he tortured the man, trying to get the safe combination."

I felt myself exhale heavily into the phone. "Oh my God. That poor man."

"You hang in there, Don. Call me anytime."

I thanked her for her help and hung up.

I wanted this to be a terrible nightmare. But it wasn't a dream, it was my life, and it was beginning to read like the script for a horror movie.

Bloody fingers ... and toes cut off ...

Hearing Diane say those words brought back feelings from my childhood when Michael caused me to boil with a rage I never knew possible. The bloody murder of the old man must have been a scene of tortuous humiliation. That image, combined with my lifelong fear of my brother's "superhuman" evil powers, caused hatred to burn white-hot in every cell of my body.

I might have been Michael's first victim, but hopefully the dead man would be his last. I knew there had been many others humiliated and terrorized by him in between.

Those recollections erupted in me like hot lava ... I remembered the first time he used his "powers" on someone other than me.

When Michael was eleven and while our parents were at work, two friends from his sixth grade class, Chucky and Larry, would come over to our house on their way home after school. Michael would order them to do things as if they were his slaves.

That day in 1959 Michael was in one of his moods. You could tell because he would pace back and forth with his shoulders forward, digging his hands deep down into his front pockets. He would stare intently at the ground like he was expecting a message to spring out from the earth. After he finished his pacing, he looked up and announced what he wanted Chucky and Larry to do.

"OK, guys, I want you to go into the kitchen." He pointed the way. "And take off your shirts."

"No way! No way!"They both retorted in unison and started walking towards the front door.

"Hey, you guys, come back here!" Michael said, shaking his head slowly side to side. "You know you guys don't want me tell your parents about … you know what … right? So get back here."

Chucky and Larry immediately looked at me; their eyes bugging out with fear that Michael would divulge their secret to me. I took a couple of steps back and stood behind Michael, praying I wouldn't be included.

He turned his head and I could see the crooked frozen grin on his face. I knew what that meant. He was about to use his powers to get them to do what he wanted.

Both boys turned around and stood together as if they were dogs ordered to heel.

"That's better," he said, still grinning viciously. "Get your shirts off and go into the kitchen, right now!"

They traipsed towards the kitchen, pulling their shirts over their heads, murmuring what struck me as swear words.

Michael followed behind them.

A few minutes went by and then I heard what sounded like moaning coming from the kitchen.

Heading in that direction, I stopped halfway, thinking I'd better not take a chance. But once again my curiosity won out, and I snuck up to the side of the doorway. I squatted down against the wall and listened.

Michael was giving directions. "I want you to squeeze your arms up like this. Now hold them there."

I heard the sound of the refrigerator door open. I took another chance and slowly peeked around the doorjamb. They were standing with their backs away from me, except for Michael, who was engrossed with what he was about to do.

Both boys were standing in front of Michael with their forearms brought up to their necks, almost like they were flexing their biceps. The milky white of their naked backs created a sharp contrast against their dark pants. They each had the same dull ashy brown hair with identical short military haircuts. A lot of people thought they were twins. They were five grades ahead of me in school and had different last names, so I knew they weren't related. I thought, as I watched them, how the absence of color made them look like they were on TV, in black and white. They stood there like statues as Michael reached into the refrigerator. He brought out a bottle of ketchup.

"What are you going to do with that?" Larry erupted, letting his arms come down to his side.

"Get your arms back up there!" he ordered.

When Larry's arms went back into position, Michael took his forefinger and ran it through the small crease of Larry's elbow.

"Don't touch me!" Larry protested, turning sideways, causing Michael to turn and look in my direction.

I quickly scooted out of sight, as fast as I could, and leaned back against the wall. I thought my heart was going to jump out of my chest. I waited ... but he hadn't seen me.

"What time will your parents get home tonight, Larry?" I heard Michael ask.

"Do you think they would mind a little visit from me? I would be happy to tell them all about ..."

"OK! OK! Do what you're gonna do so we can get outta here."

Chucky, who had been standing still all that time, finally broke his silence. "Yeah, Michael, what are you going to do with that ketchup?"

"Just hold on, Chucky! You're gonna find out soon enough!"

What is he going to do? I wondered to myself, feeling sorry for them, but at the same time feeling relief, seeing Michael abuse someone besides me. *I'm not the only one suffering*, I realized, as I kneeled back against the wall. *Should I dare look?* I made my decision and knelt forward, peering with one eye around the corner of the doorway.

I saw Michael pounding the ketchup bottle violently into the palm of his hand and then unscrew the cap.

"So you guys remember in our health class today they showed the film on reproduction and what happens to girls down there?" he rhetorically asked, pointing to his crotch.

Before they could answer, he had dug his forefinger into the bottle and started to paint the small fleshy slits on their arms one at a time. The ketchup appeared bright red against their colorless bodies.

"Here's some blood for your pussy ... and here's some for your pussy." All three of them burst out into uncontrollable laughter.

I got up immediately, confused by their guffaws. I went to my room, wondering, *What was so funny about bloody kitties?* Just the thought of little kitties bleeding bothered me so much, I decided I would ask Mom as soon as she got home.

When I told her what happened with Larry and Chucky, she got all upset and told Dad the whole story the minute he walked through the door.

I asked them again later about the bloody pussies but they snapped at me and told me not to talk about it anymore. They did put Michael on a two-week restriction, but since we were moving again, it only lasted a week.

The next Saturday, as I was waiting for the movers, I rocked back and forth on the swing. I was feeling apprehensive, still thinking about the ketchup, Michael, and how angry he was at me for telling on him.

Despite the promise of getting on-base housing within three months, we were kept on the waiting list for two years. I felt joy as I wiped away the first tear that trickled down my cheek, realizing we were finally moving onto Fort Ord. I smiled, knowing our new house would be surrounded by lots of neighbors. The afternoons of Michael burying me in a makeshift grave would be over soon. My screams would no longer go unheard.

"April showers on and off," Mom said, quoting the day's forecast and directing Michael to put the umbrellas he carried for her beside me on the porch swing. Dad was right behind her with the only thing of value our family owned, the still-life painting of the teacups. The painting was all bundled up with paper and cardboard.

"Honey," she said, pointing to Dad, "just set that down, carefully, right beside the umbrellas." I had gotten up to make room.

"Donnie, the movers should be here any minute, so I want you to keep an eye on my painting. Can you do that, honey?" she asked, taking a deep breath.

I nodded, slipping back onto the swing.

As they walked away, I glanced over at the painting. Just as I was contemplating how huge the painting looked wrapped with so much protection, Michael snuck up behind me and yelled *Boo!* Watch out for those monster teacups—they might jump out and get you!"

"Leave me alone!" I squeaked, unable to catch my breath after his disquieting scare.

After our visit to Disneyland, Michael had told me how he woke up one night and heard something in the dining room. When he went to see what it was, he found that the teacups in the painting had come alive and become as big as the ones on the Disneyland ride. "They were monsters!" He was holding his elbows and shivering to accentuate his fright.

"You saw them?" I asked, whispering with awe, believing every word.

"Not only did I see them, I'll show you which one was the biggest … and the meanest."

He took me to the dining room and went right up to the painting and pointed to the large gold teapot. I stood back, ducking behind one of the chairs.

"So whatever you do, Donnie, never come in here alone at night. They are mean monsters!"

From that time on, I had nightmares about teacups swelling up and rolling over me.

I scooted to the furthest side of the swing … away from the teacup painting. The sound of rumbling on gravel suddenly echoed from the top of our driveway.

"Look, Mom! Here comes the truck!" I called out, pointing, just as she appeared in the doorway.

The movers showed up right on time and true to Mom's estimated schedule, it took them about an hour to load everything up.

I was glad when Dad came up, took the painting, and packed it carefully in the trunk of the car. *Too bad they couldn't do the same thing with Michael*, I mused, watching him scurry around to help, pretending to be a good boy.

I stood up and swung around the porch post once and then sat back down on the swing, realizing I had almost forgotten the promise Mom had made! Today was my seventh birthday—she had apologized to me the week before for our having to move on my birthday and promised we would celebrate after the movers had us all moved in.

I so wanted to tell her not too worry about a celebration—moving was the best birthday present I could ever have, since, in our new house, I would be safe from Michael's grave.

Again Michael snuck up on me, but this time, he grabbed the swing from behind, causing me to fall to my knees. "Remember, Donnie, if you ever tell what happened in this house, I will use my magic powers to *kill Dad*. You utter even one word—and he's dead—you'll never see him again."

I believed him, especially after witnessing the power he had over his friends. I loved Dad so much because he was always there to protect me. And I would cry myself to sleep at night thinking what would happen if Michael took him away.

I looked up from the wooden porch floor to see if my parents saw what Michael had done. But, of course, he had been too clever—nobody was ever around when he abused me. I brushed myself off and went to find them. Meanwhile, I grabbed the umbrellas from where my brother had left them, and put them under the swing so they would be in a safe place in case Mom asked for them.

A few minutes later, I rounded the corner and saw Mom, Dad and Michael walking towards me. Dad was holding a big shiny blue box wrapped up with a glittery white bow. As they got closer, I could see black holes punched all over the box. The two movers crawled down from their truck, walked over to the porch, and they too joined the gathering.

Dad held out the box like it was my birthday cake and smiled broadly. "Happy Birthday, son!" Then everyone began to sing *Happy Birthday*.

I noticed Dad was having a hard time keeping the box still, and for a moment, I thought it was going to bounce right out of his arms. When they all finished the last chorus—"Happy Birthday to you"—the lid of the box popped off and up jumped a gray and white tiger-striped kitten. Everyone laughed and said what great timing the kitten had. I was so surprised I started to jump up and down.

Dad handed me the kitten and announced that *she* was a little girl.

"What's her name going to be?" Michael asked, joining in on the fun.

"Look!" Mom said pointing to the perfect white circle of fur on the top of her head. "It looks just like a crown."

"Wow, you have a royal kitten," one of the movers said.

"Oh! I've got a name!" Mom exclaimed. "I think we should call her Duchess!"

"That's a stupid name!" Michael grunted.

"No it's not!" I piped up. "Duchess is a good name! I like Duchess!"

I buried my face in her fur while Mom scratched behind her coal black ears. Mom's glossy red nails moved through her fur, exposing the kitty's pale white skin as she began to vibrate.

"Shhh …" I whispered. Duchess started her motor. "Can you hear it, Mommy, can you?"

"Yes, honey. She's purring, so that means she likes you."

"I like her too!" I purred, kissing the top of her crown.

I held her up by her tiny furry haunches and looked into her pale green eyes.

"So what do *you* think of the name Duchess?" I asked her. "Is that what we should call you?"

She opened her mouth wide and let out a loud *meow*!

"Well, that's it," Dad said. "It's settled, you are now crowned 'Duchess Kitty!'" He waved his hand over her head and with his deep operatic voice proclaimed: "Yes, you are now *The* Duchess, and probably by the end of the day, you'll be ruling this whole damn family!" The kitty meowed again; everyone laughed with appreciation for her great sense of timing.

I looked over at Michael and noticed he wasn't laughing with the rest of us. He was staring at Duchess with a curious intensity. It looked malicious to me.

His fixation on Duchess was interrupted. Dad yelled, "Michael! Can you help guide the truck for the movers so they can get out of here?"

"Sure!" he answered, smiling with the satisfaction of having been given a big responsibility.

I thought about that day in the kitchen with Chucky and Larry when Michael talked about the bloody pussies. I clutched my kitty close to my chest. Duchess crawled up under my neck and meowed into my face, sending kitty breath up my nose. "I love you too!" I cooed back and kissed her pink nose.

CHAPTER TEN

Behind the Masks 1961, Fort Ord, California

W e drove through the gated entrance of Fort Ord and I could not believe my eyes. There were houses all along the streets with kids frolicking on bright green lawns, swinging on swing sets, laughing and playing. Dogs were chasing cats, and fathers and sons actually tossed balls back and forth. I pressed my face against the car window and gazed up into the majestic oak trees that spread over the houses like giant canopies.

"Mom, look," I said, pointing to a kitty being chased by a toy poodle. "Duchess better watch out," I giggled.

"Yes, honey," Mom answered, looking at me through the house plant she was protecting in her lap, "Duchess will be just fine." She then pointed her finger, telling Dad to turn at the next street.

As we went around a bend, a sprawling golf course came into view. Dad turned sharply into our new driveway, causing the car to bounce hard as we went over the curb, and stopped in front of the garage. Staring at the golf course across the street, my heart sank as I envisioned another place for Michael to bury me.

"Here we are!" I heard Dad announce.

"Look, a golf course," Michael noticed, pointing across the street.

"A fence, there's a fence!" I joyfully declared. I was seeing a tall chain link fence running down the edge of the golf course, as far as I could see. And, to my relief, there was barbed wire strung across the top, adding one more layer of protection. I glanced over at Michael and could see only half of his face. His lips were pursed with disappointment.

I noticed the lawn in front of our house was a lot greener than the one next door.

"Wow!" I whispered when I saw the large porch that wrapped clear around to the side.

The movers worked quickly and it only took a couple of hours to unload. As they backed out of the driveway, I held Duchess snug to my chest and lifted her charcoal gray paw so we both could wave goodbye. A Monarch butterfly, with its rust, black and white patterned wings, captured Duchess' attention as it flitted in circles around the top of her white fur crown. The butterfly soon lost interest and flew gracefully to the top of the magenta bougainvillea, a charming wall-climbing flowering plant that blanketed the whole side of the flat-roofed garage.

I turned back towards our new home, walked up the two steps and through the front door, which had been propped open with my copper metal piggy bank, heavy with saved coins. I was sure Michael had put it there just to make me mad. I picked it up and let the door shut, closing off the sunlight that had streamed across the acorn-colored wood floors. My footsteps echoed faintly down the hall. After I came into the living room, Mom and Dad showed me the bedroom I would share with Michael. I was surprised by how large it was, with plenty of space between the twin beds, which were arranged side by side, with a window in the middle.

The first thing I did was make my bed. Creating the visual gratification of having the bedspread completely smooth and free of wrinkles was one part of my life I could control. I opened my dresser and took perfectly-folded socks and underwear out of my duffel bag. I placed them in the drawer, careful that they would lay together in measured rows. Once my clothes were unpacked, I began making a bed for Duchess. Dad had already cut off the top of a box for me to use, and I neatly lined it with some old pillowcases.

During the next month, I learned to play Monopoly and was amazed by the colors and designs on the game board. I loved the pastel shades of the play money. My favorite part of the game was when we got to choose our markers. There were so many to choose from. I always picked the little dog because it was the most real-looking. The intricate etchings engraved into the metal looked just like doggie fur. After we'd finish a game, I would sneak the marker into my palm, hide it in my pocket and then, when I was alone, I would pull it out and study it with amazement.

Fascination with the Monopoly pieces marked the beginning of my trinket collection. Whenever I was overwhelmed and confused about the things Michael would make me do, I would go into our bedroom closet and sit on the floor with my trinkets clasped in my hands. I would sit there and hum the happy songs we were learning in school. The melody from *"Mares eat oats and does eat oats and little lambs eat ivy"* gave me the most comfort. I would envision all the little lambs "baahing" around me, and since I loved Shari Lewis' puppet "Lamb Chop" on the *Ed Sullivan Show*, I would pretend we were together, playing within the safe embrace of the closet walls.

Once in awhile, Michael would come home unexpectedly from hanging out with his friends and I'd sit frozen in the closet, afraid he would find me. One time he brought a friend into the bedroom and they talked about how they had stolen a trench coat from a department store. Fortunately, Michael had hidden it under his bed and not in the closet. The next day I pulled it out and showed it to Mom, leaving out the part that the trench coat had been stolen. Since Michael hadn't known I was in the room when he told his story, I pretended I thought she bought it for him and asked if she could get me one too. It was rare that I could tell on him or get him in trouble without his revenge.

Somehow Mom and Dad found out he had stolen it and this time they put him "on restriction"—he could not go outside nor have any interaction with his friends. It felt good to see Michael punished for things he did wrong, especially when he was caught and punished for something that did not involve me.

Since Michael had his privileges taken away, Dad had more time to spend with me. Usually it was Michael who got to mow the lawn with my dad, but this day he was on restriction. He sat glaring out our bedroom window as my dad showed me how to make straight cuts in the grass so that they would form perfect rows. Mom looked on with a proud smile and gave me the "thumbs up" each time I looked her way, encouraging me to keep pushing the lawn mower. I was covered with sweat and pieces of cut grass and my father was following behind, raking up the grass, when she came out with her special pink lemonade. The three of us sat on the porch like a happy, normal family. Only the eerie face in the window haunted that perfect afternoon.

That day, I got away with my brother not knowing I had tattled. However, the worry and fear that he still might find out began to outweigh the pleasure of seeing him punished.

So I never told on him again.

As the months went by, people started to say Michael looked like a young Elvis Presley. Mom and Dad even let him have the Elvis haircut with the pompadour front. I would watch him as he slid the comb back into the bottom of the pompadour and whip it out create what was called a "waterfall" in those days.

With his lush chocolate brown hair and well-built body, Mom often said, "Michael's a real head-turner." There were times I was jealous of him because of the privileges he was given, since he was older. He was able to stay out late with his friends, all his clothes fit tight to his body, and of course the way he got to style his hair made me long to be older. Until I turned eleven, my own hair—what there was of it—had to be almost shaved off, into what was called "the military brat buzz cut." That was the family rule. I wasn't sure why, but since Michael had to wait until he was eleven to let his hair grow longer, he made a point of making sure my parents were going to make me wait just as long.

When I would come home from the barber shop, Michael would tease me, pointing his finger at me and making funny gestures to imply how horrible I looked. As soon as Dad would leave the room, he would grab me, put me in a head-lock, and rub his knuckles hard across my scalp, teasing me: "Oooh! Look at that … skinned … head!" And he would repeat it over and over, rubbing my head until it was raw. The painful rub was nothing compared to the humiliating torment I felt.

It would take a full week before I stopped walking around like Dracula, avoiding all the mirrors. Every once in awhile I would get to go a couple of weeks without having a haircut. Sneaking some of Michael's hair tonic, I would try to create my own "waterfall" so I could look as cool as my big brother.

Mom would go on and on about how handsome Michael was. She got so caught up with his Elvis resemblance that she would let him use her sewing machine to taper, or "peg," his pants so they had the same tight fit Elvis was so famous for.

My entire happiness began to revolve around how *my* hair looked and which of *my* clothes fit the tightest. Even then I loved design.

Unfortunately, Michael noticed my obsession. He suddenly went a whole week after my latest haircut and headlock without teasing me. I was starting to relax, thinking I had finally done some something right to manage to avoid his attention. But then one evening after dinner, he came into our bedroom, pointed at his bed, and told me to take a seat. His bed had always been off limits, so this was a treat in itself. Mom had decorated the room with bright aqua-colored bedspreads and matching curtains which hung on the window at the foot of our beds.

"I hope I can tell you a secret," Michael said quietly. "If I tell you, you promise you won't tell?"

I watched his eyes stare into mine and I felt a sense of excitement.

Nodding anxiously, I tried to assure him: "I can keep a secret!"

"Well, I don't know, this is really big …" he teased.

"I can keep a secret, Michael. Really! I *can*!"

"OK," he said, walking over to the maple chest of drawers. He opened the top drawer and took something out. I heard a crackling sound and then I saw it—a half-filled pack of cigarettes!

"Oh no, Michael!" I whispered a little too loudly, with a seven-year-old's conviction of right and wrong. "You're gonna get into *so* much trouble if Mom and Dad find out you have those!"

"Shhh," Michael hushed me, putting his finger to his lips. "They're not going to find out and you know why?"

"No …" I replied in a hushed tone, my eyes glued to the pack of cigarettes.

"Because this is going to be our little secret. You just told me you could keep a secret, didn't you?" He put his hand on my shoulder and gave it a gentle squeeze.

Shocked by seeing the symbol of the camel on the package, I nervously asked, "Are those *Dad's* cigarettes?"

"Yes," he admitted, releasing his hand from my shoulder. "But I won't have to take Dad's anymore because I have a friend who's older; he can get me as many packs as I want."

He walked over to the window and slid it open. Then he reached into his front pant pocket, took out a book of matches, and lit one of the cigarettes. His full lips puckered around the tip, causing the end to turn bright red. As he inhaled, his mouth protruded like a fish and his jaws slowly clicked up and down, silently sending out perfect little smoke rings, one at a time.

"Wow! How did you do that?"

"It's easy," he said, bringing another cigarette out from the pack. "You wanna try?"

"Really? You'd let me?" I asked hopefully. As always, I was fantasizing that my big brother and I might become friends, and, if not friends, at least I could live with him without fearing his every move.

He nodded and carefully slipped the tip of the cigarette into my mouth, whispering, "Now what I want you to do is just puff on it with the outside of your lips so you don't *nigger-lip* it." I was too engrossed at that moment in trying to do it right to wonder, as I did later, *What the heck did* that *mean?*

The heat from the smoke burned my throat and caused me to cough uncontrollably. Tears poured down my cheeks. As soon as I could catch my breath, he would make me take another puff, another, and then another, until I could smoke without coughing. He wanted to make sure that no brother of his would look like a fool.

"Good!" Michael congratulated me, both shocking and thrilling me in the same instant. "You'll be smoking like a champ in no time." He took my half-smoked cigarette, wrapped it in a piece of foil and put it back into his dresser drawer.

"Now…," he announced, walking over to the closet, "I have another surprise for you." He slid the closet door open and reached in and brought out a pair of my long pants. He held them up to show me that the flair on the muted green pant legs had disappeared. My head was still buzzing from the cigarettes, so I wasn't sure I could believe my eyes—but it was true—my little pants had been pegged!

"Wow!" I screamed, running in place.

Michael immediately put his forefinger to his lips, now our code for "Quiet!"

"I don't believe it!" I whisper-shouted. "I don't believe it! You did that for me? Can I try them on, can I?" I gurgled with excitement.

Michael handed them over to me as if they were made out of gold.

I undid my belt and felt the bagginess of my pants fall to the floor. I sat down on the bed, the way I had seen Michael do many times. They were so tight, that was the only way you could pull them on. I stood and zipped them up.

"Perfect!" I whooped, and crawled onto the bed so I could stand up and see into the dresser mirror. I balanced myself on the mattress so that the mirror reflected the tight fit around my skinny calves. "Perfect! Perfect! Perfect! You're the best brother ever, Michael!" Staring at myself, I turned one way and then the other, and gushed, "The best! The best! The best!"

"OK, Donnie. Get down," he said with a strange grin, one I had never seen before. "Now you have to do something for me ..."

"Anything, Michael, anything! You're the best brother ever!"

He made some movement that caught my eye. Automatically, I looked down. I saw his hand squeezing his crotch.

My brother turned around and opened the bedroom door to look down the hallway and make sure Mom and Dad were still watching television. He softly closed the door and grabbed his crotch again.

He walked back over to the bed, pulled his pants down and pushed them to his ankles. A small patch of black hair glistened at the base of his erection. He began to stroke himself as he told me what he wanted me to do. It sounded so weird that I froze, not able to comprehend what he was asking of me.

I remember whining ... and asking him how long I'd have to keep it in my mouth.

"So you really don't want to keep those pants, do you?" he asked, breathing hard.

"No! I want the pants. I do! I do!"

"So ... come on ... put your mouth on it." He was moaning softly.

I don't know how long I was down there, but just as I identified that the odor emanating from his crotch was similar to Duchess' breath, he exploded in my mouth. I gagged as he pushed my head down, *hard*, and then let out a guttural moan. When he released my head, I looked up at him and started to yell, "You peed in my mouth!" But he cupped my mouth with his hand so my words of shock were swallowed up into his palm.

He jerked my head back and locked his eyes on mine with the look that implicitly threatened: "Shut up or I'll hurt you!" His pupils turned totally black. I knew I needed to calm myself down. I ordered my body to fall limp and in that same moment, I submissively nodded my head. All I could think of was how much I wanted to get to the bathroom and wash out my mouth. The second he released me, I shoved myself away from the bed and staggered out of the room.

I rushed into the bathroom and wiped what I thought was urine away from my mouth, turned, and closed the door. I knelt down along the side of the bathtub, reaching over to turn on the cold water. I stretched my torso horizontally so I could get my mouth under the chrome faucet. The pale pink bathmat kept slipping from underneath my feet, so I impatiently kicked it off to the side. Over and over again, I flooded my mouth and rinsed until the bitter, salty taste began to subside. I turned off the faucet and stood up and slid the bathmat back into place. My tongue still held the bitterness and I wondered if it would ever go away.

When I looked down, I noticed how the cotton candy pink rug complemented the pea green tone of my pants and thought how pretty the two colors went together. And then I saw the snug fit around my legs and realized that the floppy flair was gone. I sighed with delight. I had pegged pants now ... and would do anything to keep them. I opened the bathroom door and stared at my ankles. I stared at them all the way back to the bedroom.

CHAPTER ELEVEN

Crushed 1963 — 1965, Northern California

I had just turned nine when we moved again. This was my favorite house because I got to have my own room. We were right by one of the base playgrounds; I swung and played on the slides as often as I was allowed.

The neighbors recognized Dad from the military night club where he was thought of as a celebrity. He adored the attention and my mom adored him for gaining it. It did not take long for my parents to start having fun with their new group of friends, most of whom earned quite a bit more. They found themselves spending money they really didn't have at the Club and on extravagant shopping sprees, trying hard to quench their shared "addiction to vanity."

The first big spending spree came only about a month after we moved in. I remember early one Saturday afternoon I was in the living room watching cartoons when my parents came barreling through the front door.

"We shouldn't have done it!" Mom cried to Dad. It was a sight to see— her arms were filled with bags, and as she dropped them one by one onto the living room couch, intense joy danced over her rouge-covered cheeks. "I can't wait to try it on," she said with guilty delight as she pulled out one of the boxes.

"Mommy, what's in all these packages?" I demanded to know as I stepped in front of her, trying to get her attention. Before she could give me an answer I heard Dad's voice calling me from the front door.

"Donnie!" My name echoed from the hallway as he exploded into the room carrying even more packages. "Here, take these,"—two small bags were dangling from his large hands. I grabbed them and watched him lumber over to the couch and release the rest of the packages. They seemed to slide in slow motion out of his arms. Mingling with the others, they almost blanketed the entire three-piece sofa.

"I still can't believe we spent all that money! We're crazy fools!" Mom exclaimed as she pulled open a box to lift out a black knit dress covered with small black sparkling beads. Holding it way up and shaking it, she giggled as the many shimmering, teardrop-shaped beads jiggled into an orchestra of happy clicks.

"Wow, Mommy ... that's so p-r-e-t-t-y!" I cried out loud.

She brought the dress down and squeezed it to her chest, taking in a deep breath and then exhaled an excited, "I just love it! I'm going to go try it on right now!" She was already halfway into her room.

I rummaged through the mountain of bags and found a small white box, contemplating whether or not to open it. I could see Dad from the corner of my eye and turned to watch him pull out a creamy white dinner jacket from a large box. He held up his present to himself, admiring it with the same enthusiasm Mom had over hers. Just as he started to say something, she came parading back into the room.

"What do you think?" Mom asked, taking a twirl with one hand on each hip.

Carefully laying his jacket over the couch, Dad reached down and took the small box from my hand and proudly announced, "This is what makes the whole outfit!" And like he was a magician ... a diamond necklace appeared, swinging from his hand.

"Let me put it on," he said as he walked over and stood behind his lovely wife, my mother.

The choker of diamonds—actually very expensive rhinestones—was divided in half by a sunburst of larger pear-shaped stones which rested perfectly in the center of her neck. With her short black hair brushed up all around her hairline and the soft lazy waves that framed her face, I thought she was the most beautiful woman in the world.

"Gorgeous! You look gorgeous!" Dad boasted as he stepped back to stand beside me, letting out a long wolf whistle. "Doesn't she look beautiful?"

There we were, father and son, standing side by side, staring with complete awe at the most important woman in both our lives. She was our rock, our strength, and we both loved her unconditionally.

After five months of living high on the hog, my parents found out that nothing in the world could deliver them from the wrath of their first-born. On the day before Michael was to start back to the eighth grade, he and his friend Daryl stole Dad's Chevy Impala, intending to drive it to San Francisco, over a hundred miles away. As luck would have it, they were picked up for running a red light.

I stood beside Dad, holding his hand, as the police car drove up to the front of our house that night and let Michael out. The silent fury Dad exhibited when the police told him they had impounded his car and it would cost a hundred bucks to retrieve it was something I'd never forget. There was no yelling, only his strong voice telling Michael to go to his room. The next day Dad took him to the barber to get his head shaved. The moment he entered the house, I saw his brown eyes had already become that now-familiar stone-cold black. They were in striking contrast to the almost-white, bald shadow which had replaced the lush dark "waterfall" of wavy hair I once had envied.

I believe this was the day my brother determined to destroy my father.

Michael stopped having conversations with our parents. He began to hang out with a new group of friends who were older and had a strange wildness about them. They wore clothes with holes in them, smelled like drunks, and talked too loud when people on the street passed. Mom said they were just like Eddie Haskell from *Leave it to Beaver* on TV—nice to your face, but somehow you knew they were up to something. Time after time, Mom and Dad were called down to the police station because Michael and his buddies had gotten caught for doing something illegal. Because of his shoplifting binges and the numerous days of skipping school, they decided we needed to move yet again, to a different neighborhood, so they could get Michael away from what they called his "hoodlum friends."

Although the move was only three miles down the hill, this put us in a new school district. And since the new house was in a cul-de-sac where most of the neighbors were higher-ranking officers, the rent we had to pay was a lot higher than before. This put a serious strain on our budget.

The malignancy of Michael's behavior began to take a toll on each of us. The new school and new friends did not distract him from abusing me, nor from treating my parents like they were invisible. There was an incessant feeling pervading the house now—a sense something terrible might happen any minute—and I was not the only one feeling it.

Soon my parents could not afford the diversion of shopping sprees and frequent fancy evenings out at the club. Even when they did go out, the fun was no longer deadening the pain. When they came home after a long day at work they turned to vodka and whiskey. Dad would pick up a pint of Mom's favorite, Smirnoff's, and a pint of Calvert's for himself, and together they would cook dinner, discuss work, flirt, and solve the problems of the world. Drinking seemed to help for a while. And they did not need an excuse—this was still the '60's and the "cocktail hour" was standard for many.

For eight months in the new neighborhood Michael stayed out of trouble. So it was a shock when our parents made an announcement one night at dinner that we would be moving again. The shock deepened when they admitted that this time they were the ones who had gotten into trouble—they were deep in debt from their reckless spending and the higher rent. The only solution was to move away from the military base to a less expensive house. They had already found the place and informed Michael and me that we would be moving at the end of the month.

I was ten years old. When we went to see the new house, it seemed like we drove and drove before turning off the highway into a small community that consisted of six blocks of houses, with each street dead-ending into miles of sand dunes. The name of the community was Moss Landing. The neighborhood was well known for the large cemetery that lined one side. And, of course, the cheaper houses were the ones with their backyards facing the rolling hills of gravestones. A blanket of fog hovered over the stark white grave markers as our family stared past the broken-down wooden fence that separated us from what looked like a movie set for a horror film.

As we turned to go into the house, Michael came up behind me and whispered in my ear, "I think this is going to be my favorite house. Ever!" And then he groaned with a low growl, literally dripping saliva down the back of my neck.

I was a year older but still under Michael's spell of terror, so I continued to retreat to the closet with my trinkets, doing my best to stay out of Michael's way.

Two weeks after we arrived, I met two sisters who lived down the street from us. I thought they were lucky; they didn't live on the side with the cemetery. Judy and Stella were two years apart. Judy had just turned fourteen and Stella was almost seventeen. They were as different as day and night. Judy was on the small side with long chestnut brown hair that hung down to her waist. Her hazel green eyes changed color depending upon what she wore. We hit it off right away and she told me I could be the little brother she had always wanted.

Stella, on the other hand, treated me like I had some sort of disease. I overheard her say once, "Little boys are nothing but germ carriers!" She was taller and heavier than Judy and her almost-black hair was cut short, with long straight pieces plastered along her full cheeks. Her bangs rested along the top of thick black eyelashes which framed the darkest brown eyes I'd ever seen. Unlike Judy's, they were slightly beady and shifty. Whenever she would look at me through her veil of bangs, I felt like she was scanning me for bugs.

The more I went to their house to play with Judy, the more they felt like family. At fourteen Judy still enjoyed playing with her Barbie dolls. The first time she showed me her collection, she lifted up an unopened box which was covered in a camouflage pattern.

"Here, Donnie," she said, placing the box in my lap. "His name is GI Joe and he's Barbie's boyfriend."

I held up the box and glared at him through the clear cellophane window. "It looks like you've never opened him up," I muttered, fumbling with the box. "Can I take him out?"

"Sure," she said, struggling to get the hot pink sequined top over her Barbie's protruding chest.

After I rescued Barbie's boyfriend from his place of confinement, I held him up and turned him over and examined his green and black fatigues. "Where are his *other* outfits?"

"That's the only one," Judy answered nonchalantly, and continued putting the finishing touches on Barbie.

"What? He has only one outfit?" I blurted out. "No wonder you never opened the box."

How boring, I thought, and returned Barbie's boyfriend back to his box.

One of the boys Michael liked best in our new neighborhood was interested in Stella as a girlfriend. His name was Terrence but everyone called him "Tarzan." I didn't understand why until he came over to see Michael one afternoon. As he rode his bicycle up our driveway, he bellowed out a loud jungle call to alert Michael that he was outside. Dad was in the living room reading the newspaper when he heard the bizarre sound.

I could hear him shout, "What the hell is that?"

An instant later Michael came running through the living room, announcing, "Oh that's just Terrance. He thinks he's Tarzan," and blasted out the door.

At Judy's the next day, she told me that Stella, Tarzan and Michael had discovered an old abandoned barn across the highway. Sitting like a pyramid in the center of the barn were stacks of hay piled up so densely that the teenagers had constructed little rooms within them. Not long after Judy shared their description with me, the trio invited her to see the hideaway. They were so proud of it that Michael didn't even seem to care that I had tagged along.

The dash across the highway was a challenge for me, because I could not run as fast as everyone else. Tarzan seemed to be the one in charge, so we followed him, single file, to the back side of the barn. Most of the building was a dark pink color; the traditional dark barn-red now faded with age. A row of old wooden slats along the back barn door were cracked just enough for all of us to squeeze through, except for Stella, who knocked off a board just as she stepped inside.

Somehow we ended up standing in a circle and all of us simultaneously looked over at Tarzan. His eyes opened wide, his mouth opened even wider, and out came the familiar "A-h-a-h-a-h-e-h-a-h-a-h-a-e-h!"

It's funny to think of him wailing at the top of his lungs into the rafters and none of us giving it a second thought. He was just being Tarzan.

After he finished his daily auditory christening, we followed him as he crawled up on a ledge of haystacks and disappeared into a cave-like opening. There were several hollowed out spaces with bales of hay staggered one on top of another, creating tunnels connecting room to room. One of the rooms was almost tall enough to stand up in. On our way out of the biggest room, I overheard Michael say he was going to bring some army blankets from home and spread them out so everyone could lie down.

On our way out of the tunnel, Tarzan began to tell Judy and me about an old man who had almost caught them the week before, when they were all inside the pyramid of hay bales.

"The old man—must be the owner—actually, we never saw him so we don't know if he's old. But he sounded old … right, Michael?" Tarzan asked. Receiving a nod, he continued, "We heard him yell *'Who's in here?'* Oh my God, we were so scared! We just sat there inside the big room and stared at each other, frozen with fear. And then he yelled again!"

Both Judy's and my eyes were as big as saucers as we leaned into each other and hung onto every word.

Tarzan lowered his head and finished, "Thank goodness he gave up and left."

"Boo!" Michael screamed in our ears as he grabbed Judy and me from behind.

"Ahhh!" We both yelled and fell into each other's arms. That was the first time I noticed what must have been the sweet smell of Judy's perfume. My nose sank deep into her neck, filling my innocent ten-year-old nostrils with the sensual scent of exotic flowers. My head felt dizzy as I pulled away, unaware that I was experiencing a moment little boys never forget—the onset of my first crush.

CHAPTER TWELVE

Michael's Powers 1964, Northern California

A week had passed since our barn adventure and I was hurrying to finish up my Saturday morning chores so I could get over to Judy's. We had planned an afternoon down at the sand dunes and we didn't want to get off to a late start. Just as I got out to the sidewalk, I heard Michael come running up behind me.

"Going to see Judy?" he asked, catching up to me and then slowing down to match my pace.

"Yep," I answered, staring straight ahead.

"So what do you two do together? You know she is awfully pretty ... you're sure she's not your girlfriend?"

"Leave me alone! I'm not bothering you."

"So you do like her—I knew it!" he chortled, stepping in front of me.

"Let me by," I begged, my head dropping in embarrassment. I stared down at the sidewalk and noticed a large crack that ran in a perfect diagonal. *"Step on a crack and you break your mother's back,"* raced through my mind.

"It's OK if you like a girl. And anyway, she's got some nice titties on her."

"S-t-o-p it!" I cried back.

"All right, little brother ... but I just can't stop thinking about those titties. Maybe I'll come by later and pay you two a visit."

"No!" I shouted. "She doesn't like you! Stay away!" And then I bent forward, dropping my head down like a bull, and charged past him down the street.

"I'll s-e-e you la-ter, Donnie!" His sing-song voice was no cover for the implied threat—not to me, not anymore. That wicked sound echoed all the way down the street to Judy's house.

I knocked on her front door. When she opened it, I could see she was ready for our day at the beach.

"I'll be back later," she yelled to her mother, who peeked into the hallway, probably wanting to see who was there.

"Don't be too late, honey." Her mother's voice faded away as she softly closed the door.

Michael's "titties" comments were still bothering me for most our walk. I found myself only halfway listening to Judy as we went through the motions of our usual small talk.

Reaching the edge of the dunes, we both looked up at the solid blue sky and blazing sun. We shaded our eyes with our hands and remained quiet, not needing to comment about the obvious—a beautiful sunny day.

Judy immediately zeroed in on a long wooden log that had been placed in front of a pile of charred wood. She took three gazelle leaps and then spun around to sit down. I watched her slip off her shoes and found myself looking at her in a way I had never done before. The pounding in my head remained as I recalled Michael's lewd comments about how pretty she was and her already-developed breasts.

"He can't hurt her!" The voice in my mind shouted. *"He can't!"*

The crashing waves and Judy's joyous giggles finally drowned out the phantom scenarios painfully playing on the movie screen of my mind.

Hours flew by as we laughed and ran over the sand dunes looking for gullies to shield us from the ocean winds. I was a lovesick puppy, falling harder and harder for the fantasy girlfriend I had created in my mind, a secret she would never know.

Over the next few days, whenever I was at Judy's, Michael would show up and pretend he was there to hang out with Stella. Each time, he acted unusually nice, behaving like a perfect gentleman.

He was so consistent that I began to think he actually *might* be changing. He had even stopped dragging me over to the cemetery to roam the graves when our parents were not home. But my reverie of "the new Michael" was shattered as I put it together: the last time there, he made me walk on a newly-dug grave, and when I stepped into the softened soil, I was so frightened, I peed in my pants. Michael probably figured that explaining to my mom how my pants got soiled was more hassle than his terrorizing me was worth.

The more time Michael spent at Judy's house, the more I could see she was becoming mesmerized by his charm. She only wanted to talk about him; I realized she was slipping further away from me. She would ask me over and over again if he had said anything about her. This got to be so annoying I would make something up, just so she would stop asking.

And becoming equally obvious to me was that Michael had a plan to steal her innocence. I knew it was beginning to work when she started ratting the top of her hair and wearing heavy eye make-up. But the worst change was the white glossy lipstick that made her look like she had forgotten to wipe her mouth after drinking a glass of milk.

With her new look and efforts to act older, I knew I was losing her.

On the morning of the first day of summer vacation, Michael stopped me in the hallway after I finished eating breakfast.

"Donnie!" he called from his room as I came down the hall. I was startled by the familiar manipulating voice; I had just been trying to figure out how long it had been since he last picked on me.

"Hey there, little brother, I have a job for you to do."

"Oh?" I replied, avoiding looking at him.

He came out of his room and directed me up against the hall wall and put both his hands behind me, creating a cage with his body.

"Don't you want to know what your job is going to be?"
I looked away and stayed quiet.

"Oh, that's OK if you don't answer; you just need to listen anyway. I want you to go across the highway and wait for me inside the barn."

"What!" I shouted, looking into his eyes. "I can't do that. What if that old man comes? I can't be in there all by myself!"

"Pow!" Michael slapped the wall behind me with both his hands. "I guess you want to go over and visit the ghouls today," he said, staring down at me. "Let's see ... how long has it been since we've been over to visit the ghouls? That's right, you little shithead, if you don't do as I say, I'll just bury you there ... and leave you."

I started to cry thinking about the graves nearby … and the one he had "built" for me back in Marina.

"Is that what you want?" Then he added snidely, "You know I'll do it, don't you?"

"Yes, Michael, I know," I whimpered, sliding down to the floor while looking up into his growling face.

He grabbed my shirt, pulled me up from the floor, and began to dictate his plan to me. "You will go to the barn and wait for me and Judy. You will wait in the big room until I get there. Then you will be the lookout for the old man or anyone else while I'm inside the pyramid with Judy."

I knew it, I thought as I fearfully listened, *he's working his special powers on Judy.*

"You got that?" he sneered, letting go of my shirt.

I shook my head yes and wiped away the stream of tears covering my face. Dazed with fear, I managed to get my jacket on and walk briskly out the front door. The barn was about four blocks away; I decided to walk by Judy's house on the way. Through the big picture window, I could see her and Stella standing in their living room, having what looked like an intense conversation. I studied Judy talking and wondered what she and Michael were planning to do at the barn. The sisters both stopped talking at the same time and looked out the window.

I took off at a run, hoping they hadn't seen me.

Once I got across the highway, I slipped through the wooden slats and stood looking up into the barn's high rafters.

"Whew!" I said out loud, smelling the strong stench of cow manure. I quickly held my nose and then, out from nowhere, a loud "M-o-o!" blared out a few feet from me.

I jumped and was almost out the door before I spotted a cow standing by itself in a stall behind me. Relieved, I stopped and took a deep breath, realizing everything was alright. I continued walking back toward the pyramid and then managed to crawl up on the bales of hay, finding my way into the big room. The entire floor of hay was covered with army blankets so I decided to take a seat and rest against one of the walls of golden straw. My eyes traveled along the frayed border of scratchy wool and I noticed, tucked into the corner, a nest of baby mice. In a flash, their mother appeared, leaping on top of them while glaring up at me with her pink beady eyes.

"I'm not going to hurt you," I started to say when I heard Michael's voice calling my name.

"Donnie! Donnie! Where are you?"

I pulled the blanket up against the nest and leapt up, answering, "I'm right here, Michael," and made my way out to the tunnel.

"Are you sure this is OK?" I heard Judy ask in a quivering voice. "It's a little scary. And what if that old man comes in?"

"Judy, I told you, that's why Donnie's here, so he can be our lookout."

I paused, listening to them, and then moved around the corner to find Michael kissing Judy hard on the lips. Seeing this, I felt like the roof of the barn had completely collapsed right on top of me. I shook my head a couple of times, cleared my throat, and happily interrupted: "I'm right here, Michael."

"Oh Donnie," Michael responded with a sly smile. "What I want you to do is stand here and keep a lookout and let me know if that old man or anyone else comes."

He bent down, taking a step in front of Judy, so he could talk to me face to face.

"If anyone *does* come, just call me and don't come back to the room. You got that?"

I nodded. And then, as if he had practiced his next line, he said, "I have the best little brother ever," and patted me on the head like I was his little puppy. I watched him turn and place his hand in the small of Judy's back, guiding her towards the cave opening. They crawled in together and disappeared.

The thought of Michael burying me in the cemetery flashed through my mind, sending a chill over me as I kept watch. A heavy fog had rolled in after Michael and Judy arrived, making it difficult for me to see if anyone was coming.

A cat's meow sounded in the distance. Out of the darkness emerged a tabby-colored cat, slinking towards me like she was walking out from a smoke-filled dream.

"Here, kitty, kitty," I called, holding out my hand, hoping to fool her into coming over for something to eat. I reached further through the opening and stroked her furry spine all the way to the end of her snakeskin-patterned tail. She obviously forgave me for pretending to have food, because she let me pick her up. She nudged her gray and white striped face under my chin.

"I wish I really did have something for you to eat," I whispered, hearing her motor start to purr. The way she melted into my arms brought back memories of Duchess.

Michael had killed Duchess by chasing her into the street during heavy traffic, while I was in the front yard playing. That was his way of getting even with her. He had taken her up onto the flat roof over the garage and thrown her off to see if she would land on her feet. She not only landed on her feet, but as Michael was crawling down off the ladder, Duchess waited until he got to the last step, and bit into his bare foot. I knew at that moment that he would find a way to kill her.

By the time the driver slammed on the brakes to try to avoid hitting her, it was already too late. Duchess was thrown like a rag doll and landed on the sidewalk in front of our garage. All I remember is screaming and running into the house. Michael went into the garage and got a blanket and wrapped her in it. When Mom and Dad came home, they believed what he told them about the accident; I knew better.

"You stay away from the highway," I told my new friend, kissing the back of her ears.

"Stop it!" I suddenly heard Judy scream from inside the pyramid. "I said, stop it!" she cried again. "Donnie, help me!" The echo of her voice careened through the rafters.

I carefully set the kitty down and hurried my way through the tunnel. When I got to the big room, I saw Judy half-standing with her arms crisscrossed over her bare breasts, searching for her clothes. Michael stood behind her, shirtless, with his pants hanging off his waist and dangling her bra in the air.

"I told you not to come back here!" Michael grunted at me through his teeth. "Now get out of here!"

He dropped Judy's white padded bra down on the blanket and reached for his blue flannel shirt. I knew I should get away but I couldn't stop staring at Judy. What I saw made me feel sick to my stomach. As I turned to leave I saw one of Judy's rosy pink nipples pop out from underneath one arm. The way her breasts were mashed against her chest looked like two white deflated rubber balls. I was surprised ... I felt so disgusted.

The whole scenario of Michael using his powers to make Judy like him haunted me as I crawled my way through the tunnel and out into the light.

A chorus of meows greeted me as I exited the barn.

"You have to stay here and not go near the highway," I said to the kitty, pointing my finger with authority. She looked at me like she understood every word and then took off running after something that had stolen her attention.

Just as I got to the highway, I turned around and looked back to see Michael and Judy appear, slipping out from the wooden slats.

The kitty had traversed the field beside the barn and perched herself on a large mound of dirt. She sat back on her haunches, posed like a statue, and peered back at the array of unexpected strangers leaving her turf.

A bundle of mist floated mystically across the mound, slowly covering her like a heavy curtain closing on a final act.

CHAPTER THIRTEEN

Hurricane of Bad Luck

1964, Northern California—1965, Southern California

I was almost eleven. I do not think my parents had taught me to be superstitious, but under my brother's influence, it seemed natural. I started to believe that living next door to a field of the dead might have caused the hurricane of bad luck that came blowing through our house. After living in that house for less than a year, Dad was hit the hardest.

It was three o'clock in the afternoon when I saw Dad's car pull into the driveway. *It is Monday,* I reminded myself. *Why is he home so early? Maybe he has a surprise!*

I jumped off the couch and hollered, "M-o-m-m-y!" as I sprinted down the hallway.

My mother had just finished a load of laundry and was in her bedroom folding the last batch of whites.

"Dad's home!" I announced, pouncing on their bed, but carefully avoiding the neat stacks of clothes. She was opening and closing the dresser drawers, methodically placing underwear and socks into them.

"He's home already?" Mom gasped, automatically turning to the dresser mirror to see how she looked. She spent just a moment fingering the loose curls around her face and then made a quick exit.

I got up off the bed, still careful not to disrupt Mom's system. Just as I turned the corner, I saw Mom and Dad holding onto each other in the middle of the dining room. I stopped, puzzled—it wasn't their natural "welcome home" hug. I decided to take a few steps back so they couldn't see me.

Dad sounded like he was going to cry as he spoke. I was mesmerized; I had never seen my father cry. He was saying that he had to quit his job and that he was lucky they didn't put him in jail. I heard something about "mishandling of funds," but I didn't know what that meant.

"Well, then I guess we'll go ahead with our plans to move," Mom said gently, grasping the side of Dad's arm.

"And you know what, Betty?" Dad's usual strong baritone seemed to falter. "It's not all bad … at least they said I'll be getting an Honorable Discharge."

They continued their embrace, in silence. The sight of them together in the hallway, both in tears, inspired fear in me. Suddenly, the doorbell rang, and I thought of Dad's words moments before, about going to jail. I was sure the police were there to take him away. So it wasn't a surprise to me when I looked out the living room picture window and saw a police car parked in front of our house. With a sense of doom, I turned back and saw Mom follow behind Dad. They opened the door together.

"Mr. Don English?" a policeman asked.

My dad nodded his head, "Is there a problem, Sir?"

The policeman was taller than Dad and had a big book in his hand. He opened it and asked if they knew where their son Michael was.

"No," Dad replied, turning back to look at Mom with a questioning look.

"Well, I'm afraid your son has been arrested for knocking down two old women and snatching their purses."

"Oh my God, that's unthinkable!" Mom blurted out, covering her mouth with her hands.

"All they probably had was their money from Social Security," Dad said sullenly, shaking his head and staring down at the officer's boots, planted firmly on the front door steps.

"One of the victims suffered a heart attack and has been hospitalized. The outcome—whether or not Mrs. Garrison lives—will determine what your son gets charged with." Both my parents were aghast.

Mom managed to find a piece of paper and quickly wrote down what the policeman was saying about where they were holding Michael and what my parents needed to do. The policemen left and Dad shut the door. He turned to Mom, sadly pounding out each word, "Where did we go wrong, Betty? Where did we go wrong?" Mom stood stoically beside him and shrugged her shoulders, chewing frantically on her lips painted with her candy apple red lipstick.

I dashed back to the couch and could see the officers were still standing outside their car, smoking cigarettes. As I watched them, I could hear Mom and Dad in the kitchen, mixing drinks. The familiar noise of cocktail glasses clanking and the golden amber and the crystal clear liquors flowing over crackling ice resounded all the way into the living room.

"Donnie?" I heard Dad call from the kitchen.

"Yes, Daddy?" I answered, getting up from the couch.

Mom and Dad came through the kitchen door with their droopy eyes totally fixed on me. I reluctantly turned from the window and shuffled my way over to them.

"Sit down, son," he said, pointing to the sofa. Dad quietly began to explain what was going on.

He couldn't hide the sadness in his voice as he told me about losing his job. After he finished the painful confession, he stared down into his drink and stirred the ice slowly with his forefinger. "Our next step," he said, continuing to stir, "is to move down to Southern California, to a place called San Bernardino. Your mother and I have heard through the grapevine that there are a lot more jobs there."

"A fresh start," Mom interjected, looking at me and trying to hold back her tears. She downed the rest of her drink, stood up, and went back into the kitchen.

When I told Judy the next day about what had happened with Michael, she seemed relieved. She said she never wanted to see him again. I felt like strutting around the house, knowing that Michael could not pop out and terrorize me. However, my relief and glee about having Michael out of the house were soon overshadowed by the dark, dreadful moods my parents were in. Their gloom affected me, and I began to feel like we were running out of places to escape. Although physically absent, my brother's presence still loomed—his unspoken terrible deeds making us anxious and uneasy.

A few weeks later, it was just the three of us who packed up the car and waved goodbye to the two nice men in the Mayflower moving truck. This was the first time we moved anywhere without Michael. He had been sentenced to six months in a juvenile detention center. When I heard he was being taken to "somewhere north of San Francisco," I thought to myself, *Wow, Michael kept wanting to go to San Francisco— I wonder if he got to see any of it on the way ...*

Even with Michael gone, the bad luck continued. My dad's eighty-year-old mother was dying. We moved again, but this time to Long Beach, so we could live closer to my grandmother. My parents' frantic search through the rental ads in the newspaper paid off—they found a place that came rent-free for the manager. They decided this would be a perfect job for my mother. Fortunately, she was hired without a hitch and we moved in. The complex consisted of fifteen units in a two-story brick building, with stairs leading up to a rooftop deck.

Dad, however, discovered that without a formal education, twenty years in the military didn't mean a thing; yet the extra income was desperately needed. He was only 50 years old, sent out into civilian life, and branded in his own mind as a failure. After searching for two months, he finally found a job—driving a taxicab. It seemed that was one of the only jobs he was qualified for. This sent him into a serious depression.

I did my best to enjoy every single minute of the six months Michael was gone. When he got out of detention and joined us in Long Beach, he was happy to see our father suffer. He had never forgiven my dad for shaving off his Elvis-like waterfall hair. I hated that Michael reveled in Dad's humiliation. Once again, I feared that he was planning to hurt our father. If there was one thing I had already learned about Michael, it was that you never, ever crossed him.

Never.

With Mom not working, except for managing the apartments, she began to drink in the morning and stayed drunk the whole day. Tenants complained from time to time when she would approach them smelling of alcohol, slurring her words and babbling on, not making any sense. Ironically, her impaired state was not what caused her to get fired; it was Michael's.

Hallucinating from sniffing glue, Michael believed he was Superman. He went up to the second story flat roof and began walking along the edge like it was a tightrope. Dad was now at work. Just when I got home, the tenant from Apt. 3 came running up to tell me that Mom was drunk and, with a butcher knife in hand, had chased Michael up to the roof. "She was yelling something about him stealing money from her wallet," Apt. 3 reported hastily, not wanting to miss any of the action. But when I found Mom, she was staring up the side of the building and shouting at Michael to come down. She was not on the roof and the knife she held in her hand was not a butcher knife; it was a dull cake spatula.

By the time the police arrived, Michael was standing on one foot on the six-inch wide ledge, singing the Beatles' song "Hard Day's Night" at the top of his lungs. He'd locked the door to the roof, so the officers had to remain on the street as they attempted to coax him down. Several tenants were mingling nearby, absorbed in the drama, and no doubt exchanging all kinds of rumors back and forth.

Coaxing wasn't working. "We're going to call in for more police officers if you don't come down this instant!" one of the officers roared through a bullhorn. Michael stopped singing the Beatles song and hollered, drawing out each word, *"OK, Mr. Policeman! Here I come, ready or not!"* as he prepared to jump.

Everyone gasped.

"Fooled ya!" he yelled, stepping back onto the roof. "OK, OK," he laughed, and then called, "I'll be down in a minute."

Michael finally appeared, sauntering through the front door of the apartment's foyer.

I hid behind one of the cypress bushes that flanked the apartment building's entrance and listened to the strict lecture the policemen gave my mother and brother.

I watched my mother twitching her arms, finding it hard to stand upright without swaying.

"You son of a bitch!" my mother screamed at Michael, when he told the officers she was a drunk.

"Well then, that makes *you* a 'bitch,' since you're my mother, doesn't it?" He was enjoying provoking her.

"Now stop it!" The chubby officer ordered them both, but had to grab my mother's arm to block the slap she was about to deliver.

It took a good five minutes for the officers to get Mom and Michael to stop yelling at each other, threatening them both with arrest if they did not settle down and make up. The threat worked. Michael went for a walk and Mom went back into the apartment. Before Dad got home, the two of them came to me as nice as could be and told me not to tell Dad about what happened with the police. Coming up with this lie together was the first time I ever saw Mom join sides with Michael in wrongdoing. I was devastated.

The next couple of hours felt like ten, as I waited for Dad. When he walked through the door, he could tell something was not right. Mom was walking around the apartment, staggering less than she had been a few hours before, but her speech was still a bit slurred. That part was normal, but the way Michael was helping her in the kitchen and their being nice to each other? That was not normal.

Dad looked at them, eyebrows raised, like he'd walked into the wrong apartment. "Donnie," he quickly said, "let's go to the store."

"OK!" I exclaimed, picking up my jacket. I turned around to see Mom and Michael standing together.

"I'm almost out of vodka," Mom called to Dad. Catching my stare and then squinting, she gave me a hard look, adding, "Donnie, you be a good boy now."

It was not until we pulled up to the store that I decided to tell Dad about Mom, the knife, and Michael acting like Superman. He reached for the key and turned off the ignition. When we got out of the car, he came to me and leaned down, studying my eleven-year-old face, with his brows knitted together.

"Donnie, I pretty much know what's happening," he assured me, lightly holding the outside of my shoulders. "But you keep letting me know anyway."

"OK, Daddy," I responded, feeling helpful.

We walked into the store. I clasped my father's hand, hoping he would forget Mom's bottle of vodka.

The proverbial winds of bad luck continued to blow, with Michael taking over the helm of the household. Just seventeen years old, and he had already driven a divisive wedge into our parents' eighteen years of marriage. Then he found the key to domination.

Soon after his balancing act on the roof, Michael discovered that our father, as they put it back then, "had homosexual tendencies." He threatened to reveal everything he knew. I overheard an argument Michael and Dad were having outside of Dad's car one brisk winter evening.

"I saw you kiss a guy," Michael said, jeering.

I found it hard to understand what they were talking about. Dad? Kissing a man? How could Michael have seen something like that? The only place Michael saw Dad was at home. For a moment I thought his special powers might include x-ray vision. When Michael said the word "queer," I thought Dad was going to hit him.

Michael stepped back and laughed in my dad's face. He started to walk away, but then looked back. He could not resist one last taunt: "See you later, *Daddy Queer.*"

After that confrontation, Michael came and went as he pleased. Mom would argue with Dad, saying that he was letting Michael walk all over him, but Dad just hung his head. At the time, I could not really comprehend what Michael was accusing our father of when he called him a "queer." I didn't know what that word meant. And as far as my dad kissing a guy? I couldn't imagine it and didn't want to think about it, so I just dismissed it.

Only a month went by after the kissing argument before Michael was arrested again. This time, he had robbed an appliance store with two other guys. When the police were booking them, Michael escaped. Miraculously, he did it by simply walking casually out of the station. "A damn Houdini!" the captain told my father during their phone conversation. "We took our eyes off him for one minute, and he was gone! A Goddamn escape artist, if you ask me!"

Dad regrettably agreed with the officer and finished their conversation without saying goodbye. I watched him hold the phone to his ear for a moment before putting it down like it was a heavy anchor hanging around his neck.

CHAPTER FOURTEEN

A Broken Heart 1981, Los Altos, California—1965, Southern California

"**A** damn Houdini!" That's what the police had called Michael at seventeen years old, and now he'd gone and done it again, but this time as an accused murderer from a heavily guarded cell.

It had been a month since Mr. Sanders broke into my peaceful world with his news of murder. I sat in my office with my morning cup of hot chocolate, once more listening to Mr. Sanders' voice on the phone. He began, "Mr. English, I'm calling to let you know that Michael has escaped."

"What? How?" I asked, almost in disbelief. My blood immediately began pulsating with the fear that he might show up at my door.

"He had help from an outside accomplice who tied a gun, a hacksaw and a few other things to the end of a rope so he could pull them in through his cell window."

"Michael's on the loose?" On auto-pilot, I went immediately—dragging the phone's cord behind me—to lock the salon door.

"This escape has not and will not be reported. It has to stay out of the papers."

"Because of the gag order?" I asked, reeling with the undercover feel of all of this. I wanted them to send the police to guard the salon and my home. A murderer was on the loose—and they weren't even reporting it? I wondered if that accomplice had given him money for the bus.

"Again, Mr. English," Mr. Sanders reiterated, clearing his throat, "what I am telling you is confidential. When he escaped, he freed other prisoners." I shook my head at the absurdity.

"This has all become very embarrassing. And since your brother hasn't been found yet, we have to keep it quiet."

"You don't think it prudent to inform the public?"

"Not yet."

"Because the D.A. might be *embarrassed*?" I was livid. They knew how dangerous my brother was and yet they weren't flashing his face all over television? After I caught my breath, however, I was flooded with relief—so far there had been no news of the murder in the Bay Area papers and none of my clients had discovered my family's secret past. It was a strange feeling—experiencing fear and relief almost simultaneously.

After I finished talking with Mr. Sanders, I called Debra. She had sent me the first article about my brother's arrest and promised to send anything else she found in the paper. So far nothing else had been written.

However, she said, there was a buzz going around town. Most residents believed the Humboldt County District Attorney hit the jackpot when he "scored" my brother's case. A death penalty trial for the murder of one person, committed by two people, was a rare occurrence. Given the specific facts and the heinousness of Michael and Mona's crime, it was almost as if they had intentionally checked off every box necessary to be convicted of capital murder followed by a death sentence. It seemed certain to me that this elected prosecutor would receive national attention and become famous.

Doing a little research, however, I found out that Diane's friend, this D.A., had also developed a bad reputation. It was rumored he had tampered with the testimony of witnesses and had personal dealings with unsavory people. Rumor also had it that somehow he had been embezzling money from the State. Mr. Sanders and the other attorneys in the Public Defender's Office were aware of these accusations. The last thing they wanted was for the D.A. to receive any positive media attention which, politically, might impede any possible misconduct investigation.

Later, I finally understood how perfect the scenario was for Michael to be able to avoid getting a death sentence. Michael's escape, if publicized, would create sufficient publicity to taint the local jury pool, thereby forcing the case to be transferred to another jurisdiction, and quite possibly eliminating the opportunity to try "two killers for one murder." That sensationalistic aspect would be lost, the D.A. would not become famous, and the investigation against him could proceed with less stress. In addition, if the local officials wanted to keep quiet the jailbreak by Michael and the others he helped, they probably—once he was caught—would want his case to be wrapped up as quickly and unobtrusively as possible. I understood all this to mean that it was likely that they would offer a life sentence, saving him from the death penalty, if he was willing to plead guilty, *and* that there might not be a lot of publicity after all. I could only hope …

I knew I needed to call Mom and tell her what had happened. The more I rehashed all that Mr. Sanders had shared about Michael having an accomplice to his escape, the more I believed that he must have used those "special powers" on whomever helped him. I reflected for a moment: *Those "special powers"… as a child I really thought my brother could actually make magic, that he had superhuman abilities, and chose to use them in evil ways. I know now that they are not superhuman powers, but actually very real, human powers—to charm, deceive, manipulate, and dominate. But all along I was right on one point; for Michael, it was natural to exercise them in evil ways.*

Once again, a sense of panic enveloped me, knowing he was out there roaming around.

I went to the phone.

"Mom … Michael escaped from jail."

"What?" she stammered.

I explained about the accomplice and how Michael had let some other prisoners free, and that now he was on the loose.

"Remember when he was seventeen and that policeman called him Houdini?" My mom asked.

I remembered feeling the same fear—that he might show up at our house.

"Mom, I'm worried he's going to find us."

"We aren't in his plans, Don. Michael doesn't do anything without a plan."

Mom was quiet for a few seconds and then she asked if I recalled *that* time when he escaped. Before I could answer, she began to relay the story from years before.

"He didn't care that the police were looking for him—after his escape he caught a bus to San Francisco."

As if in a trance she spoke of how Michael told her later about his plan to steal money. After he so cleverly walked out of the police station he remembered what his roommate at the detention center told him about "rolling queers" in San Francisco. Mom said it disturbed her how nonchalant he was when he told her what he'd done.

I gripped the phone and listened to her recount Michael's casual description.

"There's this street in San Francisco that's crawling with queers," Michael had said, confessing to her what his roommate had whispered down to him from the cell's upper bunk. "I think it's called Polk Street. All you have to do is wait for one those Goddamn old men to approach you, and then, when they take you somewhere to suck your dick, you just steal their wallet."

It was uncomfortable for me to hear this, even though I was a grown man now, but she said those were his exact words.

And that is just what he had done. After a week of "rolling queers," one of the victims described him so well that it matched the police bulletin that was sent out after the escape. When Dad got the call that Michael was in San Francisco and heard what horrible things he'd done, he left Long Beach right away and drove all night to San Francisco.

I could no longer stand to think about the past, nor the present. "Mom, I don't want to talk about this anymore."

"Don't *worry*, Don, we are not in his plan," she said as we hung up. But the entire scene of his arrest for robbing that appliance store was clear in my mind now. The next evening Dad had called home from San Francisco and said he'd found Michael, but he had gotten away again.

A damn Houdini at seventeen.

I remember being eleven years old and sitting in the living room when Dad came through the door the next day without Michael. One of his eyes was a dark purplish blue and a strip of white gauze, half-pink with blood, was taped across his head.

"Oh my God!" Mom gasped, staggering towards him with a drink in her hand.

"It's OK. I'm fine," Dad insisted, taking the liquor bottles wrapped in a brown paper bag from under his arm and placing them on the kitchen counter.

I listened intently from the living room, hoping to hear the scoop about what had happened with Michael. Dad mixed his drink and carried it over to the oval beige Formica kitchen table, sat it down and mumbled that he had to go to the bathroom.

"Donnie," Mom called.

When I came around the corner into the kitchen, she handed me the tiny brass mailbox key and asked me to go get the mail. The apartment's metal boxes were two buildings away and normally it was a treat. But now I was afraid I would miss Dad's story. I went running out, leaving the front door ajar so I could easily slip back in.

When I got back, I crouched quietly behind the big aqua rocking chair that I usually loved to swivel in. Dad was standing at the table talking with Mom, who was slumped in her chair, reflexively running her fingers through her short black curls as she listened, resignedly. When I came in, he was saying he had found Michael on the street talking with an older guy.

"Betty, I couldn't believe this was our son. The way he was dressed … my God … his clothes were so tight they looked like they were painted on. When I approached him his eyes pierced me like they were black daggers." Dad paused and took in a deep breath. "He just stood there and stared at me. And then when he finally spoke, he said, 'What do *you* want, old man?'

"He said that to me … his own father. Can you believe that? And right in front of that guy he was with … probably one of his Goddamn *johns*."

That's weird, I thought, as I repositioned myself behind the chair, *how did he know the guy's name was John?*

For a few long moments, I watched my father study the ice cubes in his glass, a far-off look on his face. Then it was as if he snapped back to reality, and with one quick swallow, gulped down the whiskey.

"Betty, it was awful," he said, setting the empty glass on the counter.

Mom uncrossed her arms and perched her elbows on the table, resting her chin between her cupped hands as she pressed her fingers up into her cheeks. Dad came around to the table, pulled out a chair and sat down beside her. I could see Mom focused hopelessly on the vase of plastic flowers in the center of the kitchen table. It almost seemed like I was watching in slow motion.

105

Dad continued with a leaden voice. "When I scolded Michael for calling me an old man, he spit at me and turned to walk away. The guy he was with had already left, so it was just Michael and me standing on the sidewalk."

I shifted my weight causing the rocking chair to creak, but they didn't notice.

"I felt a stab of pain in my heart, then I grabbed Michael's arm and began to shout at him," Dad said, wiping the first set of tears from his eyes. "And then all of a sudden, I felt his fist … punch my eye … and then I felt another punch … in my gut."

Dad got up, wiping his face, and went and stood at the kitchen sink. Placing his hands on the counter, he hunched over, peering into the stack of dirty dishes.

"I must have blacked out," he continued, staring down, "because when I came to, an ambulance driver and a policeman were standing over me."

Mom exploded, swatting the vase of flowers to the floor. "That Goddamn son of a bitch!" she yelled, getting up and stomping into the living room.

Hoping not to be discovered, I crawled further behind the chair.

"Well, did the bastard get away? Did he? What'd he do … just take off and leave you bleeding on the ground? Is that what he did? Is it?"

Dad stayed quiet, letting her rant and scream. When she finally stopped, he answered. "Betty, he did take off, but the police said that now that they know who he is, they should be able to find him. He's just seventeen, for God's sake," Dad groaned. "He can't get too far."

CHAPTER FIFTEEN

Dear God   1965, Southern California

J ust when I thought God was listening, my parents got the call that Michael had been picked up by the San Francisco police.

"Can't you take my brother somewhere and keep him!" I had been praying, before finally falling asleep. Many of those nights I would lay awake, negotiating with God into the early morning hours. I'd cover my head, creating a tent from my blanket, and then beg with my whole heart:

Dear God, if you will take Michael away, I will be the best boy ever. I'll do all my chores and try not talk back to Mom ... I promise ... I promise ... I promise.

The longer I begged, the longer my list grew. Yet I wondered if God could hear me.

Every so often, Dad would notice my droopy eyes. "What's wrong, Donnie?"

"I wish Michael wasn't coming home. We would all be so much happier," I responded, never wanting to reveal the cruel things Michael had been doing to me all these years. Even though I was a bit older, with each new crime Michael committed, I had become more and more afraid that he would follow through on his threat to kill my father, if I told.

"Michael has learned his lesson ... everything will be OK."

My dad did not know that I was living like a caged bird behind the mental bars Michael had built with his threat of using his special powers. I was surer than ever that his powers had finally gotten to our father. Dad came home a different person from his trip to San Francisco in pursuit of Michael. Maybe it was because it had ended with such a humiliating fight.

My father purchased a small white transistor radio and escaped into his own world, listening to it through a tiny plug he would tuck into his ear. I rarely saw him without it, which soon became a problem with my mom.

"Goddamn it!" she would scream. "Take that plug out of your ear and listen to me!"

Dad would just look at her and grin, and then walk away.

When I'd hear her complain, I thought to myself how clever he was to have found a way to drown out her constant drunken complaining. I was envious.

Dad had quit driving a taxicab after we moved to Seal Beach, a few miles from his mother, who was still living in her home in Long Beach. He picked up a few small handyman jobs here and there, but since Mom was now working full-time, he became more and more sedentary. Mom would yammer at him for not looking for what she called "a real job." And Dad would repeat his usual line: that he was tired of having the employment door hit him in the face.

I noticed his frustrations were causing him to withdraw more and more, and for a long while, the only conversations he had with Mom turned into screaming matches. During one of these, Dad told her he thought she needed to go to an Alcoholics Anonymous meeting.

"Oh! You're a fine one to talk," Mom snorted. "You drink as much as I do!"

I was in the bedroom listening and decided not come out.

"The hell I do! You can drink me under the table!"

Drinks under the table ... I didn't even try to figure that one out.

"You are a Goddamn drunk, Betty! And if you don't shape up ..."

She didn't even let him finish. "Me shape up? You should try looking in the mirror sometime ... you don't even have a Goddamn job. I'm the only breadwinner here!"

I heard Dad shout back, "That was a *low blow*!" The sound of the front door slamming reverberated throughout the apartment.

I noticed for the next month Mom was cutting back on what she drank after the argument they had about her "*drinking under the table*." She was limiting her drinking binges to evenings and weekends. The job she held over my father during that argument was as a civil service secretary position at the Seal Beach Navel Weapons Base. We were living in a small one-bedroom apartment Dad had found for us two blocks up from the beach, where I slept on a pull-out couch. Not having my own room did not bother me at all; I had fallen in love with the barnacle-covered pier and the two-mile stretch of pearly sand. Breathing in the salty air as I watched my footprints appear and disappear in the sand became my salvation.

By the time we had moved here, I had only two weeks left of the sixth grade. Once summer arrived, I was home by myself, so I would wake up early and take long walks along the beach. I would greet the seagulls with small pieces of bread, in exchange for their listening to my woeful tales.

One of the seagulls, with particularly shiny black feathers, was more attentive than the rest. Amazingly, when I talked, he would stop eating, tilt his head, and look at me as if he were interested in my every concern. So of course he got the bigger pieces of bread.

It was good to have a friend … even if it was only a bird. I decided to name him "Charlie," after Charlie Chaplin. I told him that the other Charlie and he had the same waddle.

Soon my pale complexion deepened into a golden bronze and my dull blond hair bleached to platinum, allowing me to fit in with the rest of the "beach boys." I not only began to look the part, but I was able to make friends with one of the beach groups. These groups formed at the beginning of summer, and pretty much stayed the same from year to year. I could not believe that the most popular group wanted me! It started one day when a girl named Paula, who lived with her sister Carla in a house across the alley from our apartment, introduced me to their family cat, while I was emptying our garbage. Paula and I hit it off right away. One thing led to another, and the following week she told me she had recommended me to become a member of the group.

Finally, it seemed like life was good.

The two sisters, Carla and Paula, had the greatest parents. They turned their garage into a playroom with couches, a piano, and even a full-sized pool table. To me, Carla and Paula were the luckiest—and prettiest—girls in town.

Gary, who was the boy captain, and Paula, who was the girl captain— both the most popular of the clique—began to like each other, and everybody knew it by the way they became inseparable.

Paula was prettier than Carla, but what made her more popular were her adult-sized breasts. All the boys talked about them. Whenever they did, I would get upset and leave their conversations.

I had developed a secret crush on Paula, not because of her breasts; she just happened to be the most beautiful girl I'd ever seen. Her jet black hair glistened even when she wasn't in the sun and the blue-gray of her eyes turned lavender when she would wrap herself in her navy blue beach towel. "She looks just like Elizabeth Taylor," my mother had commented, after meeting Paula in the alleyway one morning.

Every chance I got, I went over to Paula and Carla's garage. One day, Carla taught me how to play "Chopsticks" on her piano and invited me to come over the next day, so she could teach me another song. Dad had already left that afternoon to go spend the night with his mother, who was not expected to live out the week. Mom was already what Dad called "three sheets to the wind," so I knew I needed to ask permission before she passed out.

She was sitting at the kitchen table, sipping a drink. "Mom?" I approached her almost in a whisper. "Can I go outside and play for awhile?"

"What!" she blasted back at me. "You're going over to those Goddamn girls' garage again! Aren't you?"

Oh my God! Where did that come from? I thought to myself, as I stood in front of her with my mouth wide open.

"You don't like me being over there?" I asked cautiously. I pulled out a chair and sat down at the table, hoping she would consider that a gesture of my concern.

"You're always over there and you don't spend any time with me anymore." She whined like a little girl.

"I spend time with you. But I just want to go over and play with them for a little while. Can't I, please?"

"Go!" she almost snarled, rising from the table and dramatically waving her hand in the air as if she were swatting flies. "Go! Just go! And be home early."

I knew I didn't have to come home early. Before long she would be passed out in her bedroom. But for a brief moment, I felt guilty about walking out and leaving her. The feeling passed; I went out the door.

When I got to the garage, Gary was shooting pool with Paula. Carla asked if I wanted a coke and I graciously accepted. She reminded me about the new song she was going to teach me.

"Since you've got "Chopsticks" down, Donnie, we're going to move to a harder song, "Heart and Soul.""

"The piano is for sissies," Gary interrupted, as he concentrated on rolling the pool balls back and forth in the triangle-shaped rack.

"It is not!" Carla shot back, sticking out her tongue. "Come on, Donnie." She took my arm, leading me to the piano. "Let's let that turd play his stupid old pool."

After Gary and Paula finished their pool game, Paula announced it was time to play "Spin the Bottle." I think they all assumed I knew what that was when they called me over to make a circle. Just before we sat down, Gary whispered in my ear, "Carla likes you, so you better get ready for a long kiss."

I felt dizzy trying to figure out what kind of game it was that we were about to play that might include a kiss.

"Maybe after a few rounds of Spin the Bottle, we can play 'Strip Poker,'" Gary laughed, with an almost sinister undertone in his voice.

"Whoa! Oh, I don't know about that, Gary … there are girls here," I mumbled, certain that my nervousness was more than apparent to everyone.

"Of course there are, Stupid! Why would you want to play strip poker with a bunch of boys?" And then all three of them fell into hysterical laughter.

Boom! Boom! Boom! Suddenly, we heard a loud pounding at the garage door.

"Donnie! Are you in there? I know you're in there … Goddamn it!"

We all leapt up from the floor and looked at each other, not speaking, not knowing what to do. I found myself shrinking into a corner of the room.

"Donnie!" My mother was yelling again. "I know you're in there!" Carla looked perturbed, but went to the door and opened it. She barely missed getting hit by the flying fist of my mother, who was lurching heavily into the room.

"O-O-OK!" Mom slurred, catching her balance. "I knew you were here!" she cried, spotting me stepping out from the far corner. "Get your ass home!"

There was my mother, standing half-naked in a skimpy black slip with most of her hair matted down on one side. Her lips were smeared with bright orange lipstick, making her appear clown-like, as she continued to spew obscenities. Bending deep at the waist, I lunged forward and sprinted by her, drenched in humiliation.

Everything was a blur.

I don't remember how I got across the alley, but as soon as I got into the apartment, I locked myself in the bathroom.

"Aghhh! I hate you!" I wailed, falling to the floor and crawling to the cold, white enamel edge of the bathtub. I flung my elbows on the ledge, and pressed my head into my hands, squeezing violently at my temples.

"Donnie!" I could hear her angrily approaching the bathroom door.

Boom! Boom! "Unlock this door! Right now!"

It's her! A voice spoke from inside my head. *It's the monster!*

"Go away!" I screamed at the top of my lungs, getting up from the tub and stumbling to the door. "Why me?" I shouted, pounding back on the door. "Dear God! Please make her die! I want you to die!"

My palms continued to slap the door as I slid to the floor, leaving a trail of tears and saliva. I lay across the cold linoleum. Bringing my knees up to my chest, I curled into a ball.

This is a dream! I told myself and closed my eyes. "A dream," I whispered, weakly.

Mother's voice began to fade and soon everything was still.

I am not sure how long I was lying there, but eventually I pulled myself up, opened the door and stepped out into the hallway. Mom's bedroom door was ajar; I could see her lying diagonally across the bed. She was passed out.

I gently grabbed the bedroom doorknob and pulled it shut. "Good!" I hissed. "I hope you never wake up!"

The days that followed were warm and sunny. But it didn't matter. I had been banished from the beach group because of my mother's embarrassing behavior. The story spread all over town, and of course the more it spread, the more bizarre it got. I was tarred and feathered with the same brush of shame as she. The only difference was that Mom was oblivious to feeling shame, while I was immersed in it.

After that no one wanted to be friends with me except for one girl whose name was Ruthie. She and I had one thing in common, unfortunately—her mother was also a drunk.

Ruthie was a rather large girl; "big boned," my mother called her. She was the only girl I had ever known with red hair, actually copper red, and she had freckles to match. Her personality was a lot like a guy's. She was tough and liked to play rough. She almost broke my arm once during a wrestling match. I started to tell her off: "If you ever try to wrestle me again, I'll … I'll …"

"You'll do what?" she shot back. "Come on, tell me what you'll do to me. Come on! Tell me!"

I caved in, knowing I was no match for her and that she could beat me up whenever she wanted.

The week before, Mom did something that shocked me more than anything I could ever remember. Dad was taking care of his sick mother in Long Beach. Ruthie and I were sitting at the kitchen table playing a game of blackjack when my mom and a strange man came pouring through the door. Staggering towards us, they were both obviously drunk.

"What'er … two … doin'?" Mom slurred.

"Who is *he*?" I demanded, ignoring her question.

"Oh-h … you just never mind, Donnie." She paused, looked at the dark-haired man who looked much younger than she did, and then snickered, "What was your name again?"

"Oh, brother!" Ruthie exhaled, getting up from the table. "I got to go … I think I hear my *cat* calling me."

"Your cat?" Mom said, with a puzzled look, totally clueless that Ruthie was being sarcastic.

After Ruthie exited the apartment, Mom took her bar friend into the bedroom. I stood outside the door and heard strange noises. It sounded like they were kissing, and then I heard moaning. I sort of knew what was happening, because I had heard the same noises once before, coming from a room where Michael told me afterwards that he had been "fucking" a girl. When he explained exactly what he had been doing to her, it sounded so strange. What ran through my head at that time was:

113

Why would someone agree to do this with him, someone who was not forced, like I had been? I rapidly moved away from the door and escaped the apartment, trying to forget who—or what—my mother, whom I had totally adored, had now become.

When I tried to have a conversation with Dad about all the bad things Mom was doing, he immediately changed the subject, muttering that he had already given up on her. I heard Mom accuse him once of sleeping with one of her friends, but Dad vehemently denied it and told her she was crazy. When I saw them in shouting matches, realizing they were never kissing or holding hands like they used to, I thought that my dad might have a girlfriend. But after Michael's accusation that my father had kissed a man, I tried not to think of either of my parents with each other, or with anyone else.

Mom and I hardly saw my father during those weeks he was taking care of his mother. And when he did come home, it was to get some of his clothes. All he would talk about was how sick Grandma Gay was, and how he was sure she would die soon. It upset me to hear this. The thought of her dying, and leaving us and going to heaven, disturbed me even more, because I had only gotten the chance to know her a short while ago.

I had been sick with the flu the first time we stopped off to meet her on our way from Virginia to Monterey, after our trip to Disneyland. I had no recollection of that visit because Mom spent most of the time with me in the car. Even then, Grandma Gay's health was in a fragile state, so they couldn't take any chances with spreading my germs.

I remembered that whenever Mom would talk to Dad about Grandma Gay, she would say something like, "Your mother is hyper-in-the-attic." Of course, years later I found out the word was "hypochondriac." Ah, her pretending to be sick made a lot more sense than Grandma buzzing around in an old attic!

I finally got to meet my grandmother after we moved to Southern California, which was partly to be closer to her. She gave me the nickname "Don-Don" as soon as she met me, since Dad and I had the same name. The way Grandma said our names sounded funny. Dad said it was because she had a thick English accent, having been raised in Liverpool.

"Yuck!" I cried out, when he told me. "She lived in a pool full of livers!"

"No, son," he chuckled as he explained. "Your Grandma is from the same city as the King and Queen of England, and so is her husband."

She married Grandpa Attwood after Dad's father had died, and supposedly, this husband had royal "blue blood" running through his veins. Hearing about his blue blood explained why he was so quiet. Whenever I would come to visit, Grandpa Attwood was like a ghost; he would be there in the room one minute, and then be gone the next. I was sure it was because his blood was blue.

The first time Dad took me to meet Grandma, he explained that she probably would be in bed because her doctor had recommended bed rest for what was wrong with her. Mom said the doctor didn't have a name for the illness she supposedly had, because Grandma made it up.

I was in awe when I walked into her room. It looked like a miniature palace with dark velvet drapes and a large canopy bed draped with shiny fabrics that glittered from the lit lavender crystal sconces which hung at each side of her bed. Her carrot red hair was thin, but curled tight, so it stayed perfectly coiffed as she sat up against the mounds of pillows that rested all around her.

"Come here," she said. "Come here and give your Grandma a kiss." I looked at Dad as I stood at the foot of her bed, surprised she wanted to kiss me. He nodded his head, and as I stepped forward, a fluffy white kitty sprang out from beneath a purple throw that was balled up against the bed's foot board.

"O-o-h-h, gracious me," she sang, ignoring the kitty, and holding out her arms for me to come to her. The bed set up higher than my bed at home; I practically had to climb up, and then literally fell into her embrace. Her white skin was translucent. The scent of lilac filled my nostrils as my lips rested in the hollow of her cheek.

"Let me look at you," she said, squinting as she held the side of my shoulders with her frail hands.

I smiled, noticing her smile was exactly like Dad's. Later, I asked him why, when Grandma Gay talked, there was a clicking sound. He paused, chuckling, and then told me the clicking was from her false teeth, something else they had in common.

Every time Dad took me to visit my grandmother, she would share stories of her life in England. She had, indeed, seen the Queen and went on with details I didn't fully understand.

Her house, which was more like a cottage, had oil paintings hung on almost every wall; she had painted a good half of them. My dad pointed those out as we walked around, with pride in his voice. The largest and most dramatic of her work hung on the wall opposite the foot of her bed. It was a scene of white-feathered angels in a battle with dark angels. The top of the painting was full of white clouds and beautiful, floating, blond-haired angels who were guarding the sky. The bottom was dark and gray with naked, bleeding people falling off cliffs where black-feathered angels waited behind huge rocks, watching as they fell.

"What do think, Don-Don?" my grandmother questioned me the first time she saw me studying it.

"Uh … uh," I was caught off guard; she had caught me staring at the painting. "It kind of scares me." I respected her enough to try to give my honest opinion.

"When I painted it, it frightened me too. I'm going to tell you something I've never told anyone. Not even your father."

She moved the pillow by her side further away and patted the bed, motioning for me to sit. "Don-Don, the Lord Jesus comes and talks to me. He appears and sits at the end of the bed. Sometimes he has a cup of tea, which he sips periodically during our conversations."

She took my hand and made a sandwich with hers. She softly rubbed the top of mine with her soft, almost weightless, hand, as she continued to tell me about her conversation with the Lord.

"He was adamant about me needing to paint what he called "The War between Good and Evil." He said that war goes on constantly, and that was why I needed to create this painting. The world needs to know that we can't give in to the Devil. He's here tempting us all the time trying to grab us and pull us down into Hell."

"Grandma," I whispered shyly, not wanting to interrupt her.

"Yes, Don-Don?"

116

"Those dark angels with the black feathers," I began, looking at the painting. "Why do you think God lets them hurt and kill people? Can't he use his *power* to turn them into good angels?"

"Hey, you two," Dad said, appearing in the doorway. "I hope you're not telling Donnie any of those angel and devil stories, Mother."

He was chuckling, so I knew he was teasing her.

"Oh, you just mind your own business," Grandma warned Dad. "Don-Don and I are doing just fine. He's my little gentleman."

"Do you want some more tea, Grandma?" I asked, slipping off the bed and reaching for her cup, which was sitting on the nightstand.

"Yes, I think I would, thank you."

Dad patted the top of my head as I walked past him.

I stopped halfway down the hall before I reached the kitchen and turned around to see him sitting at Grandma's side, chatting with her so joyfully. *He is so lucky*, I thought. *So very lucky*.

CHAPTER SIXTEEN

A Vacancy   1965, Southern California

My father might have been lucky to have a mother who loved him, but he was unlucky to have a drunk for a wife. About two weeks after my experience with Mom's drunken performance—the one that ruined my young life—I overheard her and Dad arguing in their bedroom. I was in the living room watching TV, but could still make out the big phrases that punctuated the fight.

"I want a divorce!" Dad shouted.

Frightened, I got up from the couch so I could hear what they were saying. By the time I got to the hallway, Dad came rushing out, calling Mom a whore.

"Donnie told you about my friend," Mom cried with anger. "He told you, didn't he?"

Dad yelled back, "Kiss my ass!" and then traipsed into the kitchen to get the white shirt and black tie he earlier had draped over the kitchen chair.

I slowly emerged from behind the recliner.

"Daddy, are you alright?" I picked up the tie that had fallen to the floor.

"Yes, son." He took the tie and thanked me with a nod.

"Can I go with you, Daddy?" I anxiously pleaded with him. "I'll be good. I promise. And I want to see Grandma again."

His face froze for a moment and then he replied with a forced smile, "Sorry, Donnie ... not this time."

I watched his face slowly unfreeze as he walked towards the door. He stopped and turned around, and flashing me a big wink, he purposefully added, *"You be a good boy, OK, son?"*

The sound of the aluminum screen door hitting hard against its frame echoed as my father walked out into the night.

Opening my eyes the next morning with a pit in my stomach, I remembered that Dad was gone. Hearing my mother in the kitchen, I joined her at the table. Her eyes were swollen from crying and there were dark circles beneath them. She motioned for me to sit.

"Dad and I are thinking about getting a divorce." Her arms reached for me. She rested her head on my shoulder, shedding tears on my blue and white plaid pajama top. My stomach sunk and I felt like vomiting. *Did that mean I would be left to live with her?*

I had heard the word "divorce" the night before, and I knew what it meant because several of my friends had divorced parents. But Mom and Dad? I had thought they were just mad at each other and that it would pass. Divorce was incomprehensible.

When her tears didn't stop, I suggested we take a stroll down to the beach.

"It will make you feel better, Mom," I said confidently, knowing how much walks on the beach always helped me.

"No."

"It's Saturday, and look how blue the sky is!" I pointed out the kitchen window and tried again, "Please?"

Turning her head slowly, she glanced towards the window and softly said, "OK, just a quick trip."

While I was dressing, I realized she had not had a drink all morning. "Oh God," I whispered to myself hopefully, "Please don't let her take a drink before we go."

"I'm ready." Mom came out from the bathroom, blotting her lipstick with a tissue. I finished zipping up my shorts and noticed we had on the same colors. She was wearing bright white cotton pedal-pushers and a lemon yellow short-sleeved blouse that cinched tight at her waist. As she turned to pick up her purse, I reached up to adjust the collar on her blouse.

"Your collar's up," I said, fiddling with it. "There. Now you look perfect."

As I headed for the door, I turned around and saw Mom walk sheepishly towards the kitchen.

"Mom, come on," I whined.

"I just want a little."

"Mom!" I said sharply, "Let's go!'

Hers eyes squeezed shut and she sighed heavily. "OK, but let's not be too long."

The morning was crystal clear and the sky and sea were both sapphire blue, creating an invisible horizon. The sandy shore shook as we walked. We watched shore breakers crash down like huge white vertical walls before us. When the waves were like this, no one dared to body surf. Locals knew these waves could break your neck. Walking alongside Mom, I turned and noticed the clumps of lumpy seaweed, a haze of rainbow colors gleaming across the tops.

I spotted my friends, the seagulls. As soon as they saw me, they swarmed around us, startling Mom so much that she stumbled and almost fell. I was hoping the sight of the birds would make her troubles leave, as they did mine, but instead she looked angry.

"Oh my!" she squawked. "What are they doing?"

"Stand still, Mom. They're just waiting for me to feed them."

"They're what?"

"Shoo!" I hollered at "Charlie," the black seagull. He was my favorite, so I hated to yell at him, but I could see that Mom was frantic. "Stop that! Leave Mom's purse alone!"

"Shoo! Get away!" Mom demanded, as we both swatted at Charlie again.

I ran a few feet away from my mom with food in hand, trying to lure the gulls away from her.

"I knew this was a bad idea!" Mom cried. "We shouldn't have come down here!"

I poured the last of the bread pieces on the sand and watched her dance clear of the birds, turning towards the street at a fast walk. Moments later I caught up with her.

"Mom, I'm sorry!"

"We're going home. Right now!" she yelled at me.

"What? We just got here. I dropped the food so they're not going to bother us anymore. We can go that way, towards the pier, and finish our walk."

The desperate look in her eyes told me everything. She wanted—she needed—a drink.

"You just want to go home and get drunk!" I screamed. "I hate you!"

When we got to the curb, we glanced at each other, but avoided direct eye contact. One look at her distraught expression and puffy eyes, and I reverted back to being the *dutiful* son. Silencing my own protest, I accompanied her the rest of the way home.

Mom's pace sped up as we turned towards our apartment. We both came to a halt when we saw a tall gaunt-looking policeman leaning against our front door.

"Can I help you?" Mom asked uncertainly, walking towards him.

"You're Mrs. English?" the officer asked, looking from her to me.

"Yes?" Mom answered, gulping nervously.

"I'm sorry to tell you this, but your husband died last night."

"What?" she shrieked, throwing her hands up in the air.

"He must have had a heart attack in his sleep," the officer said softly. "The report says he was sleeping at his mother's residence. Is that right?"

"Oh, I see now," Mom sighed with great relief and stepped back to stand beside me. "You're mistaken. I see what's happened now … it's his mother who's died. I'll just call him."

The officer removed his hat and spoke a little more firmly, "Mrs. English, I'm sorry. But this is about your husband. I am certain."

Mom's shoulders sank.

I held on to her arm and stared at the man. An hour before, her tears were staining my pajamas while I was thinking about what the divorce would mean. Now, we were being told he was dead, gone forever, not just living in another apartment where I could visit. My head felt crowded with confusion: How could this happen? *Dad wasn't even sick or anything.*

"This is the name and phone number of the mortuary handling the arrangements," he said, tearing off a piece of paper from his notebook and handing it to her. "Again, I'm sorry for your loss." The policeman placed his hand on my shoulder and nodded at me. "Take your mother inside, son."

I took the keys from Mom's shaking hands and opened the door. Mom dashed past me and went towards the kitchen.

I rapidly reviewed what the officer said, and then thought: *It couldn't have been Dad he was talking about it, it just couldn't have. Maybe Mom was right ... maybe it was Grandma that died.* For a moment I rallied, convinced the man was wrong. The officer had been misinformed; he hadn't even been there to know if it was a man or woman who had died. He was just given the address and told to come here. It was all a mistake. Certain, I went back towards the door, hoping to talk to the policeman one more time.

"Donnie! Where are you going?"

"I think I should go and talk—"

"No ... don't do that. I am sure that they got your father and grandmother mixed up. I'm just sure it was your Grandma Gay that died." She began mixing a drink.

"But they said it was Dad. We have to find out, Mom. I'll ride my bike there."

"No, I'll find someone to drive me to the mortuary so I can get this all straightened out. Don't you worry, Donnie."

By the time she finished her second drink, she said she was going to call her supervisor at work to see if she could find someone to give her a ride—Mom had never learned to drive. She remembered that boss mentioning she had a daughter who was going to school to become a social worker.

"Maybe her daughter can help me figure this mess out."

I sighed as I pulled out the kitchen chair and sat down beside her.

Her eyes seemed locked in a dazed sort of stare, not moving off the phone in front of her.

"What if Dad really did die?" I asked quietly.

"No!" she exclaimed, turning to me. "It wasn't him! I know it!"

She finally forced herself to make the calls, soon reaching Annie, her boss' daughter. We sat together, both torn between denial and shock, for what felt like an eternity, but probably was only five minutes. I thought about my dad leaving the night before; I could still hear the sound of his hard-soled shoes across the linoleum.

The shrill ring of the telephone gave me a jolt of reality. It was Annie, the social worker.

She had investigated—my father *was* dead.

Mom remained seated at the table after hanging up the receiver. She had given Annie our address and told me Annie and her fiancé were on their way over.

"They should be here in a few minutes," Mom murmured, solemnly standing up. "Let me see. I need to …"

Mom's voice faded into the background. I turned and looked at the front door, seeing my father looking sadly at me and hearing the last thing he ever said to me: "You be a good boy, OK, son? *You be a good boy …*"

His face. His smile. The tie I handed back to him. I could see everything perfectly on the movie screen in my mind. It played mistily in slow motion, over and over. I don't remember how long it was before I heard a knock at the door. Every sound I heard seemed to bounce around in my head; yet at the same time, I felt like I was standing outside my body.

I numbly started towards the door, but Mom darted in front me, calling out, "Just a minute."

I watched her answer the door, I saw her standing there, I could hear her talking, but all the voices seemed far away. She turned back to me and said I would have to stay home while she went to "take care of things." The couple at the door poked their heads in and said they were all going to the morgue to identify my father and not to worry; they would take care of my mother. I don't recall what my answer was, but as soon as they left, I remember feeling like I was going to explode. I had nowhere to go. I was trapped.

"Dad's dead," I said out loud. I stood in the middle of the living room. "Dead!"

"Oh my God!" I exclaimed, horrified. "God, did you get it mixed up when I prayed for my mother to die? You took my father instead?" That seed of thought—the possibility that I could be responsible for my father's death—sent a sharp pain through my heart. I bounded out of the house, sick to my stomach.

I ran to the beach as fast as my feet could take me. When I got to the water's edge, I stopped, caught my breath, and stared out over the indigo ocean. The sun shone high in the sky, spotlighting the sea's surface, creating sparkles like a veil of twinkling diamonds. Tears flowed down my cheeks and the sun glared on my face. A rainbow of colors blanketed my eyes. It was like looking through a giant kaleidoscope.

"*Your father's dead*," played over and over in my head, the officer's blunt words like a broken record.

"It can't be!" I cried, falling to my knees and burying my face in my hands.

Slipping my fingers down from my eyes, I looked around and realized I had run all the way to the other side of the pier.

I felt truly alone.

A wave came crashing through a row of black pilings, rolling powerfully onto the shore. The white foam swirled around my knees, circling a few times before flowing slowly back out to the sea.

Flashes of memories sped before me: Dad's quick, handsome smile; his warm embraces; the way he always listened to me and seemed to understand me, even when I couldn't understand my own thoughts. But he had changed in the end. Michael, over time, had used his powers to ruin our father, I was sure. Yet I was the one who … who had made the catastrophic mistake with that prayer. I killed him!

"I'm so sorry, Daddy!" I cried my apology to the heavens. "It was *Mom* I wanted to die. Not you! Please forgive me. Please!"

I wandered home from the beach in a daze and was startled to see the front door of our apartment wide open. I approached slowly, and then realized that I must have been the one who forgot to shut it, when I ran out. The second I walked inside, the phone rang. I started praying that the ringing was an alarm clock that would wake me up from a horrible nightmare. After about the tenth ring, I gave up that hope and whispered a cautious, "Hello?"

"Is this Donnie?" A lady's voice asked delicately.

"Yes …?"

"Honey, this is Annie. Remember me? We picked your mom up earlier?"

125

"Yes, I remember," I answered nervously, fiddling with the coiled phone cord.

"I'm going to put Jack on the phone so he can give you directions to where I live. Your mom said it was alright to call you a cab so you can come over to my house."

"Oh," I said softly. "My mom's there? Can I talk to her, please?"

"We gave her some wine, so she's lying down."

"You mean she's passed out," I uttered, automatically angry with my drunken mother who had pushed my father out of our house the night before he died, destroying the last night I could have had—should have had—with him.

"Well, she's been through a lot, honey. Here, I'm going to have you talk to Jack. Hold on."

Before I knew it I was standing in front of Annie's little house, which was one of three cottages lined up in a row. The colors looked like Neapolitan ice cream. One was painted pink, one was cream, and the end one was a light chocolate brown. I looked at the description I had written down and searched for the cream house with the faded red door. As I stepped onto the brick porch, Jack opened the door, hurrying past me to pay the taxi driver. Annie appeared right behind him, coming out onto the porch. She squeezed her tiny fingers lightly around mine. After exchanging weak smiles, we fell into an awkward hug. Her white gauze sheath dress felt soft, and as I released her waif-like body, a light scent of honeysuckle emanated from her long blond hair. I turned around and saw Jack's long legs take the three porch steps in one leap, landing him directly behind me.

"That taxi driver must have taken him the long way around," he complained, and then muttered something about "three dollars" as he walked back into the house.

"Are you hungry?" Annie asked, as she snapped off a few sunburnt flowers from the large stone flower pot sitting by the door.

"I guess," I mumbled, realizing I hadn't thought about my stomach since early that morning.

She gracefully lifted her right arm out from the folds of her dress and directed me through their weathered door.

The aroma of freshly baked cookies filtered through the small crowded living room, which appeared more cluttered than cozy. Two black kitties scurried frantically in front of me and darted under the sofa, knocking over the stack of books which were leaning against the claw-shredded upholstery.

"Would you like a sandwich? I have some ham, or peanut butter and jelly?" Annie gently asked, bending down to re-stack the books.

Glancing around, I saw one bedroom door was open a crack—I caught a glimpse of my mother lying down on a bed. Preoccupied, I responded, "Uh, I guess peanut butter and jelly's fine."

"Save room for my famous chocolate chip cookies," she said, struggling to reach a crystal platter from the mahogany buffet that overpowered the small dining room.

"Oh … of course," I was starting to say when Jack came out of the other bedroom.

"What kid doesn't like chocolate chip cookies?" he boisterously interrupted, before plopping down on the sofa.

Annie put her finger to her lips, signaling him to be quiet by directing her gaze towards the room where Mom was. He gave her a pouting grin.

"Donnie, that's your name, right?" he asked loudly, obviously ignoring Annie's implicit request. "Take a seat." He pointed to the dark pink throne chair.

Just as I sat down, one of the kitties jumped into Jack's lap.

"Get down!" he demanded, swinging his forearm under the kitty's legs. "Damn cats!" He swore under his breath and then glanced guiltily towards the kitchen.

"You don't like cats?" I asked, sensing he wasn't very nice.

"Yeah, I like cats. I just don't think they should be in the house."

"Here, kitty," I called, bending forward and holding out my hand.

I was surprised that the little kitten immediately came to me and jumped into my lap. I noticed a white patch on the top of its head, instantly reminding me of Duchess. I ran my hand over the white crown and felt her begin to purr.

"Looks like you've met Queenie," I heard Annie say from behind me.

"Her name is Queenie?" I hesitantly asked.

"Yes, because of the white crown on her head. You see it?"

I sank my face into her fur and began crying. Duchess was dead and now so was my father.

"Annie!" Jack called out in a high-pitched tone.

I guess that from where Annie was standing, she had not seen that I had started to cry.

"Oh, honey," I heard her say and then saw her kneeling in front of me. She reached forward and put her arms around me. "Go ahead and cry, Donnie. It's OK, it's OK," she comforted me.

It felt good to let go, to cry, to have someone hold me, even if it was a stranger. She held me for a long time, until it seemed that no more tears would come.

After Annie served my sandwich, Mom got up and came into the kitchen. She thanked Annie for taking care of me and then asked Jack if he could take us home.

On the ride back to the apartment no one spoke.

The next day, the only time Mom got out of bed was to get a drink, or to talk on the phone with Annie about the logistics of Dad's funeral. Every time I heard her mention anything about how Dad was going to be buried, I froze, remembering the many times Michael put me in the canvas-lined grave. Much later, I realized that nobody had even thought to try to reach Michael; for once, he was the last thing on our minds.

I wish I hadn't asked my mother, after we got home from Annie's, if she had seen Daddy at the mortuary. Her descriptions of his cold white body—and how she had shaken him, desperate for him to wake up—were worse than any horror film I ever could have imagined.

For all those years, I had done exactly what Michael wanted, no matter what. I experienced all those awful things just to protect my father from Michael's special powers. I believed that I had kept him alive by not telling on Michael. And now my father was dead anyway.

And the suffering wasn't ending there. All my fears were coming to the surface: What does it mean to die? What happens when you are buried? What will happen to me, if my father dies? All my imagined agony and heartbreak were about to be played out ... and I was only twelve years old.

CHAPTER SEVENTEEN

Charlie

1966, Southern California

I held the purple bunny Dad had repaired the week before he died. The wires in the ears had come undone, so Dad had restrung them. Once he was finished, they stood up like they had on Easter morning three months before. Mom said that now, at age twelve, I was too old to have stuffed animals—but the bunnies were a tradition my dad had started when I was four. Every Easter he had given me a new one, and with every move we made, I took pains to find the right place in my room to line them all up. I rubbed my lips against the soft lavender satin that lined the inside of Mr. Floppy's now-erect ears, and cooed into them how much I loved him.

Today would be the day of my father's funeral. Jack and Annie were coming to pick us up at 10 a.m. sharp. I paced nervously around our small apartment. I finally ended up kneeling against the back cushion of the couch, watching through the window for them to arrive—the same position I had taken so many times, in so many homes, waiting for my father to drive up …

"What time are they supposed to be here?" I asked, getting a whiff of Mom's White Shoulders perfume before she even entered the room.

"Stop kneeling on the couch like that!" she commanded, ignoring my question.

Just as I started to hop off the couch, I did see Dad's red Dodge convertible drive up, and for a split second, I almost forgot. Of course, it was not my father behind the wheel.

"Mom!" I shouted, "Jack's driving Dad's car!"

She paused, and then nonchalantly explained, "The battery will go dead if someone doesn't drive it. So I decided to lend the car to Jack." She blithely went off to the kitchen.

I stared at the car, my heart breaking to see someone else sitting in the seat that belonged to my father. This car was the only thing left in our lives that reminded me of the happy times I'd had with him.

I watched her gulp down what must have been her third drink that morning.

She turned to the mirror and dabbed the corner of her mouth with her little finger, making sure the apple red lipstick was perfect. "Come on, Donnie," she called, picking up her clutch and tucking it snugly under her arm.

As soon as we stepped outside, Jack offered Mom his arm and then helped her into the back seat. I walked in front of the car and saw Annie through the windshield. We both smiled at each other.

I rode in the back seat with Mom, thinking how odd it was to be riding in Dad's car without him at the wheel. I pressed my cheek against the car window and left it there for a moment, enjoying the coolness against my skin.

But then the stench of stale cigarettes rose up from the full ashtray in the car door. *Eck! They must be from Jack's friends. Dad smoked a lot, but he always kept his car in immaculate condition.*

My thoughts were interrupted when Jack looked at Mom in the rear view mirror. "Is your husband's casket going to be open?"

My mind suddenly went blank, not wanting to deal with the thought of seeing my father's dead body.

"Yes, and he'll be dressed in his Army uniform," Mom said.

As if reading my mind, Annie asked with touching concern, "Donnie, are you doing alright?"

"He's jus' fine." Mom answered with a slur, reaching over to pat my leg before I could answer. "He'sh my little man, now … r-r-i-g-h-t, honey?"

I chewed on my lower lip, terrified of seeing Dad in his uniform. *Seeing him dead.*

When we pulled into the parking lot, Jack opened Mom's door and helped her up the mortuary stairs. The building looked like a small church, but I could see no religious decorations. The moment we entered the chapel, my eyes went directly to the front of the room, where Dad's coffin sat on top of a burgundy skirted platform flanked with flowers that cloyingly scented the air.

"Annie," I said, coming to a halt. "Is he in *there*?"

"Yes, honey," she whispered, and took hold of my arm.

I could feel my eyes grow big as saucers; I began to hyperventilate. I turned and began to walk quickly in the opposite direction, winding up in the foyer.

"Donnie! Donnie!" I could hear Annie's voice; it came from somewhere off in the distance. "Breathe! Breathe!" Annie ordered, rushing me back outside.

"I'm not sure I can go back in there."

"It's OK, I'll be with you."

As we stepped back into the chapel, I saw Mom standing by herself in front of the casket. Her knee-length, sleeveless black cotton dress was a perfect match against the coffin's charcoal pearl finish. She reached her arms forward as if she were about to touch my dad. Within an instant, a bald man with a gray beard came from behind to see what she was doing. When he saw she was only straightening Dad's tie, he stepped back and calmly walked away.

Another man I did not recognize tapped the silver microphone sitting on top of the wooden podium beside Dad's coffin, and asked everyone to take their seats. He introduced himself as the chaplain and proceeded to talk about my father, referring to him as *Dan* instead of *Don* every time he said his name. I was angered by his lackadaisical way of doing his job; he couldn't even make certain he had the right name.

With each mispronunciation, Mom dropped her head and shaded her eyes with her hand. The chaplain spoke for ten minutes and finally ended by reciting the Lord's Prayer.

Immediately after the recitation was finished, Jack came over to me. "Have you gone up to pay your respects to your father?"

The shock must have been obvious from the look on my face because he immediately interjected, "Donnie, you should at least walk past him and say goodbye."

"I can say goodbye from here, Jack. Really, I can." I tried to sound assured, but I wasn't even sure I could keep holding myself upright.

"Donnie, you *need* to do this." I barely knew him, and it seemed like he was giving me an order, with his arm stretched out, directing me towards the casket. I was about to resist, but then Annie nodded her agreement, which somehow softened the demand.

The moment I stepped in front of the casket, I scrunched my eyes up, trying to blur my vision. I could see a fuzzy image of Dad, lying in what appeared like a white cloud, but was actually the white satin lining of the coffin. When I mustered the courage to fully open my eyes, what I saw was worse than I had expected. He looked like a wax mannequin, with brightly-rouged cheeks and coal black eyebrows drawn heavily across his pasty white skin.

I quickly closed my eyes and imagined the face of the father I remembered. I thought about the waxy white body that looked nothing like him, which would be closed in a box and put into the ground. Oddly, the waxy image of him was a small comfort—it allowed me to convince myself that everything would be alright, since it wasn't really Daddy. I turned around and couldn't see anyone or anything as I walked out of the chapel, thinking of Grandma. I wished she were here, but I knew she was too sick.

"Donnie," Jack called. I turned around and saw Jack and Annie on each side of my mother, helping her walk down the steps. "Your mom wants to talk to you," he said, motioning with a nod to come to her.

With her voice sounding very weak, my mother told me that I would not be able to go to my father's burial.

"They just told me, Donnie. I have to ride in the hearse with your father and there is no room for you."

"Where are they taking Dad? Can't Jack and Annie take me?"

"No, honey. We have to drive all the way to San Diego. That's where the military cemetery is. He is having a military burial service."

I walked up to the large vehicle, glanced inside, and pleaded with her. "It looks like there's room … *please*, Mom?"

The sun had just found its way through the fog, lighting Mom's pale, sullen face while she continued to explain, "You need to go with Jack and Annie. I'm not sure how long I'll be, but I promise that as soon as I get back, I will tell you everything."

I wanted to see where they were taking my father—I could not imagine him buried alone, all by himself in the cold dark ground.

"I just need to get through this, Donnie, and ..."

"Mrs. English," the chaplain interrupted, as he appeared at one of the glass doors directly behind her. "The driver is ready to go."

How scary, I thought. *Mom's going to ride with Dad's dead body.* I felt a shiver go up my spine as her hand slipped from mine and she nodded towards Dad's car.

"Please, Donnie, be a good boy and go."

Jack and Annie dropped me off at our apartment. The last thing I wanted was to go inside, all alone. Dragging my feet, I walked toward the door. I turned around to wave—to try to get one more look, imagining Dad driving away, a grin on his face and his hair flying to one side—but they were already skidding around the corner and out of sight.

The front door was ajar so I didn't need to use my key. The incredibly thick beach fog had returned, creating a white wall outside the living room window. I stood and stared, mesmerized by the lack of visibility. I looked down and picked up from the floor the red pillow that I must have knocked off the couch before we left. As I picked it up, I glanced over at the couch and remembered the times Dad fell asleep there and then woke up mad because his false teeth had slipped out and landed on the carpet. I giggled at the memory. *But he's dead and gone now.* That thought swept through my mind—the awful reminder that I no longer had a father. I sat down on the couch and began to weep. I lay down, knees to my chest, and sobbed into the red pillow.

Close to five hours passed before Mom returned.

The minute she stepped inside and closed the door, I flooded her with questions. "What did the cemetery look like? Were there any trees or flowers? Tell me what happened when you got there."

She looked at me blankly, clearly drained of all emotions. Her eyes were so puffy from crying, they were almost closed.

"I'm too exhausted. Tomorrow we'll talk." She handed me a folded American flag, stating forlornly, "This was on the casket, honey. You keep it."

She promptly mixed herself a drink, and kept on drinking, until she passed out.

Night after night, I woke up in a cold sweat. Haunted by the rouge-cheeked face of my father, I had nightmares of the hole Michael used to put me in. I could hear the dirt, which kept me from escaping, being shoveled on top of the plywood.

The coffin, with the flag sitting on the top, also appeared. The most chilling part was seeing Dad scratching at the roof of the coffin, trying to get out!

Finally, I decided not to sleep at all; I sat up staring into the dark, clutching Mr. Floppy to my chest.

I felt totally helpless, betrayed, and deserted, both in the dark of my dreams and in the light of day.

After going without sleep for three nights, I finally collapsed from exhaustion. That night, the dream was so real that when I awoke from it in the predawn hours, I was convinced I actually had been with my father. It felt so real …

It was morning, and I was storming out of the apartment, mad as hell at Mom.

"I hate you!" I yelled as I stomped out the door. "You should have been the one who died …" I mumbled under my breath, knowing she couldn't hear me.

Just before I reached the beach, Charlie Seagull spotted me and swooped down, leading the way. I almost lost sight of him because the cloud cover thickened before I reached the trail. My sandals flicked the wet sand behind me as I quickened my stride through the path laden with sprouts of ice plant and pieces of driftwood. After walking blindly for twenty feet, a strong breeze cleared the mist, revealing the slate blue ocean. I inhaled the salt-filled air, mesmerized by the waves that looked like paneled drapery whipping in the wind. I noticed the cool damp sand pouring over my toes when I unintentionally stepped into the middle of a sandcastle, probably built by partiers the evening before.

Charlie landed and slowly waddled towards me. We were alone. I looked around for the other birds, but they were nowhere in sight. Just as I was apologizing for not having any scraps of bread, a patch of heavy fog engulfed us, causing me to lose sight of him. The lack of visibility startled me at first, but when it cleared, I could not believe my eyes.

"DAD! Is that you?" I asked, swallowing hard.

"Yes, son." He gave me one of his movie star smiles.

The fog slowly dissipated, allowing me to see it really was my father. His pleated blue-gray slacks billowed in the breeze as he stepped forward, reaching his arms out wide. My feet must have left the ground, because it was like I was four years old again. I was up in his arms with my face buried against the smoothness of his starched white shirt. Tears of joy poured from my eyes, and when I looked up, Dad's own tears fell with mine, stenciling teardrops in the sand. I sank back into his chest and inhaled his scent—Old Spice mixed with salty sea air.

"Donnie," he whispered, "I'm so glad to see you."

"I thought you died!" I cried, wrapping my arms even tighter around him.

"I know, son. What I'm about to tell you will be hard to understand, so please listen carefully. I am dead," he paused, "but I am not gone. You see, when we die, we leave our body and—"

"No!" I shouted. "You are not dead, you are here … you're here with me now!"

"I know this is confusing." He tried to explain, bringing his hand to his mouth in a contemplative gesture. "You saw me in the coffin?"

"Yes," I answered, with a painful frown.

"OK, I want you to trust me … take my hand. We're going back to the mortuary."

"What!"

"Trust me, son … this will help you understand."

The thought of seeing him dead again frightened me. But I clasped his hand anyway and we took off traveling, flying together through time and space. We landed—or materialized—at the chapel of the mortuary, beside Dad's casket. I immediately covered my face with both hands.

"I'm here with you," he said, wrapping his arms around me. "Now I want you to do something hard. I need you to look in the casket. It is the only way you'll be able to understand what I am about to tell you."

I felt Dad's warm body against mine. I fell into a state of peace as he began to clarify that the dead body in the casket was just a shell he used while he was here on earth, and that his spirit was what I was seeing ... what I was experiencing ... right now.

Once he finished explaining, my fear of death, of his death specifically, simply left *me. I fell back into my father's arms. The stark whiteness of his shirt turned into a fluffy white cloud that carried me back to the beach, where Charlie stood like a statue, right at my feet. He peered up at me, cocking his head, and stared for what seemed like an eternal moment. A gentle swift breeze ruffled his glistening black feathers. With his eyes still locked on mine, he took two small steps and spread his wings, catching the air. I watched, almost aching with gratitude and love, as he went soaring away. With the distinctive seagull's cry, he sang his final goodbye.*

I never saw Charlie again.

CHAPTER EIGHTEEN

My New Religion   1966, Southern California

The he visit from Dad was exactly what I needed to get through the days that lay ahead. The dream of being with him at the mortuary convinced me that he really had escaped and I took solace in knowing that he was no longer trapped inside the coffin. He was a free spirit now. What he left deep in the ground was just a *shell*—a vessel for that spirit to function as a human being—nothing more.

Knowing one day I would leave my shell and join him in spirit helped me withstand the emotionally turbulent rivers raging through my life.

Mom's way of coping, unfortunately, was very different from mine. Predictably, she frequented the neighborhood bar, drowning her sorrows in Smirnoff's. Often, after she thought I would be asleep on the pull-out couch, she would sneak in with some strange man and I'd hear him noisily screwing her to sleep. I don't think I saw the same man show up twice, but if I did, I tried not to remember.

Then one morning, just as my strength was beginning to wane, two ladies knocked at our door while I was eating breakfast.

"Who is it?" I called through the closed door, my mouth full of oatmeal.

"Sally," a lady's voice answered without elaboration.

"And I'm Mary," another one said in a sweeter-sounding voice. "We would like to tell you about how you can be *saved*."

"Saved?" I asked with wonderment, swallowing the rest of my oatmeal while fumbling to open the door.

"My mom is resting right now," I whispered, standing in the space between the partly opened door and the door jamb, intending to block their view into the apartment.

"Oh, that's OK," the one with the soft voice replied. "We came to talk to you."

I opened the door the rest of the way and saw they held a newspaper with the words *The Watchtower* printed boldly across the front.

"We wanted to give you our condolences about your father," they said, almost in harmony.

"My Dad? Uh … thank you," I replied, surprised. I had no idea that they had gotten our address, and others, I am sure, through tracking the obituary columns.

"That's actually what we would like to talk to you about," Sally, the older one, said in a deep, husky voice. She stretched her ostrich-like neck to peek over my shoulder. "Are you sure your mom can't talk to us?"

"I'm sure," I answered confidently, glancing over my shoulder to see what she was looking at.

"Well, honey, could you ask her if we can come in and share our teachings about the Jehovah's Witnesses with you?"

I studied both of them and thought, why not? I told them I'd be right back and went into the bedroom. Mom was only slightly dozing so I quietly asked her their question.

"Go ahead," Mom said sleepily. "I think your Uncle Ray is a Jehovah's Witness, so it's probably fine."

I went back into the living room and invited them to come and sit down. They began by telling me that if I became a Jehovah's Witness, "You could spend eternity with your father."

That notion—"spending eternity with my father"—made my mind race. I recalled Grandma Gay talking about spending eternity with God in Heaven, and about good and evil, and that when we were bad, we'd be grabbed and pulled down into Hell. I thought about my mother's description of crabs pinching bad boys, and of Michael's painful pinching. Grandma Gay never did answer my question about the dark angels in her painting, the ones with the black feathers. I still wanted to know, desperately. These women claimed to have appeared on my doorstep just to help me be "saved." That had to include being able to understand these mysteries, didn't it? So I asked, "Why does God let bad people hurt and kill? Can't God use his power to turn them into good angels?"

They never did give me a specific answer either, but during that first meeting, I *did* learn that, according to their calculations, the end of the world would come soon and the Jehovah's Witnesses would be the first to be saved. That kept me interested.

To become a member of their church, there were some things I would have to do and other things I would have to give up. I no longer could salute the flag or recite the Pledge of Allegiance. No more celebrations, birthdays, Christmases, or Easters. *And what about my bunnies,* I worried for an instant. And when I was old enough, I would get to go door-to-door and do what they called "witnessing," which was spreading the Word of God. I would also need to study with them every other week.

"We'll come here," Mary said with a bright smile. "And we'll spend an hour with you each time, helping you understand how fortunate you are to be included in the Salvation that will take all the chosen ones to heaven."

I was thrilled! As soon as they left, I spun around in a circle and threw a pillow from the sofa bed up into the air. *I would be saved, and, even better, I would be able to spend eternity with my Dad!*

The next day at school, I waited until after class to tell my teacher, Mr. Copan, why I no longer could salute the flag. He was a rather large man, Russian I think, and had big black bushy eyebrows.

After I finished explaining about my new religion, he sat at his desk, rubbing his chin and repeating the same word over and over, "Interesting. Interesting. Interesting."

I almost told him that *he* might be able to join Dad and me because he seemed so interested.

"You will be the only one not standing, Donnie, so other students may ask you why," he commented, making it sound almost like a question, or a warning; I wasn't sure which.

The thought of the other kids asking me questions was not all bad— I kind of liked the idea of being different. *Hmm, but maybe not too different.* I proposed a compromise: "What if I just stand, but don't say the pledge?"

The school bell rang, just as Mr. Copan nodded in agreement.

I was heading for the door when he added, "Tomorrow I'll have some time to work with you on your speech. Don't forget to bring it."

I stopped and turned back towards him. Now it was my turn to nod, positive there was no way I would forget.

Two students from my class had been selected to represent our school in a speech competition against three other intermediate schools. And I was one of the two students. I was pretty sure Mr. Copan had selected me because he knew my father had just died and he probably thought it would help take my mind off my grief. He was right.

The short story he recommended for me to read for the competition was "The Emissary" by Ray Bradbury. It was about a ten-year-old boy named Martin who was an invalid and had to stay inside. He lived next door to a cemetery and had a dog whose name was "Dog." Dog could play outside. When Martin's teacher dies, Dog digs her up from the cemetery and leads her ghost to the boy's home, while his parents are out to dinner.

I rehearsed my speech in front of Mr. Copan many times in the weeks leading up to the competition. This was the first time I had been able to picture a cemetery, or even mention the word, without memories of being buried by Michael crowding everything else out of my mind.

This story reminded me that even after people die, they are still remembered.

It had such significance for me that, after hours of Mr. Copan's coaching, I was able to act out the part of the grieving invalid boy with great conviction. I was awarded second place. Mr. Copan said I was a natural. Little did he know that my emotional reading came from first-hand experience with cemeteries and grave-digging.

After the award ceremony, Mr. Copan drove me home. I could tell he was proud of me and probably was surprised I did so well. But the whole time I was riding in his car I was thinking about where I would have him drop me off. I didn't want him to see Mom drunk. Or worse yet, see her drunk and hanging off a strange man's arm in front of our apartment.

"Pull over right here, please." I pointed to three tall bushes standing in a row.

"Here?" He sounded puzzled, but then made a joke, "Which bush do you live in, Donnie?"

I turned and looked at him. I held his kind gaze for a moment, overcoming my embarrassment, and then we both laughed together. He pulled over in front of the bushes and let me out.

The following week Sally and Mary came over for my fifth or sixth Bible study lesson. I couldn't wait to announce that I had won second place in the speech contest. But when I did, they didn't seem to care, so I thought maybe speech contests might also be against their religion. We immediately started reading from the Bible and what we read reminded me of a question I wanted to ask.

"I'm sorry I ask so many questions," I began, sinking back into our living room sofa. "But if you could answer this one more."

The ladies looked at each other. Mary replied, "Just one, Donnie, we have a lot to cover today."

"I've been thinking about when the *time* comes and the six trumpets start to blow."

"Seven," Mary corrected me.

"OK, seven. Anyway, you said that when this special time arrives, only Jehovah's Witnesses are going to heaven because the world will come to an end. Right?"

"Yes, Donnie. That is why you have to do everything we tell you," Mary assured me.

I adjusted the pillows behind my back. "So I've been thinking about this a lot …. The trumpets are going to blow and I'm thinking things are going to be pretty chaotic. And like you told me, the ground will open and people are going to be swallowed up." I saw Mary was about to interrupt me, so I sped up. "In all that craziness how am I going to find my father? How will I recognize him? Are you sure he's expecting me?" I took a deep breath and grabbed one of the pillows, pressing it to my chest.

"You don't have to worry about this now, Donnie," Mary answered with a tinge of frustration.

"Yes! I think you worry way too much," Sally emphatically concurred. I crossed my arms and slumped back against the other cushions. "I'm just worried I won't recognize Dad," I whined. "And I'll have to spend eternity without him."

Both women remained quiet for a moment and then Mary, in her sweet voice, carefully explained how everything was going to happen:

"OK, Donnie, because you are a Jehovah's Witness now, when the time comes everything will happen magically—and you will find your father—and he will look just as he did when you last saw him. He'll be exactly the same."

I beamed. "Really?" Then I hesitated, but this was crucial, "Can I please ask one more little question? It's very important."

"Make it brief," Sally snapped.

"You said Dad will be just like he was when I last saw him and we'll spend eternity together, right?"

They both nodded; Mary's face had a slight look of curiosity, probably she was wondering what could possibly be bothering me so much.

"Dad had false teeth and he used to fall asleep on the couch watching TV. And every once in awhile his teeth would come loose and fall onto the carpet. When he'd wake up and see his teeth lying there, he'd swear and curse over and over about how much he hated having those false teeth. So I'm afraid when he finds out he has to go through eternity with those false teeth, he's going to be really mad!"

"Are you making fun of us, young man?" Sally growled.

"No-o-o, I'm actually worried!" I retorted.

"Come on, Mary," Sally huffed as she picked up the books from the coffee table. "I think *Donnie Boy* needs to spend some time alone to think about how ridiculous his question was!"

Mary was much more patient in her response. "Sally forgot to say that you are just as you are when you die, but your body is perfect and healthy. So, don't worry, your dad will not have his false teeth."

Sally harrumphed and glared at Mary.

My mouth dropped open with disbelief as I watched them gather their things to leave. They had been meeting with me for many weeks, telling me all about how loving God was. My feelings were so hurt I didn't care if I ever saw them again.

But then another upsetting thought crossed my mind. Maybe *Dad sent them to me to make sure I went to Heaven so I could join him. But now they are going … where does that leave me?*

The screen door suddenly slammed and I jumped. Mary stuck her head back inside and murmured sadly, "Sally needs time to cool off. We'll come back in a few weeks." Then I heard the quick clicks of high heels on cement as they went down the stairs.

With disappointment, I realized that my initial acceptance of their ideas had been fading. So had my hope that I would be saved and would spend eternity with Dad.

Over the next few days, as I continued to ponder the whole situation, I gained more confidence. *I am sure my father would not want me to be connected with crazy religious ladies who were mad because I asked about false teeth. Maybe I don't need any religion to believe in God. Dad didn't have religion and he came back in my dream so he could tell me the secret of our shell bodies. Plus, I remember that Michael had a Bible, and he read it sometimes. I certainly don't want to wind up in the same place he does when we die!*

I hadn't had a chance to tell them that Mom and I were already packing up the apartment in preparation for another move—our seventh in twelve years—this time just down the street. To get back at Mary and Sally for their betrayal, I decided I wasn't going to tell them where we were moving. I wouldn't even leave a note.

CHAPTER NINETEEN

The Apartment   1966, Southern California

For the next two months I was happy. I made friends with a girl named Linda.

She was two years older than I and as beautiful as the girl on the Ivory soap commercial. Because she was fourteen-going-on-fifteen, her parents let her ride a Greyhound bus to the Roller Palladium in Long Beach. There she could take roller skating lessons from her uncle, who was a one-time National Figure Roller Skating Champion.

One Saturday afternoon she invited me to a skating matinee. I had made a practice of slipping twenty-dollar bills from my mother's purse after she'd come home from the bar, so I always had money. I realized I was stealing, but I needed money to fund my escapes, and it was because of her that I needed to escape … so it seemed kind of like fair play to me.

If I hadn't already fallen for Linda, watching her skate would have made me fall. I was determined to learn to skate backwards so we could do the "couples skate" together during the evening sessions. She was shocked by my quick progress; of course I never told her why I was so motivated. Her uncle also noticed my vast improvement and convinced me to enter the local Amateur Figure Roller Skating Contest. I didn't do very well, but found that I loved the excitement of competing. This surprised me because I had always been so self-conscious, even though I always tried hard to make friends. Apparently, my experience with the speech contest—working hard, doing well, and enjoying the attention—had helped me discover a new comfort level with myself.

Skating became my new escape, along with Linda. And the closer we got, the more I fell in love. We shared my first French kiss.

"You do this awfully well," Linda smiled, after our first try. "You're sure you've never done this before?"

"No, never! You're just a really good teacher!" Taking that lead, she taught me more.

"You have to stick your tongue in deeper, Donnie," she kept telling me.

It felt better to me when she'd come fishing around for my tongue.

"No!" she insisted. "Boys are supposed to do the fishing, not the girl!"

It seemed like a lot of work, but eventually I got the hang of it. We went on for about half an hour, until I thought my lips were going to fall off.

Girls' lips are so soft. That was all I could think about for the next few days. Whenever I'd see a pretty girl, I would stare at her mouth and wonder what it would be like to go fishing for her tongue.

Whenever I talked to Mom about how much I loved skating, she would change the subject and talk about something else. I wanted her to know how serious I was, so I decided to talk to her early on a Sunday morning, before she had a chance to have a drink. She interrupted me as soon as I began.

"You remember my friend Alice in Monterey, don't you?" She was walking towards the kitchen to mix a drink.

"Mom, I'm trying to talk to you about my skating." She ignored me.

"I've decided we're moving back to Monterey. Well, next door to Monterey. Alice has already found us a two-bedroom apartment in Seaside."

"Why?" My voice rose quickly to a shrill scream.

"Because we are! Eddie has agreed to move us up to Monterey with his truck. We'll see how it goes. I've already given him some of the money I got from selling your father's car to rent a U-haul."

"Mom, we can't just pick up and move!"

"We're moving, and that's that."

Eddie was Mom's latest boyfriend. He had lasted longer than all the others. I'd seen him naked twice because of my bad timing. I always seemed to walk in when they were going at it. The first time, I opened the door and he jumped up, staggering away from the bed—his erection standing straight up like a flagpole. It took a second for me to realize what was happening. I slammed the door and closed my eyes, desperate to erase the image.

Once Mom informed me we were leaving, we started packing and in less than a week, the three of us were riding in the front seat of Eddie's old truck, towing the U-haul with all our belongings back to Monterey.

Despite the bumpy ride, I had fallen into a trance, reminiscing about how the move had happened so fast. Just when I finished wiping a tear from my cheek, thinking about how much I was going to miss Linda, Mom poked her elbow into my rib.

"Donnie! I'm talking to you," she yelled above the rickety noise from the old truck.

I looked at her and nodded silently, my eyes cold.

"I got a call from the detention center. Michael's going to be released soon and he has nowhere to go."

"Oh, shit!" Eddie suddenly shouted, staring into the rear-view mirror. "Something's flown off the truck!"

The ropes had come loose and a pillow had flown over a couple of the cars behind us and was now plastered against the windshield of the third car back. It was swerving from side to side until the pillow dislodged, sending white feathers through the air as if a goose had just exploded. Eddie immediately pulled off to the side of the freeway and jumped out to see what needed to be fixed.

"Michael is coming home?"

"Yes," she answered, as we both watched Eddie through the rear window.

"Does that mean he'll be living with us?" I was in shock.

"He'll be home in two weeks. He's eighteen now, so we'll just have to wait and see how it goes. It's why I wanted to move with Eddie, so we'll have a man in the house in case Michael gets out of hand. Really, he has nowhere to go. Donnie, I promise, if he does one thing wrong, he's out."

I remained quiet for the rest of the trip; I couldn't begin to describe to my mother how I felt. But I knew—I felt almost as trapped as I did in the cave-in-the-ground. And it made me wonder … *would I ever tell my mother the whole truth about Michael? I had believed his threat about killing Dad; I let Michael torture and manipulate me to save my dad, and now he was dead. What are those powers that Michael has to make people suffer? And will he use them on Mom now? Or just me?*

When we arrived in Monterey, Mom directed Eddie to the address of the apartment complex. As we pulled up, she said, "I believe our apartment is over here," gesturing towards one of three two-story apartment buildings.

"Donnie, I have a surprise for you. I guess this as good of time as any to tell you." She looked at Eddie, winking, so I figured he was already in on it.

"The apartment comes furnished, but I told them we wouldn't need living room furniture."

"Oh great, so were going to sit on the floor?" I commented sarcastically.

"No, your father had a $5,000 life insurance policy with the Army, so I'm going to take some of that money and buy us new living room furniture. And ... I want to buy you that color TV Dad always promised you."

I wasn't sure if the TV could fix the pain of leaving skating and my friends, but it would certainly help. Finally, I would have something that came from Dad.

The next two weeks flew by in a flurry of unpacking and settling in. Before I knew it, Michael was standing at the front door of our apartment. I don't remember whether Mom even hugged him, but I do recall the first words out of her mouth: "Now that you're eighteen, if you get into trouble, you're going to prison."

"Oh, Mom," Michael retorted right away, "I'm not getting into any more trouble—I've really learned my lesson this time!"

He bent down to pick up his duffel bag and flung it over his shoulder as he eyed what he figured was our bedroom. I followed behind him, wanting desperately to believe his promise.

Throwing the bag onto one of the twin beds, Michael actually bothered to ask, "Which is yours, little brother?"

"Uh ... uh ..." I was stunned by his niceness. "This one here," I finally responded, smoothing down the corner of the bedspread.

"Oh, good." He moved his duffel bag to the bed by the window. "It's great to be able to look outside," he smiled, placing his hands on the windowsill. "I've been locked up far too long. I'm glad to be home."

"Ye-a-h," I stuttered." It's good … it's good to have you here."

My eyes stayed fixed on the back of Michael's silhouette as he stared out the window. He began talking about how he had started lifting weights, which explained why he was much huskier than I remembered. He had an almost perfect physique and had always loved the attention his Adonis-like body received. It crossed my mind to say something about our father's death, but I decided not to. Soon we ran out of things to say. I left the room wondering how long "nice Michael" would stay.

That night I had a nightmare about him turning into a spider.

Michael, a big black spider, crawled into my bed and wrapped me up with his bristly, furry legs, and then stung me so I couldn't move. I lay there, paralyzed, watching him construct his web as, one by one, different people appeared and got caught up in it. They screamed, struggling to break free from the sticky substance that had them glued to the silky wrappings. Eventually the numbness left my body so I leapt from my bed and rushed into the web to help all the screaming people. Darkness engulfed us. I looked up and saw Michael's spider body was growing larger and, without any warning, his long crimson red tongue emerged, dripping gobs of saliva, in preparation for devouring us.

And that's when my eyes flew open and I awoke, screaming for him to stop, my heart pounding away.

It was morning. I looked over and saw his bed was empty. As soon as I caught my breath, I realized it had all been a dream. I sat up, detecting a horrible pungent odor. I looked down beside Michael's bed and there was the culprit, a pair of black nylon socks. I guessed that while he was locked up, he had developed a case of foul foot odor. I jumped up, went to the window, and opened it all the way.

Well, at least he hadn't turned into a spider, I thought, and breathed in some more fresh air.

After I got dressed, I went outside. As I took my first step down the stairs, I saw Michael standing in the parking lot, smoking a cigarette. A lady with two little girls pulled up to the only available parking space, where he had planted himself, leaning hard against the carport's pole. He flicked away the cigarette and stepped back as she pulled into the space. One of the little girls jumped out first, with her sister following her. When the lady got of the car, she reached back, loading up her arms with groceries, and then kicked the car door shut with the back of her leg. A high-pitched scream reverberated all around us. Her daughter had been in the way of the closing door and fell to the ground, holding her arm. I stepped back up the stairs wanting to stay out of sight, but glued to what was happening.

Michael immediately came forward and lifted the groceries from the woman's arms while she attended to the little girl. It appeared she had not been hurt and, after a few "Let me kiss the boo- boo's," the girl hugged her mother and then bounded up, calling for her sister.

Later, Mom and I learned the young mother's name was Lee Ann. She and her two daughters, Jessie and Lily, had moved into the apartment building shortly before we had. Lee Ann's husband, who was in the Army, had brought her and the girls from Ohio to join him while he was on some special assignment at Ford Ord. Unfortunately, almost immediately upon their arrival, he received orders to leave for Vietnam.

Lee Ann was actually pretty, in a plain sort of way. The left side of her face was covered with thin dishwater blond hair that had been styled to mask the three-inch red scar hiding beneath.

"Sad looking," were the words Mom used to describe her. After seeing her scar, I figured that was why she hardly ever smiled.

I was afraid that now, without knowing it, she had fallen innocently into my brother's web.

After that day, we rarely saw Michael. Lee Ann was living in the apartment below us and that was where he stayed most of the time. The first week he was there, she helped him get his driver's license, but she soon came to our apartment, complaining to Mom how Michael had taken her car without asking. No surprise, I thought.

We found out weeks later that he had started dropping LSD. Not a good combination with Michael's uncontrollable temper. Several times when he was high, he came up to our apartment, and for no reason at all, started a fight with Mom, or me, or both of us, whoever was handy to bear the brunt of his rage.

An aura of familiar fear hung over us constantly. When I wanted to get away from the ugliness in our apartment, I would head for the old dry creek bed that began just behind our complex. It was about two miles long and I'd walk and throw rocks, daydreaming about someone coming to rescue me.

One afternoon in late spring, after Michael had come back and then left again, this time without hurting us, I decided to go down to the creek. On my way back, I saw an aqua-blue bath rug hanging over the black iron banister of the back balcony of one of the other buildings. People would shake out their rugs and leave them to air out. The closer I got, the prettier the rug looked.

I'm not sure what possessed me, but I ran up the cement stairs and found myself standing, trance-like, staring at the rug. I looked around, grabbed the fluffy bath mat, and tucking it under my arm, ran off. After traversing the parking lot, I charged up our stairs, two at a time, and rushed through our front door. Completely out breath, I whispered aloud, "I did it!"

I don't think I was quite aware of what I had actually done, but it occurred to me that the overwhelming excitement I was experiencing must have been what Michael felt from taking LSD.

"A rush!" I once overheard him telling someone, when he didn't know I was within earshot. "It's a wild rush!"

Mom wasn't home at the time, so I lifted the brilliant blue rug up in the air and shook it so all the velour shone together in one color. The color TV was directly in front of me, so I laid the mat down and then stepped back, admiring what a regal appearance it had given the room.

Wow! It was as though the whole apartment was transformed. *If one rug makes this much difference, just think what a few more would do!*

That was the beginning of my secret identity as "The Rug-napper."

Everyday I would scout the complexes and search for the perfect rug. I came up with a desired color theme, but the problem was an overabundance of blue rugs. I'd have to develop the patience to wait until a yellow or pink one would appear. One time, someone hung out a large white shaggy rug on a banister where many people passed by. I waited for at least twenty minutes until the coast was clear and grabbed it, almost getting caught.

That rug became my favorite.

Mom hadn't noticed the rugs until I brought home the third one.

"Oh my!" She stood in her bedroom doorway, staring at the aqua blue rug in front of the TV. "What's up with all the rugs?"

"I guess people didn't want them anymore. They were out by the trash so I—"

And before I could finish, she stopped listening and went back into her room.

I think it wasn't until the tenth acquisition that I realized I had run out of floor space. The drab, gray wall-to-wall carpet was covered completely and when I'd stand back and blur my eyes, it looked like "Candy Land," the children's board game. Finding rugs to fill our house with color gave me something to focus on other than Michael's next return.

The following weekend, we had what was a rare occurrence on the Monterey Peninsula, a 90-degree temperature.

"A heat wave! A Goddamn heat wave," was what Mom called it.

Since we lived on the second floor, our apartment was like an oven. The first day it hit, I woke up late because it was Saturday and there was no school. I jumped out of bed enjoying the warm air and got dressed looking forward to spending time down at the creek.

I found out later the heat also woke Mom up. I had left already, so when she got up she opened all the windows and then decided to give the apartment a good cleaning. Unfortunately, the next thing she did was to shake the rugs out and hang them all along our iron balcony rail. We lived in the end unit so the rugs hung clear around the corner, creating a very colorful display.

Candy Land was now outside, in the open.

After the first person recognized her rug, others came and marched up the stairs like zombies, all fixated on their stolen property. It was a good thing I had stopped when I did, because they had been setting *rug bait* so they could catch me.

Because the morning was so warm, Mom left the front door open. When she came out to see what all the commotion was, someone shouted at her, "You're the rug-napper! You're the one!"

More and more people crowded onto the balcony, shouting and grabbing their rugs, like they were their most prized possessions. And upon her arrival, the apartment manager announced proudly that she had already called the police.

Later when I heard Mom relay the rug story to Michael, she said she had tried to tell them it was her son who stole the rugs.

"Nobody believed me!" Mom told Michael. "Can you imagine? They thought I was the one who stole all those rugs!"

While I was down at the creek, the sun was getting hotter, so I decided to go back to the apartment. When I turned the corner of our building and saw all those people with their rugs clutched to their chests, I froze.

"There he is!" Mom shouted, pointing down at me from the top of the stairs. "There he is! He'll tell you. I did not take those rugs! He'll tell you!"

The police had already arrived, and spotted me at the same time. They motioned for me to come up the stairs. On my way up I heard a lady say, "How disgusting for a mother to blame her son like that. I know she did it. I saw her!"

Wow! I thought to myself, *they think Mom took the rugs.* For a moment, I did think about letting her take the blame.

"Hi, officers," I said. I was trying my best to appear calm as I addressed the two policemen, but I was certain—and terribly afraid—that they could hear my heart thumping.

"Tell them, Donnie! Tell 'em!" Mom shouted.

One of the officers told my mother to shut up and let me talk.

"Yes, I was the one who took the rugs. But I found them all wrapped up in a big bedspread down at the creek behind our apartment building."

Thinking about it now, I'm sure they thought I was still covering for Mom. They gave me a strict warning and then told everyone to take their rugs and go home.

When Mom finished telling Michael the rug story, he turned to me and said, "Little brother, from now on, if you're going to steal, you need to take something that's worth something. Not a bunch of stupid bath mats."

"Stop talking about stealing!" Mom chirped, and then got a big smile on her face. They both doubled over, laughing hysterically and repeating how stupid I was.

I turned and walked away, looking down, following the ugly gray rug back to my room.

CHAPTER TWENTY

The Lamb in the Lion's Den 1966, Northern California

W atching the color TV Mom bought with Dad's insurance money helped me escape and kept me sane when Michael-the-beast and Mom-still-a-drunkard ganged up on me, treating me like I was the enemy. My mother, in her drunken state, began to hate me—I was regularly emptying her bottles of vodka down the kitchen drain.

The first time I understood that I was completely alone in the world was on the day when she caught me holding a vodka bottle over the sink, the last drops pouring out. Swearing like a sailor, she charged at me and slapped me across the face. I threw my hand up to protect my face from the next slap and yelled, "I don't care if you slap my face raw. I will continue to pour them out! I hate you ... you're nothing but a drunk!" I bolted past her and stomped out of the apartment, slamming the door behind me.

When I returned, about an hour later, I could see through the half-closed door that she was passed out across her bed. I quietly shut her door and tiptoed into the kitchen to get a soda and some chips. It was 4 p.m., time for my favorite soap opera, Dark Shadows. I turned on the TV and sat down on a white fluffy rectangle, the only rug unclaimed the day I was charged as a rug-napper. I had placed it in front of the TV, creating the only clean area to sit. I took a sip of my Coke and began watching Barnabus Collins, the vampire of the show, emerge from his coffin. The phone rang. I sat up with a jolt, looking from the TV to the phone, debating whether to answer it. Exasperated, I decided to pick it up so it wouldn't wake Mom.

"Hello," I said, reaching to turn down the TV.

"H-e-l-l-o, Betty," a man's voice said. I recognized his accent from the night before. He was the man Mom brought home from the bar around the corner— it hadn't taken long for Eddie to see what he'd gotten himself into before he took off. This guy from last night had been wearing an Army uniform and looked much younger than my mother. After the brief introductions, I had gone outside to avoid hearing the predictable and disgusting sounds.

"Betty, you beautiful thing, you," he now seductively moaned into the phone. "Are you there?"

I remained silent. For some still-strange reason, I began to pretend I was my mother.

"Who are you? Do I know you?" I asked, making my twelve-year-old voice even higher.

"Oh, Betty, you know who I am! We made such passionate love last night, don't you remember?"

"Remind me. What did we do?" I loved putting on my mom's own Southern belle voice.

"Oh, my little kitten. You like to play games with me. You said I was the best lover you've ever had."

"I don't remember."

"You will, just tell me you want me to come over and I'll give you some of Jacques' French love."

"I'm still not sure I remember you," I responded, quickly sinking my mouth into my arm so he wouldn't hear me laughing.

There was a long pause. I was afraid he knew it was me. But he went on describing his French technique of lovemaking. When he started talking about how big his penis was, I interrupted him.

"This isn't sounding familiar. Are you sure we've met?"

"Oh, baby, don't play any more games. I'll come and remind you."

"Now?" I frantically replied, afraid he might just show up. "No-o-o! No! No!" My voice was climbing even higher, this time without my trying. "I do remember you now, and you ... you had bad breath. Don't ever call me again!"

I slammed the receiver down, not knowing if I should laugh or cry. *What a creep that guy is,* I thought, as I turned up the volume on the TV. The drama of Barnaby the vampire visiting a small town and disrupting the locals was just the escape I needed to take me away from the reality that strange men screwed my mother.

Just as the plot was getting good, I heard a noise coming from Mom's room. She jolted through the door and planted herself right in front of me, blocking my vision.

"Turn that Goddamn TV off!" she screeched. "I don't want to hear it!"

"Ohhh, God!" I groaned loudly, and then yelled at her with obvious scorn, "Mom, go back to your room and leave me alone!"

"How dare you talk to me like that!" My mother was getting livid.

And then she did her worst. She picked up the lead crystal ashtray from the coffee table and hurled it towards the TV. I bounded up from the couch and tackled her to the floor, causing the ashtray to hit the side of the wood cabinet, just missing the screen.

Enraged, I mustered up all my strength and shouted in her face, "Don't you dare touch my TV! That is the only thing I have from Dad!"

Then I grabbed the back of her nightgown and dragged her into her room.

"A-h-h-h!" She yelled back at me, "You hit me! You hit me!"

I watched her head bang against the doorframe. My mother slid to the floor. I didn't care.

"There! Stay there and do not come out!" I went to pull the door shut, kicked her leg out of the way, and then slammed it.

I stood outside listening to her groaning. Almost immediately it struck me: *Oh my God! I was just like my brother. I'd treated our mother just like Michael did!* I began trembling all over, feeling awful for what I had done.

I went over to the couch and kneeled on it, looking out the window. It was a clear day; from here on the second floor, I was able to get a glimpse of the ocean. I stared off into the distance, still trembling, still feeling unbelievably ashamed. I knew I needed to do something—right away—to make it up to my mother. I got off the couch and decided to cook something for dinner. I didn't know any other way.

"A meat loaf. I'll bake a meat loaf," I whispered to myself. Meat loaf was one of my new dishes. There were a lot of things I needed to learn since Mom had relinquished her duties as a mother. Learning to cook became mandatory—if I wanted to eat. I pulled the Betty Crocker cookbook off the shelf and turned to a page ironically titled "Betty's Special Meat Loaf."

I brought down all the spices and lined them up. I put the ground beef into a bowl and then went back to my mother's door to listen. I could hear her snoring from the bedroom, so she must have hauled herself up from the floor where I had left her. *She couldn't have been hurt too badly*, I figured.

Feeling the dread evaporate slowly from my body, I returned to the kitchen. After pouring some ketchup on the meat, I added the spices. Thyme, parsley, salt, pepper; I sprinkled the oregano on last. The special lid with the holes fell off, causing half the bottle to spill. "Damnit!" I cried out and stared at the pile of green flakes completely covering the meat.

"Oh-oh," I groaned, scooping off what I could with my fingers, convincing myself it would probably be fine. I opened the oven door and placed the pan of green- colored meat on the rack and slowly shut it, sneaking one last glance. I brushed my hands together and then reached for the timer.

"Hey!" Michael stormed through the front door.

"Agh!" I yelped. The timer fell from my hand. "You scared me!" When I saw his face, I could tell he was high. His eyes were glassy and his mouth stayed frozen with a wild grin.

"There you are, Michael!" Mom suddenly was stumbling from her bedroom. "Your brother hit me! He hit me!" she wailed.

I picked up the timer and walked into the living room, looking first at Mom and then at Michael.

"He did what?" Michael exclaimed, in disbelief.

"He would not turn off the TV, so when I went to turn it off, he knocked me down! And then he kicked me and threw me in my room!"

It has finally happened, I realized. *I'm like the lamb in the lion's den. Mom has become a lion and now the poor little lamb will have to fend for himself.*

"You did what?" Michael roared, lunging at me. I backed up and began to raise my hands in frustration. "I didn't hit her. She was—"

Bam! With the back of his hand, Michael struck my face so hard I fell and skidded on the carpet.

I yowled, holding the side of my face and feeling blood gush from my nose.

Michael's face was darkening with fury. "Don't you ever touch your mother! Do you hear me?"

I lay across the floor, delicately rubbing the rug burn on my elbow, and peered over at Mom. My mother—my once-beloved mother—stood with her arms folded across her chest, an approving smile on her face.

The pain that rushed through me at that moment had nothing to do with anything physical. I felt numb. I realized, *I have no one now.* When Michael came at me again, I said nothing. I just let him strike me. I did not even try to defend myself.

After he hit me again, I then felt his army boot crash into my ribs. I was that lamb with no one to protect him, and Mom and Michael were the heartless lions teaching the lamb a lesson.

I believe I blacked out momentarily, and when I came to, Michael was dragging me into my bedroom.

"There!" Kicking me through the doorway, he thundered, "Now you know what it feels like! Don't you ever touch your mother again!"

The door slammed shut. From the floor, I reached for the bedspread hanging down and pulled it towards my face to sop up the blood. My whole face felt like it was on fire as the soreness began to set in. I listened to their muffled voices in the other room and I could only make out that they were laughing. I lay there, experiencing a cataclysm of emotions—rage, fear, betrayal, and desperation—which led to only one thought: *I need to escape, immediately. I need to get as far away from them as I can. But how?*

Then I remembered a family that lived in Marina. Back when we lived on base at Fort Ord, Mom and Dad would take us to their house because the couple had two children around Michael's age. I remembered how their mother used to play with me while her husband and my parents sat drinking in the living room. I guess she didn't like to drink because she would sit with me in the kitchen and make tea for us. Mine was more cream and sugar than tea and I remembered she always had the best-tasting oatmeal cookies.

Now I waited until Michael left the apartment and my mother went back to bed. It must have been twenty minutes before Michael left. When I stood up, I couldn't see very well. Both my eyes were virtually swollen shut, so I had to feel my way out of the room. When I got outside the front door, the lady who lived in the apartment next to us was coming up the stairs. She gasped when she saw me. I put my forefinger to my swollen lips and looked back at the apartment door with a slight nod, trying to convey the source of the danger.

She helped me down the stairs and took me to the manager's apartment.

161

By the time the police came, the two ladies had me cleaned up. They were not sure if I needed stitches, but both policemen said I looked like I would be alright, and they didn't need to take me to the hospital.

After I told the officers what happened, I gave them the last name of the family and told them where they lived. The police stepped into another room to make the call, but I could hear anyway. I sighed with a sense of huge relief once I could tell the Willards were saying they were willing to help me.

They told the police to bring me to their house. It had been almost two years since I had seen the Willard family and wondered if they still lived in the same flat-roofed house. I remembered how small it was, with only one couch in the living room, and hoped they had moved to a bigger one. Bringing me in as an addition to the family might be a problem, but I sent those thoughts out of my mind and prayed they would keep me.

I must have looked pretty bad because when I arrived at the front door the whole family stood there and stared.

"Oh my God," I heard them say all at once.

As the door closed behind me I started to envision my new life with this Marina family, thinking I would never have to see my mother and brother again. How could the police send me back after they saw what Michael was capable of? As we watched TV that night, sharing a big bowl of buttered popcorn, I looked around the room, hoping I could be part of their family. They reminded me of the Cleaver family from the TV show *Leave it to Beaver*.

When it came time to go to bed, they made a bed for me on their one couch since there was nowhere else for me to sleep. My body hurt in so many places it was difficult to relax. But the pain I felt the next morning, when they told me the bad news, hurt even more. It would be against the law for them to keep me, so back to the apartment I'd have to go. My plan had failed; my hopes were dashed.

I told the family Michael and Mom would kill me—especially since I had called the police on them—and that they would never forgive me. The woman who had so kindly made me tea had tears in her eyes when the police officer climbed out of the squad car, came to the porch and started walking me towards his vehicle. My head turned towards their house with longing, I kept my eyes on her, until the policeman put his hand on my head to make sure I ducked before getting into the back seat.

As we drove to the apartment, the policemen assured me I would be protected.

"You do not know my brother," I insisted. "You have no idea!"

I was terrified getting out of the police car. The thought of confronting Mom and Michael—after I had turned them in—caused to me to hyperventilate.

"We'll be with you," one said, trying to comfort me. They actually had to help me walk up the stairs. When I saw our front door start to open, I turned around and tried to run away.

"No, no, no," the tall black policeman said softly. With conviction I certainly could not feel, he added, "You are going to be just fine."

Mom and Michael were standing side by side in the front room with their arms crossed tight across their chests.

"OK," the white officer began, while directing me to stand in front of him. "We have documented every mark on this young man's face and on his body."

"You don't know what he did!" Mom shrieked, interrupting him. She was obviously drunk, swaying back and forth as she tried to argue that I had beaten her up.

"Be quiet!" the black officer said, taking one step towards her. "We do not want to hear your side of the story—this boy's face says as much as we want to hear."

Michael started to say something; the officer stepped in front of him. "You are lucky we aren't hauling you off to jail."

Michael harrumphed, but was smart enough to keep his mouth shut after that.

"You are on probation, young man, and what you did to your brother is enough for us to arrest you. But we are giving you a second chance, for now. If we see even one more scratch on this boy's face, you will be put away for a long time!"

"Can I say something now?" Mom asked, uncrossing her arms and placing them on her hips.

The officers nodded for her to go ahead.

"My son hasn't been going to school," she said, wagging her finger in my direction. "I signed him up, but he says he won't go, because the school is full of *niggers*."

163

I immediately looked at the black officer to see what he was going to say. Mom was right about me not wanting to go to school, but I never used that word. My second day at this school, a group of black students did beat me up on my way home. Once I told Mom what happened, she said since there was only a week left of school, I didn't have to go back.

"Are you drunk?" the black officer sharply asked, ignoring Mom's comments.

"No," Mom responded flatly, straightening up her back and sticking out her chest.

"OK, Donnie. You have my number," the other officer firmly said, looking at me while adjusting the tip of his hat. "You'll be fine. Won't he?" he finished, having changed the angle of his vision to look Michael square in the eye.

"Yes, officer," Michael replied, looking serious. He waited until the officer turned to leave and then directed a wicked grin over his shoulder at me.

After the door shut, neither Mom nor Michael made a sound. I knew they were waiting for the officers to get to the bottom of the stairs.

As if joined at the hip, they simultaneously turned and glowered at me. All I could see were two pairs of eyes, equally filled with venom.

"So you think you can get away with what you did to us?" Michael hissed with that awful whispery growl he had perfected. He took two steps towards me and cocked his arm back. I tried to steel myself for the blow. He swung, but pulled back the punch, just an inch from my face.

"You just wait," he continued to growl, holding his forearm just above my swollen lips for a few more seconds. But then he lowered his arm; I could see it twitch.

I stood there in disbelief. But in a flash, it sunk in: *It worked! He's not going to hit me!*

The air had changed in the room. For the first time ever, I felt like I was in control. I stepped away and headed towards my bedroom. Strangely, as I passed them, they both somehow looked smaller. I put my lips together and began to whistle the only song I knew how to whistle. Approaching my bedroom door, I started to sing it instead: *"Mares eat oats ... and does eat oats ... and little lambs eat ivy.*

When I closed the door on them, I was whistling the rest of the song.

CHAPTER TWENTY ONE

I Feel Lucky   1966, Northern California

Two weeks after Michael beat me up, he barged through the front door and threatened my mother. "If you don't get me fifty dollars by tomorrow, I'll knock the hell out of both of you!" This was the first time I heard Michael threaten my mom, or anyone else, for money.

"There's no way I can get the money," she cried. He shoved her backwards, sending her sprawling across the kitchen floor.

"Tomorrow!" he roared.

I watched Mom crawl to the back wall, and just as she reached for the kitchen chair to get up, her son came over and kicked her in the leg.

"I mean it!" he growled, paying no attention to her screams.

She lay there grabbing onto her leg until he slammed the door.

"Oh, it hurts," she whimpered, rubbing her calf.

I had spent two weeks waiting for her to apologize for her part in my beating, but the apology never came. I had not spoken to her for all that time, but when I looked at her hunkered on the floor, pitifully gasping in pain, I decided it was time to break the silence.

"What are we going to do?" I reached down to help her up.

"No." She refused my gesture with surprising calm. "I need to sit here and think a minute."

Since she did not want to get up, I decided to sit down beside her. We both inched backwards to rest against the wall. It appeared that we were a team again—if only to survive Michael's rage.

"It's that whore he's staying with downstairs!" she said angrily, still rubbing her leg.

"You mean Lee Ann?" I couldn't believe that my mother was still in denial, still blaming someone else for Michael's vicious behavior.

"Yes! Her! One of the neighbors told me they've been driving to Marina almost every night to that Mortimer's, that damn gambling joint."

How my mother could love and defend Michael even when he beat her, how she could watch Michael beat me and be on his side—even though I was the good son who took care of her—was something that haunted me. I sat slumped against the wall, void of all feeling.

Moments later, her new-found energy surprised me. "I have a plan to get some money."

"You're actually going to do this? I shrieked. "We can't! If you do, Michael will threaten us whenever he needs money!"

Ignoring me, she gathered herself together, braced against the chair, and hoisted herself up from the floor. Heading straight to a mirror, my mother wiped the mascara from beneath her eyes and—ever convinced of the importance of looking good no matter the situation—she powdered her face and applied her favorite deep red lipstick.

"Tomorrow, we will take a bus to Monterey and I will ask Mary and Larry to lend me fifty dollars."

"I think we should call the police." I pulled the piece of paper the black policeman had given me. "Here's that officer's number." I tried to be the grown-up; I tried to be insistent.

"No, no, no! That will just make Michael angrier."

All I wanted was for Michael to disappear and my mother to stay sober, but I could tell my mother's mind was set, so I gave in to her plan. "Can't you just call Mary and Larry on the phone? Have them wire it?" I questioned, as I began straightening up the room. "What if we go all the way there, and they refuse?"

"I thought about that. But I think we'll have a better chance of them being willing to loan us the money if they see us in person."

Late the next morning we were standing at the bus stop. Since it was Sunday the bus was only half full, but we must have stopped at least twenty times. Mom called it the "milk run." Before we approached Monterey, she had already given the bus driver Mary and Larry's address and found out which stop we should take.

"Next stop, Cannery Row." He caught my eye and tilted his head towards the door, as his reminder.

"Mom, this is where we get off," I whispered, noticing she had closed her eyes. She'd had only one drink before we left, so I knew she wasn't drunk. The bus driver pulled over to the stop and politely nodded to us as we moved towards the door. I could not remember the last time since Dad's death that I had seen her so dispirited. Yet as soon as we stepped off the bus, she began striding the four blocks to her friends' house.

Mom knocked fervently on their screen door. "They have to be here!" she repeated, as much a prayer as a determination. "They have to be!"

"Mom, let's go." Standing a step behind her, I gently patted her on the shoulder. "I don't think they're home."

It turned out to be a good thing we left when we did to make our way back to the bus stop. We had not thought about the limited weekend schedule; fortunately, we caught the last bus home. As the driver called out our stop, I watched my mother summon up the strength to stand up and get off the bus. She turned away from the route home and started trudging in the direction of the liquor store. I thought about complaining, but the bruises on her face were starting to darken and I knew Michael had broken her heart yet again. I followed behind, without uttering a word.

With the familiar brown paper bag tucked in her purse, we arrived at our apartment building. When we reached the stairs, Mom grabbed my arm and whispered that she needed help. With my left arm around her waist and my other under her right arm, we slowly mounted the stairs, one at a time.

Thank goodness I had her in a protective grip, as she faltered when we got to the top and saw our wide-open front door. I left Mom holding onto the balcony rail. I could tell as I cautiously approached that something was wrong. But when I looked in, I still couldn't believe it. All our living room furniture was gone!

My eyes went immediately to the empty space where my color television had been.

"My TV!" I screamed, and ran to the empty space, crying hysterically.

"Michael!" Mom said his name with disgust as she stepped inside behind me. "He did this! That Goddamn son of a bitch! I'll kill him!"

Mom immediately went to the kitchen and mixed herself a drink. Then she decided to talk with the neighbors to ask if they had seen anything. One of them said she had noticed two men dressed in overalls; she assumed they were movers. She said she figured we must be moving out, so she didn't think anything of it.

After Mom came back from her investigation, she went downstairs to Lee Ann's apartment to confront Michael. Of course, he wouldn't talk to her. Shoving her out the door, he berated her, "Get out of my face, you crazy old woman!"

"He's got his money," she told me resignedly, upon her return. "I hope he and that whore lose every Goddamn cent of it!"

The next morning when I got out of bed, I stepped into the living room and froze, saddened to see the empty wall where my TV had been.

"Donnie!" My mother's voice, surprisingly strong, called out to me from the kitchen.

I walked in and saw her standing by the sink. She turned to face me and placed both of her hands behind her so she could brace herself against the aqua Formica countertop.

"I called Mary this morning and told her what Michael did."

"Did you tell her we tried to visit her yesterday?"

"No. But she said a neighbor spotted what looked like a mother and son knocking at their front door."

I noticed a half-pint of vodka sitting on the counter to Mom's left, with the cap lying along beside it. *She's about to have her first drink of the day*, I worried. She continued to relay what was said.

"We're going to move to Pacific Grove and Larry and Mary are going to help us," Mom said with a hint of excitement in her voice. "I told Mary I cannot go on like this, always scared of what your brother might do next."

Mom's eyes began to tear up and then she reached her hand up to her nose and wiped it, bringing back the stoic face I was used to. She proclaimed, "I've decided to quit drinking."

I was stunned.

"Don't say it," she added, putting her hand up like a stop sign. "I mean it this time."

She turned and picked up the opened bottle of vodka and proceeded to pour it down the drain. The clear liquid cascaded out, leaving the glass bottle empty.

"I'm through, I'm telling you," she insisted, and continued. "After I told Mary how many times I have tried to quit, she suggested we move to Pacific Grove because it is a dry town, even though it is right next to Monterey."

She sat the bottle down just as dramatically as she had picked it up, and began to explain that bars and liquor stores were forbidden there. "It's against the law for them to sell liquor. So you see, honey, I am going to do it this time!"

A solemn silence filled the room as we both stood facing each other, allowing the words to linger for a few more moments.

No bars? No liquor stores! I began to comprehend what this could mean. Hope followed me as I turned and walked back to my room.

Maybe, just maybe, after we move. How many times had we moved already since my father died? I asked myself, gazing out my bedroom window. *Maybe this move will do it ... we'll get away from Michael and Mom will quit drinking, and Dear God,* I began to pray, *please help us. I don't know if I can hold on much longer.*

Three days later, Larry and Mary called to say they found a four-plex that originally had been a large Georgian-style mansion. Someone had taken the historic building and converted it into four one-bedroom apartments. We splurged on a cab later that day to see it. I stood on the sidewalk and thought the building, with its faded beige siding crackled with centuries of paint, looked like an old lady with too many layers of make-up.

Our unit would be the one in the back. It had French doors in the bedroom facing the vacant lot next door. The lot was filled with huge oak trees, their intertwining twisted branches like limbs of dancers moving gracefully across a stage. The sun filtered golden rays through the snarled web of branches. I stepped out of the French doors and onto the rickety porch, letting the darts of sunshine play hide-and-seek with my eyes.

A few weeks later, I found myself standing in that same place with all our possessions moved in and my clothes unpacked. Everything was coming together and school was to begin that week. On my first day of eighth grade, I met a girl named Regina and we clicked right away. We discovered we had something in common; both our fathers had recently died of heart attacks.

Regina was half-Japanese and not very pretty and she wore black-framed glasses with lenses as thick as Coke bottles. The glasses almost made her look smart, but when she opened her mouth, a high-pitched whiney voice came out that made her sound stupid. At times kids would make fun of her and call her names, so I would try and stand up for her. A boy punched me in the nose after I called him a "butthead" for calling her a "four-eyed Jap." I let her fend for herself from then on.

After I got home from my first day of school, Mom greeted me at the door with a surprise. Actually the surprise was for her. Mary's mother had gone into a nursing home and the facility would not let her bring her toy poodle, Cindy Lou.

My mother had always wanted a poodle. So there we stood, Mom, me and Cindy Lou. I said right away, "Mom, we gotta lose the 'Lou.' It sounds ridiculous." *"Cindy" is bad enough for a dog,* was what I was really thinking, but I left that alone. Fortunately, Mom agreed that the "Lou" could go.

Watching Mom with Cindy was like watching a different person, especially since she had not had a drink for the entire week.

She even went so far as to ask me, "How does it feel now to have a baby sister? Don't you think she's just the cutest thing you've ever seen?"

That day marked the beginning of Mother's obsession with my "new little sister." She started spending money we didn't have to have her groomed. And along with grooming, she would pay to have Cindy's toenails painted purple, pink and every shade of red. She bought several rhinestone leashes and collars that went with all of Mom's own colored accessories. And then there was the matching bow, tied securely to her top knot—which lasted about an hour, until Cindy, the beauty queen, pawed it off and flung it across the room.

But I never complained because I thought that Cindy was the reason Mom remained sober. I never brought up how she was doing with her sobriety nor asked where she found the strength. I was afraid to talk about it, thinking that voicing it might break the spell. She never said a word either, not to apologize for past deeds, nor to talk about her struggle trying not to drink. It was as if her drinking never happened.

However, the *spell* only lasted two more weeks. On one of her long walks with Cindy, she ended up at the border of Pacific Grove and Monterey, where she found a liquor store. A mile-and-a-half of walking was all it took, and soon she was back to her old ways. She would walk an hour to Monterey during the day and take taxis to the bars at night, spending the money she got from Dad's VA pension. When Mary and Larry found out she was drinking again, they washed their hands of her, but I was sure they were the ones who contacted the Salvation Army the week of Thanksgiving, after Mom called begging them for money. Two ladies from the Salvation Army came to our door. They left a large box filled with food and a turkey with all the dressing.

The next day I remember Mom stayed sober long enough to cook us our Thanksgiving dinner. And of course Cindy had to have her own plate filled with turkey.

"We don't like that old dark meat … do we, Cindy?" she said, talking in baby talk as she watched how Cindy chose only the white meat. "She's just like her mommy."

I was mesmerized by how much she loved Cindy and by evening started to think that Cindy was the reason she cooked Thanksgiving dinner. That was the beginning of our sibling rivalry; but at least she was a dog … and that I could handle. Her snobby attitude whenever Mom was in the room was obvious. And if Mom ever had to choose between us, the winner would definitely be the four-legged one with the top knot.

The morning of Christmas Eve, Regina and I met in our usual place to hike down to the beach and explore the tide pools. It was a bright sunny day—unusually warm for the end of December—when we met at the beginning of the trail. I could tell right away that something was wrong.

"Are you OK?" I asked.

"I'll tell you when we get down to the rocks." Sulking, she shuffled off ahead of me.

Just beyond her I noticed a young man wearing a white t-shirt with black printed words across his back that said "I FEEL LUCKY." The words seemed to fit perfectly between his bony shoulder blades.

I feel lucky—now that was a concept unfamiliar to me.

As I watched him disappear down the path, I began chanting in a whisper those three words: "I feel lucky. I feel lucky." I thought it was beginning to work until we reached the rocks and Regina told me the bad news.

"My mother saw your mom picked up by the police for being drunk in public."

As I listened to my best friend's farewell speech, my eyes scanned the rocks. I thought about diving into the most beautiful tide pool I'd ever seen.

The show of bright colors was interrupted when I heard Regina say, "Donnie, did you hear what I just said? I'm not allowed to see you anymore."

I looked up with tears in my eyes, "Yes, Regina. I know my mother's a drunk. And God knows I've tried everything to make her stop!" The shame began to overwhelm me.

I found my eyes diving back into the tide pools, but my tears blurred the colors to a muddy brown.

With a soft sigh, I said, "You know, I probably should just go." And without even giving her a hug goodbye, I headed back up the sandy trail. Crying most of the way back home, my thoughts shifted to the t-shirt I had seen earlier, about *someone* being lucky, and I wondered if that would ever be me.

Making my way off the trail, I followed the old cracked sidewalk, walking in and out between parked cars. Just as I got to our street, a Pacific Grove police car passed me and then pulled up in front of our building. Both men were tall and thin, but one appeared much older than the other. Taking an official walk around to their rear door, the younger officer opened it.

I couldn't believe what I saw. My mother poured out of the back seat with Cindy clutched tightly to her chest. I could see Mom's coal black coiffed hair glistening with blood that was oozing from the white gauze bandage the police must have administered.

When I approached the car, Mom saw me and her first concern was for Cindy.

"Donnie, this is all such a mess!" she said directing her attention towards Cindy, instead of me.

Sternly interrupting Mother's silliness, the older officer asked, "Is this your son, Mrs. English?"

She nodded without looking at him and continued to put all her attention towards Cindy. "Cindy was such a good girl," she babbled on, sounding almost childlike. "I must've blacked out on the sidewalk and my little Cindy stayed right beside me the whole time."

"How many times have we picked you up now? Four … five?"

Mom ignored him and turned away.

"Mrs. English, if we pick you up one more time, I personally will see that your son is taken away from you! Do you understand?"

"No, *you* don't understand! I didn't have anything to drink," Mom responded immediately, finally directing her attention to the officers. "I was walking, and I just blacked out. I had nothing to drink. Nothing!"

The officer became noticeably disgusted. He looked up from his writing pad and began to scold her, "Did you understand what I just said? This is your last chance. If we pick you up again, you will lose your son."

His loud stern voice scared Cindy so much she squirmed right out of my arms. I grabbed her metallic purple rhinestone-studded leash as she landed directly on top of some crabgrass growing alongside the porch. With a quick twizzle, she squatted and did her business. Out of the corner of my eye, I noticed the policemen motioning to each other that it was time to leave. Making eye contact with me, both officers nodded as if to say, *"Son, take good care of yourself. And good luck with your mother."*

Cindy and I followed Mom as she walked along the rock pathway back to our apartment. Once inside, the sound of Cindy's purple painted toenails prancing across the stained yellow linoleum floor echoed louder than normal. Mom strolled by me and stopped in the middle of the living room, striking a pose of deep contemplation.

Hungry, I went to the kitchen and browsed through the cupboards, calculating the food we had left. The dreaded end of the month was approaching, and Mom would have spent all of her monthly income on jugs of wine and taxis for bar hopping. It was a good thing I liked oatmeal, because it became our main staple. Since tomorrow would be Christmas, I grabbed the Quaker Oats, leaving the tomato soup for our holiday meal.

After scouring the burnt oatmeal from the bottom of the pot, I decided to go next door and play in the small forest of trees where layers of oak leaves were divided with old bricks into secret rooms. I knew I would feel the weight of the day lift as I stepped into my secret hideaway, inhaling the botanical scents that wafted together with the fog. Each room had its own mood depending on where I would sit. My favorite was the one that looked onto an old alley fence covered with red and gold nasturtiums. I went to get my coat and a blanket to sit on. Just as I reached the front door, I heard my mom on the phone with her drinking buddy, Marianne.

"I was wondering if you could do me a favor," she said. "I just had an incident with the police and they threatened to take Donnie away from me." It didn't sound from her voice like she took it very seriously.

I stepped back towards the kitchen so she couldn't see me.

"Do you remember Lillian talking about those meetings? Well," Mom asked, "can you call Lillian and see if we can go tonight?"

Yes, tomorrow would be Christmas Day. I stepped outside and a wave of memories flooded over me of how Dad always had a way of making Christmas Eve fun. He would dress up like Santa Claus and allow Michael and me to see him placing presents around the tree. I don't know if I realized it was him back then, but the excitement was something I would never forget. The sound of the jolly, "Ho! Ho! Ho!" in his deep operatic voice reverberated in my head. Those Christmas Eves were cherished times I held in my heart. I missed my Dad so much, and felt horribly alone. I snuck back outside, sure mom and her drinking buddy had a wild night planned, and Christmas would pass with no celebration.

If loneliness had been a fatal disease, I would have never survived.

Hello, Elizabeth   1967, Northern California

When I returned from my forest, Mom was gone. *She must have of gone out,* I thought, detecting the last mist of perfume she always sprayed on just before leaving. I curled up with Cindy and jingled the one and only decoration, a sleigh bell on Cindy's collar. Even when Mom was passed out on her bed, I would feel warm knowing at least someone was there. Since Michael had stolen my TV, the only company I had was the radio. I turned it on and began listening to the evening's Christmas music. The last song I remember before I fell asleep was Bing Crosby singing "White Christmas," my dad's favorite song to sing.

I closed my eyes and sang along, dreaming about my father.

"Merry Christmas," I murmured softly to myself as I awoke, pushing Cindy to the floor and standing up from my bed—the couch—with my blanket wrapped around my shoulders. I heard keys jingling outside the front door.

"Merry Christmas, honey," Mom sang.

"Merry Christmas to you, too," I politely replied, scanning her arms for the expected brown paper bag.

No wine, I concluded. *Oh, of course, it's Christmas and the liquor stores are closed.*

"I met the nicest couple last night,"—she was still sounding upbeat— "Edna and George. They will be picking me up in a little while to take me to another meeting."

I didn't say anything and just nodded, letting her know I had heard her. I reached over to the end table and flipped on the radio. The first words I heard were, "*I'm dreaming of a white Christmas.*" I felt tears well up in my eyes. I knew it was a sign from Dad since "White Christmas" was the same song he would sing while he made pancakes every Christmas morning.

Mom hustled into her room, showered, changed, and was ready and waiting at the door when her friends came to pick her up. She happily went out the door with no mention of what I was to do that morning. I called to Cindy and we snuggled up in the array of sheets and blankets I had left unmade on the couch. We must have both dozed off, because when the phone rang, it startled Cindy. She sprang off the couch and started to bark.

It was Mom calling. Wherever she was, they had a Christmas buffet with all kinds of food and they said I was welcome to join them. She gave me the address and told me to call a cab.

"Are you sure it's OK?" I asked with trepidation, afraid they might turn me away.

"Yes, it's fine. And George said he'll be waiting outside, so tell the cab driver someone will be there to pay him."

I called for a cab and got dressed as fast as I could. While I was waiting outside for the taxi to arrive, I admired the other houses with their decorations. The brick building with the wrap-around porch had a life-size manger scene, with a plastic baby doll wrapped in a blanket portraying Jesus.

I heard a car coming and recognized the bright yellow color. As the cab driver pulled up to the curb, he reached across his seat and pushed open the door.

That's odd, I thought. *I guess he wants me to sit in the front seat.* I opened the car door and coughed, inhaling the smoke that blew towards me. I watched the driver put out his cigarette butt by smashing it into the dirty metal ashtray.

"Hello there, young man!" he greeted me jovially. "Where's your Mom today?"

His question surprised me at first, but then I recognized him from another time he had picked us up.

"She's at this place," I handed him the piece of paper with the address.

He reached over and took it with his left hand, while his right hand slipped over and patted my knee.

"Oh, I know right where this is. It's the rehab center over by the Lighthouse."

Mom said her friends were picking her up for a meeting, but had said nothing about a rehab center. After he patted my leg a few more times, his hand stayed there, resting on my thigh. "So, your mom's expecting you?" he asked, while his hand inched up towards my crotch.

"Oh, yes!" I began to sense he was someone to be afraid of.

"Both my mom *and* dad are there. Mom said some of Dad's friends are there, too." I paused for a moment, desperately thinking of what else to say to protect myself.

I felt his fingers begin to squeeze me. That's when I burst out with, "Did my mom tell you my father is a policeman?" I didn't wait for his answer and began rambling about the buffet and all the food Mom told me about on the phone.

His fingers slowly unclasped the bulge he had already thoroughly investigated, and then he mumbled, "Well, we better get over there, hadn't we?"

"It's Christmas, you know," I said nervously. "They'll probably have a turkey and dressing."

He did not say a word while I elaborated on what I imagined the menu might be. All I wanted was for his hand to remain on the steering wheel. I felt like if I just kept talking, I could keep his hands at a safe distance.

Oh no! I suddenly thought. *I don't know where we're going! What if he ...?* Just as I began to panic, we stopped in front of a three-story Victorian house.

"Here we are," he smiled, reaching for the handle on the meter. "It's two-fifty."

At first I wanted to run from the car, but I quickly fell into my normal state of denial by just "switching off" my thoughts and pretending nothing had happened.

I opened the car door and stepped out, hoping it was the right place. As I approached the house, I looked up and watched the light and dark pine green colors of the building appear and then disappear with the clouds of fog that were beginning to engulf the house.

A tall bearded man with thick salt and pepper hair darted past me, saying, "Go inside, Donnie. I'll pay for the taxi."

Mom was at the door to greet me, and after a few introductions, she led me into the old home's dining room. My eyes went right to the large table covered with platters of food. It was obvious everyone had already eaten, but from the looks of it, there was still plenty left.

"You go ahead and eat," Mom whispered, pointing to the plates and silverware. "I'll come back for you in a little while." It was wonderful not to smell alcohol on her breath.

There was so much food! I immediately went to the large platter still piled high with slices of ham. I could not remember the last time I had had a ham dinner.

Just as I finished, I heard Mom call my name from the other side of the room. "They are about ready to start the meeting," she announced. "I talked to George and he said it would be alright for you to observe, but you have to sit in the back."

"You're sure it's OK?" I asked softly, "I can stay right here, Mom, if—"

"No, honey, really, it's fine. Come on and follow me."

We entered through a large, arched doorway into what once must have been the living room. It was set up with a massive oblong table big enough to accommodate at least fifteen people. A tall bay window stood proudly at the end of the room, its built-in window seat covered with faded floral cushions.

"This is where you can sit." Mom patted one of the cushions. "If you get bored, you can slip out here," she said, directing my attention to a small doorway a few steps away.

The buzzes of voices grew louder as more people entered the room with greetings of "Merry Christmas!" interspersed with, "How are you?" and "How have you been?"

Suddenly a ring from a small bell stopped the chatter and everyone dispersed to take their places around the table. A short, stout man with very little hair took his place at the head of the table and called the meeting to order. You could have heard a pin drop when he announced the rules for the meeting. After he finished, he said his first name and then followed with, "and I'm an alcoholic." Then, in unison, the group responded melodically, "*Hello, Bill!*"

I could see Mom sitting a few seats down from him, with Edna and George sitting by her side. She looked over at me and winked, so I tried to wink back, but ended up winking nervously with both eyes. When it came time for her to introduce herself, she looked at me, then took a deep breath, and turned back to the folks at the table.

178

"Last night was my first time here." She hesitated slightly, instead of saying her name. "When I introduced myself, I didn't admit I was an alcoholic. Edna and George here," she paused, turning to look at them, "have taken me under their wing. Well, what I'm trying to say is … my name is Elizabeth, and I'm an alcoholic."

I wasn't sure what surprised me most— her admitting she was an alcoholic— or introducing herself as "Elizabeth," instead of "Betty." The room then resounded with the expected, "*Hello, Elizabeth!*"

After the introductions were finished, George came over and squatted down in front of me to apologize for having to ask me to leave at this point. "I'm sorry, Donnie, but AA meetings are for adults only."

"That's OK," I said glancing at the side door. I got up and tiptoed towards the exit. I paused to take a look back.

It was Christmas. I reminded myself, once again looking about the room. One I would never forget.

Edna and George were at our apartment almost every day for three weeks. Alcoholics Anonymous infiltrated our lives and infused us with the hope I had been praying for. I wasn't sure how long it all would last, but I began to adopt Mom's new mantra, "*Take one day at a time.*" Our lives had gone in an unpredictable direction since my father had died, so it made sense now to concentrate on each day, instead of counting on the future.

Things were going well. I was finally able to afford to take roller skating lessons at the Monterey Del Monte Gardens skating club because Mom had taken a part-time housecleaning job. She knew I loved skating and she said it was a way for her to make amends, a step she said came from a book that had twelve steps she needed to follow in order to stay sober.

One particularly memorable Saturday morning, as we ate our breakfast, she shared more of the AA philosophy. My mother was going to receive her "30 day Chip," for 30 days of being sober. We went through our usual Saturday morning ritual—cleaning the apartment—with Mom doing most of it because I had injured my tailbone trying to master a waltz jump during a skating lesson a few days earlier. When I fell, I was sure I had "broken my butt," but when I got home and told Mom my diagnosis, she made a little joke saying, "How can you break something that's already cracked?"

I didn't laugh.

"Actually, honey, you can't break your butt," she explained. "You've probably just bruised your tailbone."

She was again enthusiastically sharing her feelings about receiving her chip when the phone rang. She put the half-bald feather duster down on the desk and wiped her hands on her flower-printed apron, pausing a moment before she picked up the receiver.

"Hello," she answered, in a cheery tone.

I decided this was a good time for me to sit down. I gathered two pillows from the back of the couch and placed them carefully under my broken butt.

"Yes, I'm Mrs. English," I heard Mom say, while I wrestled to get comfortable. Suddenly, the morning cheerfulness left her voice. It was replaced by heavy-hearted trepidation, as she confirmed, "Yes, I have a son named Michael."

It was the police. Lee Ann was dead.

The officer conveyed the only available description of what had happened—Michael's. He had told them that he and Lee Ann were driving back home from Mortimer's in Marina, where they had been gambling. It was just about 2 a.m. He admitted they were having an argument while he was driving about 70 miles per hour on the highway. They had just passed the gates to the entrance of Fort Ord, when Lee Ann threatened him, screaming, "If you don't pull over and let me out, I'm gonna open the door and jump out." He didn't take her seriously because he couldn't imagine that she would ever, as he put it, "do such a Goddamn stupid thing."

Obviously, Michael had not pulled over. Less obvious, and forever a mystery to everyone but my brother, was the manner in which Lee Ann left the vehicle and landed in the middle of the highway. Much later, at the inquest, the coroner testified that he was pretty sure, given the admitted speed, that she had died instantly, right after she hit the pavement. Unanswered questions loomed, but since there were no other witnesses, Michael was not charged. Lee Ann's death was officially ruled a suicide.

Putting down the phone after the policeman finished, Mother cried out, "Those two little girls! Those poor, poor little girls."

Hearing her wails of distress reminded me of the nightmare I'd had about Michael transforming into a venomous spider. I remembered dreaming how he would draw people into his deadly web, and then slowly kill them, deaf to their cries.

I'm sure he killed her, I scowled to myself, at the same time trying to shake the image of her body flying from the car to the pavement.

Before I knew it, Mom was on the phone relaying the whole gruesome story to Edna and George. I heard her finish the call by saying she could be ready in a half-hour.

"Are you going to a meeting?" I asked.

"Yes ... I think so," she answered, staring off into the kitchen. I followed her stare and realized she was looking at the cabinet where I recently had found an old bottle of wine, half-empty, left there before she quit drinking one month ago.

I stopped rubbing Cindy, trying to concentrate on what I should say. Then, as usual, Cindy rolled onto her back and started to do what Mom called her "begging" move, pumping her front paws up and down and clawing at empty space, to let you know *you* were not finished with *her.* I complied and began to rub her belly, hoping it would help keep my anxiety from totally taking over.

"So, Mom ... when are they picking you up?"

She took a step and turned like she was going to go into the kitchen, "You know, Donnie, I think I'll call Edna and tell them I'm not going to go after all."

I watched her move towards the phone, my heart beginning to pound. *If she doesn't make it this time, she'll never stop.* I was certain.

I had to put Cindy down. I quickly lifted myself up off the couch and spoke with some noticeable desperation, "Mother, I think you should go. Really!"

She jerked her head back towards me with a puzzled look on her face and stood there, squinting at me for a moment.

Ah, suddenly I knew what to do! She liked me to help pick out her clothes—something Dad had done when he was alive.

"Come on, Mom." I softened my tone. "I'll help you pick out something pretty to wear."

Given all the chaos of our lives, I had no idea what she was going to say or how she was going to react. She just stood there, staring off into space. She emitted a short sigh, and then said firmly, almost to herself, "OK, let's see what I've got to wear."

Mom was dressed and ready to go just as Edna and George knocked at the door.

"Just a minute," she hollered at them through the door.

I picked up Cindy and watched my mother suddenly dash back to her room. She had almost forgotten to spray on her signature scent, White Shoulders.

I was incredibly happy that my mother chose to go with Edna and George to a meeting, but at the same time, I was equally shocked and saddened by Lee Ann's horrible death. I didn't know how to handle such a contradictory set of emotions. Meanwhile, my injured tailbone was throbbing. I could do something about that. I ran a hot bath, looking forward to some soothing relief.

Just as I was about to step out from my underwear and get into the bath, I heard a *thud*. It sounded like it came from the porch outside the set of French doors off the bedroom. I pulled up my shorts and froze, thinking it was a burglar. I tiptoed around the corner to where I could see through the white lace curtains.

"Donnie! Is that you?" The tall silhouette called out, peering back at me through the lace.

"Michael? Michael, is that you?" I parroted back.

"Thank God you're here!" he clamored, pulling frantically at the doorknob and still peering through glass.

"Open the door, Donnie!"

"Wait a minute, I gotta put my pants on!" I hollered back, looking around, but not seeing my pants anywhere. I circled the bed, scanning the floor, and finally saw them behind the chair where they had fallen. As I reached down to grab them, I twisted my foot and fell down, landing smack on my tailbone.

"Oww!" I screamed.

"Donnie, come on, let me in! Goddamn it! You gotta help me carry something in. I can't carry it anymore."

Listening to his groans, my mind went into a frenzy: *Oh my God! He's brought Lee Ann's body back with him. That's what that thud was. He stole her body!*

My fear of dead bodies resurfaced as I remembered being buried in the graveyard behind our house at Moss Landing. Ghouls and zombies had haunted me ever since, and now Lee Ann's dead body was right outside the door!

"Oh my God," I kept repeating, scrambling to get my pants on.

"Wait, Michael!" I screamed, trying to zip up my pants.

What should I do? What should I do? My mind raced hysterically.

"Come on, Donnie! I can't carry these duffel bags anymore!" I caught sight of his silhouette stepping away from the door

Duffel bags! Did he say "duffel bags?" Not believing I heard right, I tried to see more of whatever was outside. *Yes! That's what he was carrying! I could see two bulging duffel bags lying diagonally across the porch steps.*

I finally opened the door and listened to him explain how the police had taken him to Lee Ann's apartment so he could pick up his things and get out before her husband arrived from Vietnam.

He instantly made his way through the apartment and when he saw the tub filled with water—in his naturally self-absorbed way—he assumed it was for him. "Great!" he exclaimed, and sneakily disappeared behind the door, "A bath is just what I need."

He must have been in there for an hour, finally getting out and dressed just as Mom came home. As soon as she saw him, she yelled hysterically for him to get out.

"You don't understand!" he yelled back.

Cindy began barking and nipping at his leg, protecting Mom the best way she knew how.

"Cindy!" I screamed, trying to grab her before Michael kicked her in the head.

Their arguing continued until Mom went over to the phone and threatened to call the police. Her threat worked.

He left, fuming that even his own mother didn't love him.

"That's right!" she yelled right back at him. "And don't let the door hit your ass on the way out!"

I was surprised by her courage and even more surprised how she dealt with him without having a drink.

AA was working!

CHAPTER TWENTY THREE

Queers Are Everywhere
1981, Los Altos, California—1968, San Leandro, California

I was thinking about Lee Ann and the murdered man in Eureka one morning when my receptionist tapped on my door and said a lady from the newspaper was there to see me.

"What! What did you say?" I exclaimed, almost jumping up from my chair. I was in my office looking over the remodeling designs for an expansion I was planning. My salon—*Dorian Grey*— had finally been recognized as one of the most successful hair salons on the San Francisco Peninsula.

The reporter said she wanted to interview me for an article about the salon, for the business section of the local newspaper. But, for a moment, I worried, *Maybe she's an undercover investigator sent by the D.A., or from a newspaper wanting "the real story behind Michael English."* My silk shirt was dripping wet by the time I was through speaking with her, even though her questions turned out only to be about the business.

So, luckily, the reporter was not there to tie my life to my murderous brother's. But my nervousness made me realize I was bordering on paranoia, and if I didn't find out what was happening with Michael, I was going to go crazy. I waited until the end of the day to call Mr. Sanders, his public defender.

I was surprised he was still at his office, since I called after 5 p.m. He said my call was timely because my brother had just been found, and was behind bars, being held with the tightest security.

"They caught him?" I gasped.

"Yes, and because of the extenuating circumstances, all I'm allowed to tell you is that he did not get very far. What's really going to hurt his case, though, is that some of the other prisoners he freed are still on the loose."

I was both speechless and relieved that they had caught Michael. I could stop looking over my shoulder, afraid he would show up at my door.

After locating my voice, I cleared my throat. "What will happen now?"

"It looks like Michael wants to plead guilty, since he will be getting a change of venue due to the jeopardized gag order. That's why I'm working late, at least this time."

"Change of venue?" I didn't understand what he was talking about.

"Because of the escape and the publicity around it, he will have to be moved to another county. I've recommended to him that he plead guilty so he won't have to go to trial." And then Mr. Sanders added, with a slight triumphant tone in his voice, "This will allow him to both keep what he did out of the press and to escape the death penalty."

"No trial is good," I nodded.

He went on. "The District Attorney is upset because now he's lost the chance to try a case with two people being charged with one death. It's not likely he will ever encounter that situation again."

I was having a hard time following all the legal details. But my first reaction—thinking back to all my childhood suffering—was anger: *Once again, Michael will get away without the punishment he deserves.* Yet, almost simultaneously, I experienced a slight feeling of relief, admittedly not just about my personal safety. Michael was still my brother, my only brother. I did not actually want him to die. And I didn't, and still don't, believe in the death penalty.

That didn't stop me, though, from thinking about Lee Ann, and her two little girls, and even her husband and how tragic her death had been for all of them.

Lee Ann had been so innocent. The man in Eureka was elderly and innocent too, yet they were both dead.

Hearing Michael was back behind bars made me hopeful that this would be the last I would hear of him.

It had been thirteen years since that Christmas Day AA meeting, when I witnessed my mother's commitment to AA, and the mantra of taking one day at a time entered my life. And that was exactly what I'd been doing ever since that first day when Mr. Sanders called—taking one day at a time—constantly fearful that my life would be ruined. But now it looked like Michael's escape was thwarted and he would be put away forever, if not given the death penalty. My life would return to normal. I had escaped the front page news story I had so dreaded.

I put the phone down and sat still, staring at the plans to remodel the salon. In this state of grateful relief, I thought back to those first few years after Lee Ann's death, when I started getting serious about roller skating. Not only did I enjoy it, I became really good at it. I opened my desk drawer and took out the picture of me wearing roller skates and holding a trophy in my hands, my face shining as if I had won the Olympics.

Just as I had become known and comfortable in the skating community in the Monterey area and was starting to feel good about my life, my mother broke the news that we were going to move to the East Bay. This time moving was not connected to her drinking or financial problems. In fact it was the reverse—she had been hired for a Civil Service clerical position at the Oakland Army Base. I was happy that this would be a better job for her; nonetheless, I was disappointed about what it meant for me—having to start all over. I was fourteen years old.

When we went to check out apartments to rent in Oakland, we found the only places we could afford were in virtually all-black neighborhoods. Someone told Mom that the quiet suburb of San Leandro, next to Oakland, would have more affordable rents. We found a place there, but she had to take three buses to get to work.

I found a skating club in the heart of Hayward, a city to the south of our town. It took me two buses to get to there and three to get home, but I would have taken five. Skating had become my passion, and the glue that held my life together. I was able to practice hours a day for most of the summer. And the more I practiced, the better I got.

At the skating rink I made friends who were around my own age. When we hung out, we often talked about how skating helped us deal with our problems. Skating fast, feeling the wind blow through your hair, spinning, jumping and dancing on roller skates to fast music produced a high that we all knew. We agreed: when we were on the skating floor, there were no problems—it was just us and our roller skates. *We were free.*

I treasured my new-found freedom. I'd spend virtually all day, every day, at the rink. But this was about to end; school would begin in two weeks.

Mom reminded me I needed to go and register for my first year of high school. The school was only four blocks away, so the next day I set out to sign up for ninth grade. I loved to learn and, for the most part, had enjoyed school. But back in Monterey, bigger boys had teased me and called me a sissy because I didn't like sports. Up here in the East Bay, I had already been assaulted and mugged on the bus, again by older boys.

I couldn't help but be worried that, especially now as a freshman, I'd have problems getting along with the older boys in high school. And the moment I stepped onto the school grounds, my worries were proven true. A group of Latino boys, probably seniors, approached me. "Where do you think you're going?" the tallest boy sneered, moving right in front of me, with his chest puffed out like a peacock.

My eyes found the ground, as I murmured, "I'm registering for school."

"You want to come to our school?" And then he hollered to his friends in Spanish, something about a *Gringo*.

Immediately they formed a circle around me and started pushing me from one to the other. "Leave me alone," I yelled.

The tall one told them to stop. I stumbled as the last boy pushed me to the ground.

"Get up!"

"Yeah, get up! Get up!" they all started chanting.

Once I found my balance, I stood up. Tears were running down my cheeks.

I heard one of them mocking me, "Aw, the little boy is going to cry now."

"Go on, Gringo, you can go," the suddenly polite leader said, as he motioned for the other boys to form a line so I could walk by.

I stood and stared at them, wondering if they were really going to let me go.

"You're sure I can go?" I said with a hopeful voice.

"Vamonos!" was the last thing I heard. I took two steps past them and then felt a foot kick my knee, forcing me to the ground. The palms of my hands grated on the asphalt; tiny rocks pierced my flesh as I stuck to the ground.

A man's voice shouted from a distance, "What's going on?"

I looked up. The boys scattered in all directions.

They're just like my brother. I'll be trapped again! I silently screamed, as I got to my feet.

"You OK?" My savior, a tall husky man dressed in a janitor's uniform, had approached. "Yeah, I'm OK," I said, staring at the grit on my palms mixed with bloodied shreds of skin.

"You sure?"

"Yes. I'm sure." I replied, turning away, knowing I was lying. No doubt he knew too.

As I walked home, I carried on a conversation with myself, debating about what I should do.

Those boys are just like Michael. I can't be around them. And I won't! At that moment, I made the decision that I was not going back. Ever.

By the time I arrived home, I had a plan. I would carry a razor blade with me and if someone found out that I was skipping school, I would cut my wrists, killing myself before anyone could force me back to the schoolyard.

For the next four years, I stayed home from school and nobody noticed.

Since I never made it to the office to register that day, there was no record of me anywhere. My mother never asked to see any forms; she assumed that I had registered, as I said I would. I guess I was lucky because she really had no idea what the modern-day school schedule was all about. Her only point of reference was her own schooling—in a one-room classroom in the back hills of Kentucky. She and Dad had never gotten involved with Michael's short stint in high school. Activities like teacher conferences, career days, sports teams, after-school clubs—she didn't even know they existed. She believed pretty much whatever I made up. She had no logical reason not to.

I was sneaky. One day I went to the school to gather teacher's names from their classroom doors. I figured if she ever got suspicious and checked, at least she would see the names of real teachers on my report card. All the while, I was betting on my Mom's personal struggles taking a toll and that she wouldn't have the energy to actually visit the school to check up on me. Some nights I locked myself in my room, claiming to do my homework; fortunately, she never asked to see it. She trusted me.

Mom left for work before I was supposed to leave for school and returned home well after I presumably would have gotten out of school—I was safe on that score. Most days, I just never left the house. All day I would sit and watch TV while I played with Cindy. The soap opera *Love Is a Many Splendored Thing* was my favorite program. The game shows were alright, but I found the soap operas a lot more interesting. It was amazing to me how, on a day-to-day basis, people could make such messes out of their lives. Their lives were not so different from ours; they too kept repeating the same mistakes over and over.

While watching those daytime soaps, I began to notice how sexually aroused I got when a handsome man would appear on the screen. My first soap star crush was Bernie, the tall, dark and handsome man who was married to Laura on *Love Is a Many Splendored Thing*. I would fantasize about being his wife so we could run away together. I was also finding myself more and more attracted to guys around me, wondering what it would feel like to be a girl and have him as a boyfriend. It is interesting that I could only imagine a relationship with a boy if I were a girl. The notion of being a boyfriend to a boy was still foreign to me.

Right around that time, my skating teacher, Jimmy—who looked a bit like my soap opera crush, Bernie—mentioned to me, during one of my private lessons, that he needed to talk with me.

"Donnie, you have a lot of natural talent," he told me. "I've been thinking about it and I've decided to talk with Darren to see if he will take you on."

Darren, the head teacher at the rink, had a great reputation for creating champions. "You need a pro, someone with more experience," Jimmy explained, patting me on the back. "I teach beginners and I think I've brought you as far as I can."

I liked Jimmy and didn't understand why I needed someone else. But because I respected him, I agreed, but added, "If I don't like Darren, I want to come back to you."

"You'll like him," Jimmy said confidently with a smile. "And anyway, he has trained national champions, and I think you are going to be his next one."

A few weeks later, Darren came to our house and talked with Mom, telling her that he would pick me up after school and take me to rink. That way, by not having to deal with buses, I could get in several hours of practice each day. Mom was happy that someone, especially a male, had come into my life and seemed to care about me. Darren was 27 years old and had the job of running two roller rinks; one in Santa Rosa, north of San Francisco, and the one in Hayward, where I trained.

Over the following months, my skating improved dramatically. Competitions were all I thought about; since I wasn't attending school, skating became everything to me. Darren picked me up at home—enough after the time school let out that he had no reason to suspect my delinquency—and spent hour upon hour training me.

The night before my first competition, Mom and I said a prayer that I would skate my best. She attended the next day and I won first place in all four of my events.

After that, I won almost every contest I entered, at least for awhile …

Sometimes I couldn't understand why— since she was proud of my skill —it was not enough for Mom that I had found a sport I loved, something I was good at it. No, it wasn't enough that I was winning competitions and moving up in the skating world. She wanted me to earn a college degree. Not that she knew what that entailed, or how a person got from high school to college. I figured it was something she heard at AA, something parents should want for their kids, so she parroted it back to me. I am not sure what it was that had her stuck on education as the only way to succeed, but she often reminded me how hard it had been for her to study, and how, nonetheless, she had challenged herself. She was proud of her high school diploma and prided herself on developing new skills as well.

I dreaded Saturday mornings, standard time for one of her lectures. I thought I would go out of my mind listening to her tell me how important school was, and how proud she was that my grades were as good as they were.

She thought my grades were good because I would watch the calendar for the typical time when report cards were due, and then ask Darren if I could use his office typewriter for some class assignment. I would type up a fake report card, using the teacher name list I compiled each semester, and bring it home. Each time, I'd stand there in fear of her asking to meet one of my teachers. But I knew that was a long shot, because she had to be at work during the week and wasn't aware that parent-teacher activities were generally held at night.

Darren had no idea that I was skipping school. He did everything he could to support my education. "As long as it is for your school work, Donnie," he'd tell me, "you can use my typewriter anytime."

And I would be thinking: *If you only knew, Darren, if you only knew.*

Suddenly there was a second Saturday morning lecture topic: "Queers, and how I needed to watch out for them."

"You know, Donnie," she began, with a protective tone in her voice, "because you don't have a father, you have to be extra careful that queers don't get a hold of you."

"Mom, what are you talking about?" I was shocked. I knew what it meant, but this was the first time she had ever mentioned the subject to me, although I had heard her and Michael toss the word around derisively.

"Yes, honey," she said with the utmost sincerity and concern, as we stood face to face. "There are queers everywhere. And you have to be especially careful because you only have a mother, so that makes you easy prey for them."

Whenever she went into her "queers are everywhere" diatribe—and that was most Saturday mornings—it didn't scare me. At fifteen, my hormones were zipping around like crazy, and boys, especially the cute ones, were showing up all the time in my fantasies.

But this sexual attraction confused me and I had no one I could trust to talk to about it. All I knew was what I remembered of a priest's condemnation of "men loving men." He declared, "They are all sinners who will burn in Hell for eternity!" I recalled feeling his fury fill the chapel; it scared me.

The images of the fight between Michael and my dad—when Michael accused him of kissing a man—and seeing how humiliated my father seemed afterwards, kept floating around in my mind.

The sexual experiences I had with Michael caused me even greater confusion. Because he liked girls, I thought our sex together wasn't "queer." The sex with him was about pleasing him, and about giving in to him, afraid of his threats. I remembered that each time he made me do things to him, I felt as though I were in a trance and had to do whatever he told me. Maybe that's why I felt I was not being "bad."

But now my desire for sex and my attraction to boys were both growing stronger. Now I was becoming convinced: *I am sure I am going to Hell.*

It did not take long for Mom's prediction that "queers would be trying to get a hold of you" to come true. Darren's hands would touch me in a way that made me feel uncomfortable during my private skating lessons. Several times when we were alone in the rink, he would place his hand on my inner thigh and keep it there until I squirmed and moved away. He started telling me he wanted to spend more time with me because he really enjoyed my company. On the weekends, he would take me to the movies and out to a nice dinner. I had not had that kind of attention since my father died.

One evening when we arrived at Lyon's restaurant, my favorite, Darren parked in the back, where there weren't any other cars. I wondered why for a moment, but I got distracted and did not say anything. As usual, we sat down across from each other. But after ordering a steak dinner with fat onion rings on top, something changed—he started talking differently. He scooted around the booth so he could sit closer to me; he leaned into me as he spoke. He giggled, and began whispering into my ear. This was a side of Darren I had never seen before.

After dinner, as we were walking towards his car, he continued with our usual small talk. "I'm thinking about buying a new car."

"What's wrong with this one?" I loved the two-door dark green Oldsmobile with the matching leather seats. The way he kept it so immaculate reminded me of my Dad. And like my father, Darren smoked, so the soft leather seats were scented with the mixture of tobacco and his Aqua Velva aftershave.

"I don't know," he said, sliding into the driver's seat and pushing in the cigarette lighter. "I've had it for awhile now." As he adjusted the knobs for the heater, he patted his shirt pocket, checking for a pack of cigarettes.

"Damn! I must have left them in the restaurant." He reached across my lap to open the glove box; I assumed he wanted to look for an extra pack.

Then I watched his hand brush across my crotch.

"Careful … don't let it hit your leg," he cautioned, as the lid plopped down. As he reached in and shuffled things around, his arm was rubbing against my pants. He stopped when the now-unnecessary lighter popped out.

"I was thinking about using the same music for you that I used for Jerald's last routine. You know, the one he won Regional with."

Darren placed his hand on my thigh while he waited for my response.

"You think I'm good enough for that music?" I asked, not believing what I was hearing—that he saw such potential in me.

"Of course you are!" he exclaimed. Then he paused and stared at me with intensity I had never seen before. "Donnie, you know, you are really a special young man ... you're different."

"Different?" I nervously wondered, *What is going on here?*

"Yeah, different," he said, lifting the armrest that was between us. He scooted closer, placing his arm around the back of my seat. I tried to get as far away from him as I could, turning sideways and pushing my back against the door, while at the same time, leaning in towards the dashboard.

"Do you think boys can like boys the same way they like girls?" he asked, with a strange flirtatiousness in his voice.

"Uh, I ... I don't know. That sure would be different," I giggled apprehensively.

That was the first time I heard someone talk about boys liking boys, without the "queer" epithet attached.

"Do you think that's possible?" I asked, trying to keep an even tone in my voice. I noticed the windows were beginning to fog up.

"I never thought it was possible," he replied, lowering his head, "until I met you." He sounded so gentle, almost apologetic.

"You mean ... you think of me as a girl?" I almost squeaked.

"No!" He immediately shook his head, and then paused. He began to draw out his words. "Well ... I'm not sure what I mean. I just know you stir up feelings in me, feelings I've never felt before. And I just can't stop wondering what it would be like to ... well ... to kiss you." There was a questioning lilt in his voice.

"I don't think that's right," I blurted out. "Boys are only supposed to kiss girls." My mind was reeling with confusion. I felt excited when he said he wanted to kiss me—but I didn't *want* to feel excited, because that would mean I was a queer! So I backed away, trying to make sense of what he was saying, while also trying to slow down my pounding heart.

The only sounds in the car, while I thought about kissing him, were the low hum of the heater and Darren's heavy breathing. We remained quiet for a long moment. Then I hesitantly said, "Maybe I'll let you kiss me … if you promise to stop if I don't like it."

He dropped his arm from the back of the seat and brought his face directly in front of mine. "Close your eyes," he said. And before I knew it, his lips were plastered against mine.

Sand paper, was my first thought. *It feels like his lips are surrounded by sand paper.* I moaned as he shoved his stiff tongue into my mouth. He made large circles around mine—bringing on my second thought, *He has no trouble doing his fishing.*

"OK!" I pushed away, finding it hard to breath. "That's enough."

He moved his hand off of my shoulder and stroked the back of my head, stroking my hair like it was fur on a cat.

"I hope I haven't scared you, Donnie," he whispered, and then sank his face into my neck. "You want to go now?" he asked gently, kissing the crevice under my chin.

I nodded yes—even though what he had been doing felt good.

"I hope you're alright?" He reached over and squeezed my thigh.

We both looked down at his hand sitting beside my erection, which was pushing its way up.

"Yeah." I felt embarrassed and turned away. I slid over against the car door, shoving his hand away from my leg.

The sexual surge that ran through me was frightening. I looked across the car at the satisfaction on his face and the feeling inside me grew. *What is wrong with me?* I wondered. My lips were still tingling. I needed time to think, to figure it all out.

I could only hope Darren would be patient.

CHAPTER TWENTY FOUR

Saturday Morning: A Mother's Intuition

1969— 1970, San Leandro, California

It was the morning after Darren revealed his feelings for me. We were halfway through our Saturday morning mother-and-son cleaning-the-house ritual when Mom started harping on my life.

"I never see you studying." She tried to sound casual, while holding the spray bottle of Windex in one hand and a cleaning rag in the other.

"I told you, Darren makes me study an hour before I can take the floor to practice. That's why I'm getting such good grades, *Mother.*"

Lying like that had become second nature to me. I polished the lies I told Darren in the same way. The incident in the car was still weighing on my mind as I attacked a spot of mold growing in the corner of the windowsill. At just that moment, Mom suddenly switched from favorite subject number one, education, to favorite number two: *queers.*

"Donnie ... those men I've warned you about, have they approached you at the skating rink?"

"Oh, Mother!" I cried. Thank goodness we were at the perfect point in our routine for me to naturally turn my back on her—I had to go to the closet to get the vacuum. As I pulled out the vacuum and bent down to plug it in, I wondered, *Is Mom psychic? Or is my face flushed? Or is there something unveiling all the conflicting thoughts I'm having?*

"Honey, you know I worry about you. I hardly see you; you're always at the skating rink."

"Mom," I whined, "I have to practice, you know that."

I turned on the vacuum wondering what she would say if she knew Darren was one of those *queers* she was warning me about. I could never let her find out, I decided, or that would be the end of my dream of being a skating champion. Skating was my whole life now and I would just have to deal with Darren as time went on. I began thinking about last night. Before falling to sleep, I had let the "kissing scene" play out in my mind, just as it had happened.

But I found myself going further, fantasizing about having sex with him, wondering what it would be like. I was still confused, but I was also curious. I wanted to explore my new feelings.

I continued to vacuum, actually much longer than necessary, so I wouldn't have to listen to my mother's worrisome concerns.

A week passed and the topic for our next Saturday morning chat was one I could never have imagined. Michael, who we had not seen in four years—since the day Mom refused to let him and his duffel bags stay, after Lee Ann's death—was coming to our apartment the next day. And if that wasn't enough, he was bringing his wife and six-month-old daughter to meet us!

Mom finally admitted that she had gotten another call at work from Michael. He recently had found out from one of her old friends in Monterey where she was working. She chose to believe that Michael being married and having a child meant that he had turned himself around. I didn't buy it.

Whenever she would tell me she was communicating with my brother, I would try to change the subject. There was no question that our lives had been much better without him. But Mom was most upset that it had taken him so long to tell her about his wife and his six-month-old baby girl, her grandchild. It seemed as if she had forgotten how many times he had beaten her.

Mom was excited when the day for Michael's visit arrived. Waiting for them to show up, I was about as anxious as I had ever been so I decided to clean the apartment, even though we'd already cleaned the day before, anything to keep busy.

The idea of Michael fathering a child was fathomable, given his sexual appetite, but Michael being married and actually being a father was something I never thought possible.

Maybe this was just what he needed to straighten up, I hoped, at least I tried to hope. I heard a knock at the door and Mom went to open it. I could see from where I stood in the kitchen, mixing a glass of chocolate milk, that it was them. Mom welcomed in a breathtakingly beautiful woman carrying a baby in her arms, with Michael by her side, sporting a proud grin that spanned from one ear to the other. She was about six feet tall and had a perfect figure.

"Mom, Donnie, this is my wife Sheila."

Sheila stepped forward, "Nice to meet you, Mrs. English, I've heard so much about you."

My mother looked down at the baby in Sheila's arms, speechless.

"That's my daughter Michaela," Michael blithely said, as he walked into the kitchen, picked up the glass of chocolate milk I had just finished mixing, and drank it down in one swig.

"May I use the restroom?" Sheila asked, handing the baby over to Michael. Mom just nodded in the direction of the hall.

Michael whispered, "She's a Carmelite, you know, one of the girls from a wealthy Carmel socialite family."

My mother continued staring at the baby, dumbstruck.

"Aren't you going to say something, Mom?" Michael adjusted the baby's blanket. He was actually cooing and talking baby talk to her. Like Mom, I was stunned into silence.

"This is your baby?" she asked, trying not to sound suspicious.

"Sheila got pregnant, so I married her," he answered in a scarily detached way. "I saw blood on the sheets, so I guess she was a virgin," he added with a cocky smirk as he wiped the funny-looking chocolate milk mustache off from around his lips.

I finally opened my mouth. "How old is she?"

"Six months."

Sheila emerged from the bathroom, her blond hair falling silkily down her back. I had always counted on Michael to have the prettiest girlfriends—and now he'd gone and married one.

"Do you want to hold her, Donnie?" Michael asked.

"I'm afraid I might break her, she's so tiny!" I gasped, stepping back, not wanting to take a chance.

"What's the matter?" he challenged me, obviously insulted I didn't want to hold his child.

I stared at the baby—now cuddled in her grandmother's loving arms—froze, and began stuttering.

"O-o-h, I c-can't!"

"Oh, come on, are you afraid?" Michael demanded in a tone that was all too familiar to me.

Still, I couldn't do it. I could not imagine holding such a fragile little baby. I had no experience and was sure I would hurt her by mistake; I could only imagine what Michael's response would be like.

After that, the visit was strained and short. Mom took some snapshots of the baby and then offered to make something to eat. Michael refused and announced they were leaving.

"But Donnie hasn't held Michaela," my mom protested, not wanting her precious granddaughter to leave.

"Time to go. Let's go, Sheila," he abruptly ordered.

There was a confused look on her face. For a moment I thought Michael was angry. Maybe we had not made a big enough deal of his new wife and baby. Abruptly, he got up and escorted his family out the door.

A few minutes later my mother and I stood staring at each other, alone.

Mom sighed, "You should have held Michaela, Donnie. She's your niece."

I have always regretted that I did not hold her that day, because I have never seen her since.

Mom was excited about her new granddaughter and told me how she showed off the pictures of Michaela at her AA meetings. Still, we both remained on guard, as we always had to do with Michael. So Mom was not terribly surprised when, only a month later, she received a call from Sheila.

"I'm sorry, Mrs. English, but I have some bad news," I heard her say as I crowded in on Mom so I could share the phone's earpiece.

"An appliance store?" Mom whispered into the phone. "Arrested? Oh no," she groaned. I moved away from the receiver and watched Mom's hand cover her mouth, her eyes darting towards me.

They had spoken for a few more minutes when Mom put her hand over the phone to muffle the sound and whispered to me, "Michael's been arrested again, for robbing an appliance store. She's divorcing him."

Then I heard my mother say something that shocked the hell out of me.

"Sheila, listen to me carefully." Her voice was tremulous; she spoke slowly, with emphasis on almost every word. "I do not want you to tell me where you and my grandbaby are going. I am afraid that whenever he gets out, he will come after Donnie and me and beat it out of us. We cannot know where you are." She ended with strong conviction, but I could see her blinking back the tears.

There was a long silence as she listened to Sheila, who must have been quite shaken by my mother's fears. But she went on: "Honey, change your name, never tell him where you are going, hide, do whatever it takes. Once you divorce him, if he can find you, there's no telling what he might do to you."

Mom paused, then added, with a catch in her throat, "And, Sheila, whatever you do, do not ever let him take my grandbaby. Not even for a night."

The phone hit the cradle and bounced on the floor. There was a solitary tear running down my mother's cheek.

I cannot imagine how unbearably painful it was for my mother to arrange to never see her only grandchild again, to forfeit any future experience of being a grandmother to Michaela. What an amazing act of compassion.

I was fortunate to have my skating competitions to distract me from the constant turmoil my brother created. It was sad, yet not surprising, to know that nothing had changed—even when he was not around, Michael's negativity would linger, causing all kinds of emotional turbulence for anyone for anyone connected to him. I was determined to push the intrusions of his criminal behavior from my mind, and to solely focus on my skating.

It was around that time that I placed at the Regional competition. That qualified me to compete at the National Championships, something I had worked so hard for throughout my skating career. I tried to explain to my mother how important Nationals were, but she never could understand how the different levels of competitions worked.

The national competition that year was in Lincoln, Nebraska. A four-day trip, Darren told my mother. He thanked her for saving up the money for us to go; she was coming too. Mom had taken a weekend job as a typist at an income tax business to pay for the multitude of costs that came with what we had discovered to be an expensive sport.

My first thought was of my mother, and of how much she had sacrificed for me, when the announcer from the US National Roller Skating competition announced enthusiastically to a filled-to-capacity auditorium, "And in second place, from Skate Arena, in Hayward, California, Don English."

When I heard my name called, I couldn't believe it! My dream of becoming a National Champion had finally come true. I looked up to the stands and found my mother beaming with delight. It was a moment of triumph we both shared. At least one of her sons had made her proud.

Meanwhile, Darren had won me over after that first kiss and had sex with me whenever he could get me alone. The first time, he took me to his apartment and offered me a Screwdriver to drink. After I finished it, he asked if he could kiss me. I let him, willingly. We had sex, but it was not what I expected. I didn't feel like we were boyfriends; it was different from the kiss. Of course, since I had never been with a girl, I had nothing to compare it to. The whole experience left me even more confused. When I told him afterwards I thought what we had just done wasn't right, he told me I just needed some time to get used to it. He promptly gave me another drink and we had sex again. I still knew something didn't feel right, but I was willing to exchange my innocence for his professional expertise in training me to skate.

I was afraid that if I didn't do what he wanted, he would leave me, both as a trainer and as a friend.

Darren told me he also liked women, explaining that he was actually bisexual. And so he had several girlfriends while we were "together." For some reason, this didn't make me jealous; rather it made me feel like we had a shared secret. His one serious girlfriend during our time together was Lynette. He met her when her daughter signed up for skating lessons.

Lynette had a great sense of humor. She was short in stature and wore her black hair up in a French twist dressed with Grecian Cascade curls. Her skin was pale, even though she was half-Italian and half-Portuguese. Her running joke was that she thought her hazel green eyes were her best feature, but men always said it was her large breasts. She would wear shift-like dresses to camouflage her bust line and even made other jokes about how big they were. She'd say they were a nuisance to her, so she never understood why men liked them as much as they did.

The more time I spent with Lynette, the more I liked her. My mother, on the other hand, said that at sixteen, I acted more maturely than Lynette. But it didn't matter to me anymore what my mom thought. These were my skating friends, and in this world, I was on top. Soon Lynette and I became best friends.

Time flew by and before I knew it, we reached what was supposed to be my senior year and Lynette was asking me what I wanted to do for my high school graduation. I had done such a good job lying about attending school, when she asked about this, it was like a slap in the face wake-up call. I knew the inevitable was coming, and unconsciously I wanted to come clean about what I had done, or in this case, what I hadn't done. I had been living a lie and deep down I was looking forward to breaking out from the self-inflicted bondage.

The more I thought about how I was going to confess, the more I realized I needed to tell Darren first. I could not even imagine telling Mom. Every time I'd think about how to tell her, nothing sounded right. I couldn't even figure out how to start the conversation.

I racked my brain and this was all I could picture: *"Hey Mom, guess what? All those report cards you signed these last few years ... well ... I typed them! That's right. No school for me. I never signed up. I've been home all this time, watching TV and playing with Cindy."*

And that's when she would pull a knife from the kitchen drawer and stab me to death! Yes, first things first, I concluded. *I'll tell Darren, and then Lynette.*

I tossed and turned all night worrying about how I was going to tell him. I don't know where I found the courage, but when I did tell him, he thought I was joking. Maybe it was because I told him without any warning that some bomb was about to drop.

"I'm not joking!" I yelled back.

"Oh, come on," he replied, indignantly turning around, pretending to pout, like what I was saying was a joke to get some kind of attention from him. "Donnie, if you've been skipping school, you're just going to have to make it up."

He just would not believe me; instead he thought I was playing a game. I had to shout, "How do you make up four years of school? Can't you hear what I'm saying? I never signed up! I haven't been going to school, at all!"

The shocked expression that flashed across his face was one I'll never forget. He put his hand to his forehead, still trying to comprehend this, and then started walking around in circles, mumbling. After what must have been his fourth circle, he stopped and addressed me, "So," he said with a mix of shock and anger, "you are telling me that you have not attended school since you moved here? Is that right?"

I shook my head slowly, "Yes, Darren, that's right."

At that point tears welled up in my eyes and all I wanted was for him to take me in his arms and tell me he'd fix everything. But instead he turned away and started making more circles, fretting to himself about what kind of trouble *he* might be in.

"OK, Donnie," he said, stopping, not completing the last circle. "We need to go and tell Lynette." He stood still for a moment and then exclaimed, "Oh my God! Does she know, have you told her?"

"No," I cried, wiping tears away from my cheeks.

"For God's sake! Does anyone else know about this?" he yelled.

"No, no one. Just me," I whimpered, taking a step back.

And then he made a couple more circles and told me to get into the car. It wasn't until we drove up to Lynette's apartment complex that Darren told me I needed to tell her everything. When I walked through the door, Lynette took one look at me and asked what was wrong. Darren motioned for us to go over to the couch. After we sat down, I confessed my crime once again, but this time when I finished, Lynette took me in her arms and I cried so hard that the front of her magenta crepe blouse looked like a bottle of grape juice had been poured over it.

"Well," Lynette to Darren while waiting for me to finish my sobbing, "I guess we should talk about who's going to tell his mother."

Oh my God. She said it! I thought to myself. *Now Mom is finally going to know.*

I wiped my face and sat back against the couch waiting for what they were going to say. Darren remained motionless and then dug into his shirt pocket to get a cigarette. The click from his lighter echoed through the room.

"OK!" Lynette blurted out suddenly. "I'll go and tell her."

"Good idea," Darren eagerly agreed. "I think it's best coming from you."

Lynette shot him a look as if to say: "Why me?" And then, just as she was about to say something else, he got up and went towards the bathroom.

"What, what are you going to say to her?" I shuttered, still crying.

"I don't know, Donnie," she said, glancing down at her tear-stained blouse. "I think I'll call her now and tell her I need to come over and discuss something that has to do with you."

I stayed on the couch, watching her as she got up to go make the call. I held my breath, listening to her dial Mom's number.

"Hello … Elizabeth?"

I continued to hold my breath, and prayed.

After Lynette hung up the phone, she and Darren left the apartment together. I decided to go lie down in Lynette's bedroom. As I walked towards her bed, I saw her Bible sitting on the nightstand. She was a practicing Catholic and had taken me to church a few times. I was impressed by the dramatic décor in the cathedral and felt a sense of peace each time I went. What disturbed me though, was Christ figure nailed to the cross with life-like blood painted over his body. All I knew of Christ was what the Jehovah's Witnesses told me after my dad's death, so my exposure to Jesus and Christianity had been extremely limited.

I picked up the Bible and opened it, hoping to find the same solace Lynette received from what she called *The Word of God.*

I'm not sure why I did what I did next. I took the Bible and walked over to her closet. I slid the door open and then stepped inside, sitting down with my back against the wall facing the length of the closet. I scooted a few pair of shoes out of the way so I could sit comfortably. I left the sliding door open so the light could come in while I thumbed through the Bible, hoping to find a scripture that would calm me down. I'm not sure how much time passed, but before I knew it, I had dozed off and only awoke when I heard Lynette call my name from the front room. I leapt to my feet, bumping my head on the clothes rod, not wanting to get caught, I flung myself across the bed and I lay there, posed as if I had fallen asleep.

"Donnie," Lynette said, repeating my name as she came into the room.

"A-a-a-h," I yawned, softly rubbing my fist across one eye. "I must've fallen asleep," I said as I sat up.

She walked over to the bed and sat down beside me. "I think it was a good thing I called ahead and warned her I had something to tell her," Lynette said, looking at the bedside table for the Bible I'd left in the closet. "The first thing your mom asked me when I got there was if you were alright. I guess that was because I'd sounded so mysterious on the phone."

"Did you just tell her, or did you build up to it?"

"Well, I mentioned how afraid you were of what she might do when she found out what you'd done. And then I told her everything."

"Oh," I muttered.

"The first thing she said after I finished was, 'Where is he? I'm going to kill him!' And then, she got up from her chair and started pacing back and forth repeating, 'I'm going to kill him.'"

"Oh no!" I cried, not wanting to hear anymore.

"When she finally got a hold of herself, she turned to me and asked where you were. When I told her, she said that she needed some time to think and would come here to talk to you tomorrow."

"That's it?" I asked, getting up from the bed. "She's going to come here tomorrow?" Numb, all I could do was repeat her words.

"Yes, Donnie. That's what she said."

CHAPTER TWENTY FIVE

My Mess   1970-1972, San Leandro, California—1972-1973, San Jose, California

When my mother came over the next day, I was surprised by her calm serenity. I had been afraid my news would push her off the wagon, but she must have called her sponsor and held it together. My heart was pounding so loud, I was sure both she and Lynette could hear it.

She sat down and began to talk about Mary, the young lady who did her hair at the local beauty school, where she went once a week. "Last night, I remembered something she told me," Mom announced to Lynette and me. "Mary only has an eighth-grade education, and she's in the process of getting her tenth-grade GED so she can receive her cosmetology license."

When I heard this, I thought my mom was experiencing a nervous breakdown. It took me a few seconds to grasp what the beauty school student had to do with me.

"Since you've gotten yourself into this mess already," she continued, very formally, "all I can do is my best to help you get out of it. I'm going to call the Veterans Administration tomorrow. Since your VA benefits from Dad don't run out until you're eighteen, maybe they will pay for your tuition for beauty school. It's the only solution I can see to this mess."

I never thought of going to beauty school and was not even interested. I started to say something, but she put her hand up, a clear signal I needed to shut up. Then Mom said, as sternly as I had ever heard her—sober, at least—"I do not want to talk to you about this anymore."

My mind was racing. *My skating, what's going to happen to my skating? I am a National Champion, after all.*

My mother must have known what I was thinking, and even how I was thinking it. "It took everything for me to come here, Donnie," she stated, looking past me, over my left shoulder. "I'm going to go now, and I will let you know what the VA says when I hear back from them."

And then she got up, secured her purse under her arm, and walked out.

I felt ashamed of what I had done, to both my mother and to myself. She was very angry, deservedly so. I asked Lynette, "Would it be OK if I stay for a couple of days, you know, until things settle down?"

I was still there, more than a couple of days later, when an envelope appeared, half-slid under Lynette's front door. It was a copy of the letter Mom wrote to the Veterans Administration, which she kept and I still have:

Gentlemen:

This is a very hard letter for me to write. In requesting for this form attached to be filled out, I have learned my son, Donald English has not attended high school for the past four years, yes, he has been living with me, and I know it is hard to believe, but I did not know of this. I was fooled completely. But two wrongs will not make a right. The young man is basically a good one, and I don't intend to throw him to one side. He has never been in any trouble, and has only harmed himself by this. The first year he got in so deep and then did not know how to get out of it. The only excuse I can find is he had no father to talk to and a Mother who did not know how to listen.

He wants to take up something creative and has talked this last year about going to beauty school, but did not know how he could do it with just an eighth-grade education.

So, it proposes lots of problems for himself. He sincerely wants to go to night school for High School and to Beauty School during the day. Is there any way that the VA can help him in this. The only income I have is as a secretary for Health, Education & Welfare Department, as a GS-5, plus Social Security for the boy and your VA check.

He will be 17 in April, 1971. If I can get help for him, maybe I can teach him that the best policy is honesty. I don't intend to let him down now. If there is anything you can do to help him and me, please let me know.

Two weeks later, Mom told me, in an unemotional tone, that she had received an answer from the VA: "They said 'yes.'" And then, after a very long pause, she continued, "So now, young man, you have to get busy and study, so you can pass your GED."

"Yes, Mother. I will."

I felt intense guilt over how I had disappointed my mother, so I began immediately to search for a school of cosmetology. Also—Mom was right—at that time, having the tenth-grade equivalent of a GED was an entrance requirement. I managed to pass the test without a problem.

The only beauty school in the Hayward area was called "Don's Beauty School." *An omen*, I thought, so I immediately applied. I was accepted and began school the following month.

Having spent most of my time around adults, interacting with the patrons was not a problem at all. I enjoyed it.

Although I didn't realize it at the time, I definitely had acquired some knowledge in those few years "off." From skating, I learned poise, grace, and the capacity to stretch my limits, plus a lot of social skills, like dealing with all kinds of personalities. And from my soap opera addiction, I learned that you definitely cannot read a book by its cover—rich or poor, beautiful or plain, those TV characters had all kinds of problems you would never guess. Actually, I loved to hear people's stories—whether in real life or on TV—trying to imagine how they got into such strange situations, or better yet, how they would get out of them. Actually, it was all very encouraging to me—to see that everyone was just trying to figure out how to be happy.

What was a true surprise was how easy hairstyling came to me. I had found something other than skating that I was good at!

I heard from the other students that Don's Beauty School was the best around. We had what was called a "style section," where once you got good enough, you were able to style hair without supervision. It was as if you were already working in a professional salon. They even had hydraulic chairs, which were unusual back then.

There was a young man, the only other guy in the class, who dressed meticulously and fit the bill of "tall, dark and handsome." So of course, I fantasized about getting together with him. But I became discouraged right away—he had decided I was *the one* to talk to about the crushes he had on some of the cute girl students.

Although friends were easy to make, it was also a competitive program. The owner, Mr. Don, took a liking to me right away because I was making him a lot of money. I won virtually every product sales contest they had. I didn't know why, but selling, too, came natural to me. Customers walked out having purchased treatments and hair products they'd had no intention of getting when they walked in.

After a period of time studying and practicing on each other, you started working "the floor," serving real customers. Soon after I got on the floor, styling patrons' hair, returning clients started specifically requesting me. This was unusual for a beauty school; usually people walked in off the street and took whoever was available.

I was very good at the latest hair style, "The Artichoke." All the patrons wanted it. You used small rollers so you could set the hair in a spiral design starting at the crown, circling around the head. Then when styling, you could tease it up so it eventually looked like artichoke leaves delicately sculptured in a circle. "You style a *mean* Artichoke," my fellow classmates would say.

Most of them were like me, kids who didn't like high school and were not planning to go to college. However, over the past five years of skating, much of it competitively, I had discovered, and my coaches had nurtured, my inner drive to be the best. And I had learned well that to be the best required working your absolute hardest. Unfortunately, for the majority of at least the students in my class, that kind of drive and discipline were missing. I liked to—rather, I needed to—feel like a winner. So I guess I needed to be the "Hair Champion of Don's Beauty School." And I made it happen.

As soon as I signed up for beauty school, my mother forgave me for all the years I lied to her about high school. I knew that asking forgiveness for her own mistakes was part of her AA program. Mom let me know, in many ways, that she felt she had done more wrong to me than I had done to her and so she was willing to forgive my "skipping" high school, and wanted to forget about it and move on.

Eventually, Mom was proud of me once again, and I repeatedly gave her credit for thinking of the idea and pushing me to attend beauty school. She was especially proud when I told her Mr. Don brought his wife to me, to cut and style her hair. I made the suggestion to change her ash brown hair color to red. I worked along with Mr. Don mixing the color, and an hour later, I received "*oohs*" and "*ahhs*" for the whole new look I had come up with. The color got such raves, I talked Mom into letting me dye her hair the same shade of red. But she hated it! She made me dye it back immediately to her standard shade of beige blond, and never let me change her color again.

Balancing skating practice and beauty school was a challenge. One evening at the rink, after a full day of perming a whole group of women who arrived at the school in a nursing home van, Darren approached me while I was lacing up my skates.

"You're late again. You know we're starting a new routine."

I kept working on my boots, undoing them and then lacing them back up, so I could avoid looking at him. I knew where this conversation was headed. My skating proficiency had taken a hit because of beauty school. I no longer was winning contests; I no longer was one of "Darren's champions." Also, I had begun refusing his sexual advances, always coming up with some lame excuse about why I couldn't come over to his apartment. I knew today was going to be my final lesson. I just had that feeling.

"You know I can't get here as early as you want me to. And today I got out even later because we had to do all these—" He interrupted me before I could finish my rehearsed excuse.

"Then you must think my time is worth nothing. I have been waiting a full half-hour for you." He rolled back on his skates to give me room to stand up, but went on scolding me like I was a ten-year-old kid. He looked hard at me and said, "Maybe we need to call it quits?"

I looked around to see if anyone was listening to our argument. I was relieved nobody could hear.

"You know, Darren," I responded, crossing my arms, "I think that's a real good idea." I stared at him, trying to read his face. He actually did not seem to be upset. At that moment, the student who was scheduled after me came up and asked Darren if he was ready to start his lesson. Darren glared at me, gave the student a forced smile, and then skated away.

I went and cleared out my locker and never saw Darren again.

Now released from Darren's sway, I was able to expand my circle of friends and meet people outside of the skating world. One of those friends had figured out I was gay and introduced me to the "gay scene." He also set up an interview for me at a salon with Richard, a master hairstylist, who was looking to hire stylists right out of beauty school.

Everything in my life was speeding ahead in the direction I wanted.

I believe there are positive influences around us all the time, but that it takes good fortune—or wisdom, or sometimes both—to recognize and connect with those people who show up in your life exactly when you need them. Richard was one of those people and, somehow, I had the good fortune. He managed a hair salon in a high-end department store at the East Ridge Mall in San Jose.

My interview was at 3:00 p.m. As I walked into the department store, I couldn't believe my eyes. Between the escalators, there were glass elevators lifting shoppers up as if they were on air. The mannequins were dressed to the nines. This was the most stylish and refined store I had ever seen.

I looked at my notes. The salon was on the second floor. When I got off the escalator, I took a deep breath and walked confidently ahead, imagining I was about to begin my skating routine at a National Championship. The moment I walked through the arched doorway, Richard saw me and called out my name.

"You must be Donnie!" He enthusiastically stepped out from his office, rushing to greet me. "I'm so glad this time worked for you," he said, his smile lighting up the room with the whitest teeth I'd ever seen.

"Hi. It's nice to meet you." I deepened my voice, trying to sound professional.

We shook hands and then he turned around, directing me to follow him through the reception area. He stopped there and motioned with a sweeping gesture of his arm, encompassing the entire space. "This salon was designed by Billy G—he's one of the top decorators in the business."

A tall gold oriental vase stood off to the side of the entryway, filled with long-stemmed pussy willows that reached halfway to the ceiling.

"Notice the wallpaper," he commented with pride, as we walked through the reception area. "It was all hand-painted. And the same artist painted the flowers you see here on the glass partition." The wallpaper had a metallic silver background with pale lime green and citron yellow colored flowers abstractly painted from floor to ceiling. The same flowers were glazed across the glass divider that separated the reception desk from the stylists' areas. It was very elegant, and very enticing. Richard had a right to be proud. I noticed though, that it came across more as confidence than arrogant pride.

After Richard finished with the tour, we went to his office and sat down. He shuffled through some black and white photos and began to tell me about a new haircutting concept the company had hired him to launch. They had decided to use the newly-built department store to introduce what he called "blower styled cuts."

"Women will no longer need to set their hair with rollers; they'll be able to blow dry their hair themselves."

I had my doubts. But of course I kept my thoughts to myself.

"Here is Jane Fonda," Richard said, showing me one of the pictures. "See how her hair was cut short on the top, almost standing up to give height, but still remains long on the bottom. We call that a "Long Shag."

"That was styled without rollers?" My voice rose a notch unintentionally—I didn't believe it could be done.

"Yes. And you'll be able to do all these cuts," he continued, showing me the other pictures. "You see, Donnie, our haircutting team wants stylists who aren't attached to the 'old ways' of cutting."

I thumbed through the pictures, shaking my head with amazement.

"That is why we want you, because you're just out of beauty school, and I've heard you have natural ability. We have found it's easier to teach people who have the knack, who don't have a lot of experience."

He excitedly described the last picture, "These styles are cut with scissors … not razors." I was taken aback—cutting with a razor was the only way I was taught—I could not imagine anything else. I guess the look on my face told him exactly what I was thinking.

"You have your doubts, I know … but you just wait and see. After you get through with our Master Stylist training, I promise you, you will be one of the top hairstylists in the business."

To my shock, he made an offer right then. "So what do you think, Donnie? You want to join our team?"

"Yes," I enthusiastically replied, still staring at the pictures. *Wow … they want me!* was all I could think.

I watched Richard put the pictures back into the side drawer and then open the middle drawer, pulling out a long piece of paper that looked like a form. "So now what I want you to do is fill out this application and take it to the office on the third floor. I've already told them you would be coming."

He also handed me a brochure about the mall. I turned it over and noticed the bus schedule. Darren and Lynette had broken up, but I remained very close friends with Lynette. Weeks before my job started, she let me move in with her, generously covering the expenses until I started earning money. No question, though, I would have to use public transportation to get to work.

I tapped the brochure on my knee. "Thanks, I don't have a car, so this will help."

"Where do you live?" he asked, as we walked out of his office.

"Santa Clara."

"Well, that's right on my way. I'll schedule you on the days I work so I can pick you up and take you home."

"Are you sure? I mean, I don't want to …"

"No. It's fine, Donnie. Once you learn my styling tricks, you'll be earning enough in commissions to buy your own car."

He guided me through the arched doorway and walked me to the elevator.

"It's on the third floor," he reminded me, as he pushed the brass button.

This looked like a perfect place to kick off my new career. Then two weeks went by without a word. I was getting skittish; it had sounded like getting hired was a *fait accompli*, what with Richard talking about a schedule and all. And now—nothing.

So I was very excited the next day when I heard from a woman in the company's Human Resources Department. She sounded upbeat when she said she was calling about the hairstyling position.

"Mr. English," she went on, "I am the one that is processing your information. And there is a problem."

My heart sank. I had lied on the application. Afraid they would not hire me if they knew I only had an eighth-grade education, I had put down that I graduated from Pacific Grove High School.

"Oh?" I managed to say calmly, even though I felt like I was going to be sick.

"You forgot to write down your Social Security number."

"Oh, I'm so sorry," I said, swallowing hard. "I forgot to mention that I don't have one yet. But I was planning to go tomorrow and apply for one."

"Well, that is all we'll need to finish processing your application. Just call me with the number and you'll be all set."

After that, I completed the application process without a hitch. I would be starting my professional career on the 13th of April, the day of my 19th birthday.

When Richard picked me up for my first day of work, I was as nervous with anticipation as when I was about to do a triple waltz jump at the end of a routine.

I paced back and forth along the sidewalk with my hands clasped tightly behind me. My back was turned when I heard a short honk. I spun around and saw it was Richard, smiling. His teeth even glowed through the car windshield.

As I got into his car, I commented, "This is really a cool car. Is it new?"

"This is the car everyone is talking about, Donnie. It's Datsun's newest sports car—a 240Z. I just picked it up yesterday, so you're my first passenger."

"Wow, it shimmers like no other car I have ever seen."

"Yeah! That's the metallic paint. It's the latest thing!"

By the time we got to the mall, I learned that Richard and his partner of three years, Mitchell, were both hairstylists. Mitchell worked at another high-end department store; his was in the town of Palo Alto. I was definitely impressed. Richard was only 27; he had money, a partner, a new car and probably owned his house—all things I thought would always be out of my reach.

As I listened to him talk excitedly about his work and all he was going to teach me, I started to dream of a real life—not my typical fairy tales and fantasies. A real life, *a life that just might be mine if I worked hard enough.*

CHAPTER TWENTY SIX

A Formula for Success

1973, San Jose, California—1974 -1978, Los Altos, California

I thought our first lesson for the day would be about hair, but it wasn't. "What's a Gucci?" I asked, interrupting Richard, who was explaining how he and his partner had become so successful.

He did not immediately answer my question.

"Donnie ... I think you have a very nice sounding name, but you know, 'Don English' sounds better, more sophisticated, than 'Donnie English.'" I thought for a moment, said that I agreed, and then waited for him to continue.

"There's a lot more to being a master hairstylist than getting that certification and giving great haircuts." Richard then said, "See my belt? This is a Gucci belt."

He was so trim that even in the confines of the sports car, I could see the large double intertwined "G's" connected to a two-inch wide strip of navy blue leather.

"This belt was made from the finest Italian leather and these gold "G's" tell people that you are *in the know* and can afford to buy whatever you want."

I was still staring at his waist. "Well, the belt looks great, but you could wear anything and look good. You're already gorgeous," I gushed.

Richard did not even skip a beat. "No! That's not good enough, Don. You have to look—and—dress the part. That's the formula for success, remember that." He again spoke with such confidence, I was determined to absorb everything.

"Most of our clientele know what a Gucci is. And those who don't, well ... they will at least *sense* you have good taste."

He's absolutely right, I thought. *Because when I met him the first time, I thought he looked like a movie star and I didn't know what a "Gucci anything" was.*

That first day, as each client of Richard's arrived, I could see what he was talking about. Most of them wore expensive clothing and flashed some of the biggest diamonds I had ever seen. Later that night, I mentioned them to my friends. "I guess I'm going to have to wear sunglasses to work tomorrow," I said, trying not to laugh. "I think some of those huge *rocks* caused some serious damage to my retinas!"

Each client I met was as nice as Richard had assured me they all would be. The women were of all ages, and he even cut a man's hair that day. My head was so full of information, I was glad to see the day come to an end. I needed to take some time to absorb all that I had learned. But Richard did not stop. While he was showing me how to close up the salon, he shared more about his winning formula. "Don, you are not just a hairstylist now." He paused to point to a row of switches, and then flipped them off, glancing at the ceiling. He picked up his leather checkbook off the desk—I noticed the red and green fabric stripe with a gold double "G" clasp that held the fold of the wallet.

As he directed me through the reception area, he shared the cornerstone of his formula. "*Now*, what you need to do, is to become a fashion expert. And not only that, you need to travel in the same circles as wealthy people. Go to the same restaurants and vacation in the same places."

By the time we got to the parking lot, my head was swimming.

"How long do you think it will take before I'll be able to afford to do all these things?" I timidly asked.

"Don't worry about that, Don. You're going to be making a good salary now. And once you get started, you will be surprised how much more money you can make."

He smiled and placed his hand on my shoulder, giving me a fatherly pat. His belief in me was intoxicating. "But now you have got to start saving your money and invest in that image I was talking about."

"Thanks for the ride, Richard. I feel so lucky to have you helping me." I wanted to say more, to tell him that I would make him proud, that his belief in me gave me the hope I needed to overcome all I had been through—all the things I wanted to tell my father, but never had had the chance.

He continued to grin, nodded modestly, and waved, "See you tomorrow."

The more time I spent with him, the more I learned about the things in life that I needed to focus on. For one, he was adamant about me getting a tan.

Richard said, "You need to lie in the sun, so when you wear those gold necklaces, they'll sparkle against your bronzed chest."

So I spent my weekends tanning.

"And talking about sparkles," he mentioned later that first week, "I want you to go see my jeweler Rene. His store is in Cupertino. Check out his selection of diamond rings and tell him I said to give you a good deal. He has a lay-a-way plan."

Diamond rings? I thought. *Is he crazy? I don't even own a car yet, and I'm supposed to buy a diamond ring?*

"Don't worry, Don." He seemed to read my mind. "You have real talent; you'll be able to afford these things in no time."

Worry was an understatement. I sure hoped my new mentor was right.

Within the first month, Richard let me know how pleased he was with my progress. He was especially excited when I came back to the salon with my first gold necklace. I had gone downstairs during one of my lunch breaks and made friends with the woman who worked at the fine jewelry counter.

"I am interested in looking at gold necklaces," I said, pointing towards the case. "I work in the hair salon here."

She smiled, "You know you get a discount if you use the store credit card, right?"

"They haven't issued me the card yet," I replied. "But they gave me my account number, so I guess I can start charging right away."

"Sure. And what is your limit?" She was already following my eyes, which were focused on one particular necklace. It had a pendant shaped like an upside-down pyramid, about two inches tall. There was an abstract stick figure hanging in the middle.

"You like that?" She was already forgetting the question of my limit.

"I've never seen anything like it," I sighed. "And the chain ... it looks like glitter."

She reached in through the glass door and pulled out the midnight blue velvet pedestal it was lying across. "This just came in. I don't even have a price for it yet."

She picked it up and held up the necklace, letting the pendant dangle in the air, causing the stick figure to sway.

"What do you think that's supposed to be?" I asked. We were both staring, waiting for it to stop moving so we could see it better.

The stick figure's arms stretched across the wide part of the V triangle and the legs looked like they were crossed together at the bottom.

"*Jesus!*" we gasped simultaneously.

"You think so?" I was upset that I had fallen in love with an abstract crucifix.

"Here, put it on." She was already undoing the clasp and motioning for me to turn around.

I felt the coolness of the gold "V" against my chest. When I looked in the mirror, I could not believe how beautiful it was.

"Wow, that's looks really good on you," she exclaimed.

"But I'm not Catholic," I whispered, feeling a bit sacrilegious.

"I don't think it matters," she whispered back. "And anyway, I don't think anyone could tell what it is. It's definitely not obvious."

I gave her my card number and she went to ring it up. The price came up five dollars under my limit! As I walked away from the counter, I grasped my fourteen carat gold Jesus hanging from my neck, feeling dizzy with excitement. I could not believe what I had done—I had just spent three hundred and fifty dollars. That was more than two months' of my part of the rent for the apartment I shared with Lynette.

I turned the corner and caught a glimpse of myself in the floor-to-ceiling mirrored column. I could see the sparkling chain and Jesus peeking out from under my shirt. I had made the right decision, I decided, admiring my purchase in the mirror. *Yes ... definitely the right decision,* I mused. And then I hurried back to work.

A diamond ring was the next item I needed to get on the "Richard says Don needs this" list. I remembered that awhile back, Lynette showed me the wedding ring she kept hidden in her underwear drawer. She said she would never wear it again because it reminded her of her failed marriage. When I told her about Richard's diamond ring suggestion, she insisted on giving me the five diamonds from her ring. One of them was almost a half carat. Right away, I took the gems to Richard's favorite diamond shop and spoke to his friend Rene about designing something original for me. He designed a gold nugget band with Lynette's diamonds randomly set among antique golden craters, which were etched in black. When it was finished, I proudly showed the ring to Richard.

"Nugget gold is the latest thing." Richard seemed pleased when I showed it to him. He hesitated, and then went ahead with another recommendation. "Not now, but eventually, I would have the antique black polished out."

I looked at the ring, a bit upset that in choosing the black antique finish, I had made the wrong choice. I went the very next day and had it polished to gold. I wanted the formula to work; whatever Richard said, I followed.

Now, with my newly-purchased necklace and ring, Richard declared that I was ready to hit the gay club scene. The movie "Saturday Night Fever" had just come out and John Travolta was igniting disco dancing everywhere. Disco became the rage among the gay population. Something about this era of freedom of expression helped many folks burst right out of the closet.

But not me. As willing as I was to be "openly gay"—simply put, relaxed and comfortable—among my newly-acquired gay friends, I was still far, far away from admitting my sexual preferences to my mother and to my clients.

On my first night out with Richard and his friends, we went to one of the most controversial nightclubs in San Francisco—controversial because it was the largest openly gay club in the country. The three-story building stood around the corner from the Financial District, and just a few blocks from the tourist mecca of Broadway, where "straight" strip clubs were heavily frequented.

I remember the excitement I felt when I started walking down the steep hill and could see the disco's name, "Cabaret," flashing in lights, and hear the thunderous music roar from the second-story windows.

I had spent hours shopping for my outfit. I wore a pair of beige polyester flared pants with a skintight long-sleeved burgundy pullover, and to top it off, a thick wide black belt wrapped around my small waist. The long line snaked around the block; gay men decorated the streets with sequined tops, light colored pants, and, of course, the latest style, black platform shoes. My shoes, because they were new, had trouble holding traction as we dashed down the hill. By the time we got to the bottom, there was a group of guys at the end of the line practicing the California Hustle to the music blaring out into the cold, misty night.

Richard had introduced me to Mario, the manager of Cabaret, earlier that week. Mario had given me his personal card and instructed me to flash it to the doorman and say that I was his boyfriend, to avoid being carded. I had a fake ID, but Mario said this would be better, in case his own security people were on the lookout for underaged police decoys. When I handed Mario's card to the muscle-bound doorman and stated who I was, he took a step back from the podium to question me.

"Mario's boyfriend is already here," he grumbled, confused. "Oh! I get it. Come stand over here." He directed me behind the podium while motioning for the other doorman to take his place while he went inside to find Mario. I smiled at the guy who took over for him, noticing how handsome he was. He didn't have the bulging muscles the other one had but sported a golden tan. He had a sexy way of chewing his gum while keeping an eye on me and trying to check IDs, too. Twenty people must have had gotten through while we flirted, before I heard Mario's voice behind me.

"Don...? There you are!" he called, entering through the black curtain. I quickly turned and looked back at Mr. Handsome Doorman, making sure he saw me walking into Cabaret with Mario.

I loved showing off.

As I followed behind my host, the vibration of the music pounded the walls, reverberating through every cell in my body, making me feel I was already intoxicated. Strobe lights shone through the screen of cigarette smoke, as we wove our way between the walls of bodies—feeling the effects of the current epidemic, "Disco Fever."

After the tour, Mario led me back down to the first floor and into a tasteful entertainment lounge where you could escape the commotion upstairs and watch drag shows. They had the most real-looking and flamboyant female impersonators—"world- famous," the Master of Ceremonies announced. They were all stunningly beautiful. I had never seen so many sequins and feathers in my whole life. The entire experience made me feel like I was back at Disneyland, when I was four years old: *whimsy and fantasy surrounded me.*

From then on, my weekends became all about partying at Cabaret. When I wasn't going to the city, Richard and his partner would invite me to join their social group on the Peninsula. I was able to see first-hand how truly successful people lived. I was hooked and I could not *wait* to climb up the ladder and join them. I was certain that if I worked hard, and followed everything Richard told me, it would only be a matter of time.

Ten months later, when Richard was promoted to a newly-built store with a salon across the Bay, he made it clear to the other stylists that he was turning over all his clients to me. His belief in me paid off.

"They know Don now," he explained to the other stylists. "While I was training him, he got to know all my clients."

Later, I figured out that he had known about a possible promotion, which was why he raced through my training. I was Richard's clone, just a younger version.

"Don is really talented. And my clients like him," he ended his surprising announcement.

Because of this, nobody in the salon liked me. They talked behind my back, claiming I did not have the experience, status or seniority to get all of Richard's clients. I decided my only hope for having a friend at work would be if we hired a new stylist who knew nothing about the controversy surrounding Richard's decision.

One day the opportunity presented itself while I was sitting at the receptionist desk, going over my schedule.

"Hi!" a young woman said, very energetically. She startled me, breaking my concentration.

I looked up and was immediately struck by the intense sapphire blue of her eyes.

"Oh ... I'm sorry," she apologized after seeing me jerk with surprise.

"That's OK," I gulped, as I clasped my hands together letting them rest over the pages of the opened appointment book.

"I have an appointment with Kathy for an interview," she stated, with a mysterious smile.

"Oh, you must be Debra," Kathy said over my shoulder, as she stepped behind the desk. "Here's some paperwork for you to fill out."

Debra took the clipboard Kathy handed her, stretching her arm over my head. I ducked out of the way and did a quick inventory of Debra as she turned around to sit in one of our white rattan reception chairs. Her long chestnut brown hair—natural, I concluded—was pulled back in a tidy ponytail, showing off her flawless, ivory white skin. She was a little on the chunky side— not fat— but not thin either. Her height, about 5'6, helped balance out her larger-boned figure, and she was pretty in her own way. I was giving her my internal approval, just in case Kathy did happen to hire her.

After Debra left, Kathy asked me to come into her office. She was on the fence and wanted to know what I thought of Debra.

"I got a good feeling about her," I answered quickly, thinking this might be an opportunity to have an ally, untainted by jealousy, working here.

Debra was hired. We did not start out as friends—but our lives seemed to dovetail together, after the rumor floated around work that I was planning to move to a privately-owned salon and take all of Richard's clients with me.

I was taking a break in the back room, waiting for my next client, when Debra walked in and lit her cigarette. She swung the door closed.

"S-o-o-o, Don," she whispered, while blowing smoke out the side of her mouth to avoid my face. "Is the rumor true?"

I was caught off guard. "What rumor?" I asked dramatically, like a novice actor.

It had been almost a month since I had made the decision to move to a salon north of San Jose in the sleepy, but affluent, bedroom community of Los Altos. It was ripe for a master stylist to come and release women from being slaves to their weekly shampoo and sets. I didn't realize it at the time, but because I had such a large following—due to Richard's generosity—this salon was jumping at the chance to have me. They offered a fifteen percent higher commission rate than I had been receiving. If only half of my clients followed me, I could double my income.

Even with all my attempts to keep things quiet, people found out. Of course, I had denied I had any plans to move until the day came when I handed Kathy my two-week notice. The tension was high those last two weeks, but I made it through without a scene.

It amazed me, that first day at my new location, to see how many expensive cars were filed neatly into the slanted parking spaces lining the quaint storefronts on the few blocks that make up downtown Los Altos. *So, this is what "affluence" looks like*, I chuckled inwardly.

I was thrilled that fairly quickly, over half of my clients followed me to my new, exclusive location. I really appreciated their loyalty—for many it meant lots of extra miles and extra time.

Within three months, my commission rate was double what it had been at the old salon. I now had the money to upgrade my zip code. I moved into an apartment near the border of Los Altos and Mountain View, a much larger bedroom community.

When I told Mom the exciting news, she offered to go with me to pick out furnishings for the first apartment that would be all mine—the decorations, the furniture, the dishes; the you-name-it. We had so much fun traipsing through stores, plopping down on sofas and trying out mattresses. At the end of the day, I surprised her. The last store we went into was a jewelry store. I bought my mother a designer watch. She loved it, but of course complained about the cost. "I can afford it, Mom!" I boasted, and gave her a hug. It felt good to buy her something we were never able to afford in the past.

I was changing our destiny.

As I was developing my new image, I decided that I was tired of parking my little beige Toyota Corolla alongside Jaguars, BMWs, Mercedes and, yes, even a few Rolls Royces. I knew I needed an upgrade. I kept thinking of Richard's formula for success: eat where my clients eat, drive their kinds of cars, travel with the elite set.

It just so happened there was a small used car lot run by a Mercedes auto repair establishment in town. Most of their "pre-owned" vehicles were Mercedes and I found one I liked, a brown two-door coupe sedan. It was five years old and had 49,000 miles on it, but was in mint condition. The price, I was told, was negotiable. However, I had never negotiated anything in my life, so I am sure I would have been an easy mark. Luckily, I was able to enjoy one of the benefits of working in a small town—the owner's wife, who was also his receptionist, was a client of my salon.

She gave me a loan officer's name from a bank down the street and said she was certain they would work with me.

Could this be happening to me? I screamed silently, as I walked out the door. *Could I be driving a Mercedes, parking alongside all the well-to-do Los Altos residents, tipping parking valets generously to be sure they would take good care of my very own Mercedes!*

Just like everything else that had been falling into place of late, so did the purchase of my "new" car—new to me, anyway. And I never got tired of the heavenly smell of leather every time I got in. I thought to myself, Mmm, this is just like what I breathed in when I entered a Gucci store, "the aroma of rich."

Richard's formula for success had worked. My mentor had given me everything I needed, before he moved on to his new salon across the Bay. We didn't talk much after that, not for any particular reason. I did soon realize, though, that I no longer needed someone else to believe in me—to believe that I could succeed.

I believed in myself. I had arrived.

CHAPTER TWENTY SEVEN

An Opinion   1979-1980, Mountain View, California

I was spending most of my Sunday afternoons with my mother, who now lived in Walnut Creek, a small town across the Bay. It was about an hour's drive from Mountain View and it was totally worth it because she regularly cooked me wonderful food. I could picture my father and mother together in the kitchen when I was little; they loved preparing creative dishes. Since Mom stopped drinking, her creative, joyful cooking had returned and I got to reap the rewards. I didn't like to cook, so I was happy to sit at the counter and chat while she did her magic with her many recipes. I was 21 years old and glad our relationship was growing into a friendship. She would share with me news of her activities with AA. Many times, we also reminisced about past events.

One afternoon, I asked if she ever heard from Michael's ex-wife, Sheila. I had wondered about this often, but never had the courage to bring it up. On this particular day, she seemed especially relaxed, so I chanced it.

Her sharp retort was immediate. "Of course I haven't heard from her, you heard me tell her to disappear."

I waited a moment and then decided to apologize. "Sorry, you don't need to get so mad, I was just wondering about her. I didn't—"

She interrupted me, "You know that Michael and everyone associated with him are dead to me. How he could have had a baby and then go back to his old ways by robbing that appliance store." She shook her head. "He's just dead to me now. Dead!"

"I know Mom, I'm sorry," I replied, standing up from the barstool. I glanced over to the stove. "Something sure smells good." I attempted to change the subject. Then I grabbed some condiments and walked out the patio door to her deck, where she had the table set for dinner. She followed behind me with a large glass bowl, summer vegetables heaped high inside it. "My goodness, who else did you invite?" I teased.

She grinned and shook her head. "Nobody, it's just for you. You know you need to eat your vegetables."

"I know, Mom ... and my spinach, too, so I can grow up and be big and strong ... just like Popeye, right?" I kissed her on the cheek, and sat down.

The late afternoon sun darted through the huge pine branches, sending spears of sunlight across the deck. I loved that deck. It was built around the tree and kept us shaded, even in the current 100-degree heat. After we finished what might have been one of her most delicious meals, she stood up. I noticed her mood had begun to turn melancholy. She began to clear the table, stacking each dish along her arm. Just as I was about to ask if she was still upset, she interrupted my thoughts.

"Wait 'til you see what I made you for dessert." She spoke with a forced sense of excitement. "It's your favorite."

"Oh you didn't, Mom!" I exclaimed. "Not in this heat!" I was relieved that she was not going to sink back into a bad mood because of the *Sheila* question.

"I baked it last night," she smiled, passing through the sliding glass door. "And I have some French vanilla ice cream to go with it."

"You are the best mother!" I shouted, so she could hear me from the kitchen. "Mmm," I purred with anticipation of her special strawberry rhubarb pie.

I was still a bit concerned about her mood, but I decided to go ahead—I had a proposition, or rather a great big favor, to ask. Debra and I wanted to open our own hair salon, hopefully in Los Altos, and we had calculated that $10,000 would allow us to create the most elite one in the vicinity.

We both agreed the only way we could manage it financially was to borrow money from our parents, and we both knew that they, in turn, would have to borrow to get the $5,000 each. Therefore, this was a big deal.

I found the courage to ask Mom for the loan. It turned out that she was in full agreement with the idea, adding that she would be happy to work together with Debra's parents.

My mother had worked her way up the ladder at her Civil Service job, so her improved financial situation made it relatively easy for her get a loan from a federal credit union. Debra's father was able to do the same, through his local credit union in Humboldt County.

In the months that followed, we began putting Dorian Grey, our salon together. We leased space in a newly constructed office building, and when we started planning, we discovered that I had a natural talent for interior design. Debra loved my ideas and was fine with letting me to pick out everything. I searched antique stores for mahogany dressing tables to use as styling stations for the stylists. The effect was stunning; Dorian Grey eventually became known as one of the most elegantly designed salons in the Bay Area.

Through all this combined effort, my relationship with Debra grew stronger—we became like best *girlfriends*. We even moved into a condo down the street from where the salon was being built, to be closer to the action.

That was when things between us began to get murky. Debra knew I was gay, but because I wasn't out of the closet to my clients, we led them to believe we were together. From all appearances, we were the perfect couple. We knew that in the process of promoting a likeable image to our client base, we also would be silencing questions people might have, based on assumptions about male hairstylists. It was 1980 and I did not want those stereotypes to become an issue in building my business.

I helped Debra with her own "make-over." I picked out her clothes and taught her everything Richard had taught me, from hair styling to his secret formula for success. I even made sure she kept her weight down. The situation was a perfect ruse for me.

Debra, on the other hand, had a hard time.

Only nine months after we had opened Dorian Grey, Debra approached me and—in a very serious, almost sad, tone—said that we needed to talk. She wanted a "divorce" from the salon; she could not continue living this lie. She wanted to eventually marry and have a family. Her plan was to move back to Eureka and open a full service salon, with the hopes of meeting the man of her dreams and getting on with the next phase of her life.

I wasn't sure what that really meant at the time, what "living this lie" was like for her. Now I am able to appreciate how emotionally draining it must have been—putting up a front while needing, as a young adult, to claim who she really was. Yes, I have certainly come to understand that.

After Debra left, I still kept up the "straight" façade with my clients. I worked hard to maintain all the secrets I had been harboring for so long.

My insecurities were numerous. What would they think of me being an eighth-grade dropout, with no real education. Interestingly, I never even mentally gave myself credit for passing that tenth-grade equivalency test. What if they knew that when I was twelve, there were days that I had gone hungry because my falling-down-drunk mother had spent our food money on taxi rides to the local bars? Or that some nights, I had to escape our apartment to avoid the sounds of my mother in bed with one stranger or another? And that we even needed the Salvation Army to rescue us with a meal? (For which I am still grateful.)

That was certainly not the image Richard would have approved of.

I kept my sordid past in the closet with me. I dressed like a straight man, acted like a straight man, and avoided at all costs the stereotype of the flamboyant gay hairstylist. I was going to follow Richard's example, no matter what; I believed walking in his formulaic footsteps was the only way to fulfill my dreams of success.

What I didn't know then was that many of my clients and straight friends had figured it out—the gay part, that is, not the unimaginable suppressed horrors of my life.

When clients would sit in my styling chair and share the events of their lives, I would listen, smile into the mirror, and ask more questions. It became second nature for me to chime in with stories about my imaginary past. Many of my clients had children attending prestigious colleges, such as Princeton, Harvard and Yale. It was easy to add in snippets from my made-up school experiences. For some reason, many of my clients or their husbands had graduated from Princeton; frequently their children carried on the family tradition. I had one client who was getting her hair done for her third child's Princeton graduation.

"My son, you know, is graduating this weekend from Princeton, so I have to look good."

"Not a problem." I repeated my signature refrain. "Your son is so lucky you're going to be there. I remember my graduation; it was great having my mother there. Family is so important," I sighed.

"Yes, my father-in-law will be there as well—another Princeton graduate. He has so many great stories about when he went there." She smiled into the mirror.

I smiled back and—big mistake—went on with my fantasy, deciding to say something about my dad and my graduation.

"I missed having my dad at my graduation. He died when I was twelve." I stopped cutting her hair and glanced back into the mirror. "But my mother came. She still tells me how proud she was seeing me walk across that stage."

"So you went to college?" she asked, without a moment of hesitation or a lilt of surprise in her voice.

"No, that was my high school graduation. I graduated from Carmel High, where I grew up."

"So you're a Carmelite?" she asked with a twinkle in her eye. "I grew up in Carmel also. What year did you graduate?"

I quickly changed the subject.

From then on, I learned to be careful about my lies and, of course, never mentioned a word about having a brother, nor even that I was a military brat. I worked hard to convince people I was educated and that I had grown up in a sophisticated environment. I lied about the backgrounds of both my mother and father, perpetuating a fantasy family history rooted in the wealthy side of the tracks. When I talked about my father dying when I was twelve, I described my mother as still enjoying a life of comfort. Nobody would ever find out that the police literally picked my drunken mother up off the street more times than I could count. Nor would they know that my brother terrorized me with threats of killing my father while shoveling dirt onto a plywood-covered grave.

I lied so much, I truly started to believe my own stories. Later, mental health professionals determined that I experienced some of the symptoms of dissociative disorders, a category of common, psychologically protective responses to trauma. One of the effects was that I virtually convinced myself that I was the person my imagination had created. I enjoyed that, and life went on.

Everything was going pretty well, until a year after Debra left.

One day I was served with papers; I was being sued by a client. Clara Binge, a well-known psychic, was claiming that I caused a serious burn on her scalp, leaving bald patches.

It was as if the earth opened and I was being sucked in. I was consumed every waking minute by the fear of having anything to do with the law, and particularly the chance that Michael, or any part of my past, might be revealed. What I feared most was that somehow, the case would show up in

231

some newspaper and Michael would see it. He would know where I was, and he would come find me. My mother and I had gone to such great lengths to leave no trace behind when we moved from the apartment where he had visited us with Sheila and the baby. As Mom had told Sheila, we expected Michael to be infuriated with her disappearance and we did not know what he might try to do to us whenever he was released from jail for the robbery.

By the time my deposition was scheduled in the case, I had lost five pounds, which made me look more like a refugee than the fit, fashionable, straight man I was pretending to be.

My attorney had informed me that the deposition—where Mr. Keller, the lawyer for the psychic, would ask me questions under oath—would be held at Keller's office in downtown Palo Alto.

When I walked in, I saw Ms. Binge for the first time since she had last been at my shop, some months ago, on the "day in question." The room was stuffy, making me uncomfortable; that did not bode well.

I sat where I was directed, across from Clara. She was wearing a black Yves St. Laurent-style suit. Her age was still a mystery, because of all the cosmetic surgery I knew she'd had. I was fairly sure she was at least fifty.

Clara had been a client of mine for about a year before that last appointment. On that day, she had scheduled two chemical services—hair coloring and a perm. Her claim was that the treatment irritated her scalp, causing a blister to develop, which then led to a staph infection. She was suing me for $77,000 for a nickel-sized bald spot on the top of her head. Yet even though her hair was thinning, this spot was not visible.

My attorney, Mr. Ware, had prepped me for what he expected would be the questions Keller would ask me, and explained that I should keep my answers brief. "Don't elaborate," he sternly directed me. "Too much information can get us in trouble. Just answer with as short a response as you can."

"I'm sure I can do that," I had responded, hoping I really could.

However, I was not prepared for her attorney's first question.

"For the record, Mr. English, what is your formal education?" Mr. Keller kicked off with what may well be a standard question. Mr. Ware had not mentioned it, probably because, for most people, there is a very straightforward answer. Nonetheless, I was not positive what "formal" meant in regards to education, a touchy enough subject for me.

"Formal?" I finally asked.

Her attorney furrowed his brow in a look of disdain and said, "Your years of education, college, training."

"Oh!" I quickly interrupted him, "I went through high school and graduated from beauty school." By now, lying about high school had become second nature to me, so I answered it right away.

Considering that Clara had recently received acclaim for finding a missing boy in the San Joaquin Valley through her psychic abilities, I was afraid my brief sojourn in beauty school was going to pale in comparison. She had also bragged about her interview on the *Merv Griffin Show* and about some guest appearances on the local morning programs.

"Mr. English, in your opinion, what do you think caused the burn on Clara Binge's head?" For some reason unknown to me, he stressed the word "opinion" in such a way that I got defensive.

Was this a trick question? I instantly thought to myself, avoiding eye contact with my accuser. *Opinion? What would it mean if I give my opinion? Could I be incriminating myself?*

I went ahead and looked at Clara Binge, scanning her short fire-red hair, and her head, the subject of this lawsuit. Her expression was statue-like.

"What is the definition of opinion?" I asked, then noticing that everyone in the room seemed surprised by my inquiry. Even the court reporter stopped typing and looked up, with an expression on her face I could not read.

"Are you serious?" my inquisitor shot back.

"Wait a minute!" My attorney interrupted him. "If he wants a definition, then give it to him."

"OK," Mr. Keller said, taking a deep breath, attempting to calm himself down.

He went on giving obvious meanings of "opinion" and when he finally got through, I answered very confidently, "I don't have one. I do not have an opinion about what caused her burn."

It wasn't intentional, but I could tell I had caused Mr. Keller's hackles to rise. I noticed the court reporter looking up again, so I glanced at my attorney.

"That's it. I think our time is up," Mr. Ware announced, stepping over to me as he patted me on the shoulder. "We can go."

I got up from my chair feeling proud of myself for avoiding the trick question. That would not be the end, of course; the trial was still to come.

Three months later, we sat in a courtroom. That morning, the judge called Clara Binge and the attorneys into his chambers to see if she might be willing to settle without going to trial. She wanted $25,000 to walk away. My attorney—who was actually the attorney for my insurance company—was willing to go to $15,000, with no admission of wrongdoing. I was not crazy about settling, because I strongly believed I had done nothing to cause the injuries she was claiming. And I certainly did not want to lose—I did not want my name besmirched by a finding that, essentially, I had committed some form of malpractice.

No agreement was reached, so the trial began. It was the Tuesday before Thanksgiving.

Mr. Keller started out showing a video of Clara Binge appearing as a guest on the *Merv Griffin Show*. "See how thick her hair looks, and how happy she is. This is before Ms. Binge lost the hair on top of her head," he dramatically pointed out and then turned towards me with a sneer he intended the jury to see.

I got angry as I realized what the attorney was doing—he was trying to imply that I was responsible for her losing hair "all over her head!" This was supposed to be about the one bald spot they claimed my actions had caused, not about what anyone could see was her thinning hair.

The physician who treated Clara testified. She had taken pictures and made slides of the oozing staph infection and the now-nickel-sized bald spot that she said the infection caused. When I saw the blown-up slide of her scalp, I noted there were a number of spots where hair had not grown back— wherever she had scars from plastic surgery. The larger scars were from the most recent round, done that year. She had had two facelifts, and the scarring from both caused areas of hair loss—hair cannot grow in scar tissue. That was the reason why her hair was looking so thin. Of course, her attorney did not bring out any of that. Moreover, these other areas of baldness were bigger than the one I supposedly had caused.

I whispered my observation to my attorney as the doctor was testifying. "What!" he muttered under his breath.

"Yes—she had *two* face lifts," I repeated. "It's the scarring that is her problem."

"Good. Very good," he said, sounding like he had just found the goose that laid the golden egg. "We'll use that later. That's good, Don," he whispered as he patted me softly on the back.

It was now Wednesday, so we adjourned early that afternoon for the Thanksgiving holiday, and did not return until Monday.

My attorney, Mr. Ware, began that Monday with his cross-examination of Clara Binge. He began by asking her about the slides of her scalp, which had been put back up. With a long stick, he pointed to one of the scars; the area around it was as bald as "my" spot.

"Ms. Binge, can you tell me what this scar is from?" he queried, in a boisterous tone.

"Yes," she began, and then seemed to hesitate a moment. "That is from some minor plastic surgery I had."

"And this scar over here, again, where there also is no hair?" Mr. Ware asked, moving the stick to the other side of the screen.

"Yes, that one is from the surgery also."

Looking directly at her, my lawyer asked, "So can you tell me this, are those *other* scars, where also there is no hair, from the first face lift you had, or from the second face lift?" Gracefully, he swiveled towards the jury so that he was facing them as he completed the next question: "You have had more than one face lift, haven't you, Ms. Binge?"

She glared at me, and then nodded yes. I wondered what the jurors thought about the vanity of a woman who had already had two facelifts by age fifty.

When it was her attorney's turn to question me, he had me read from my deposition testimony. When I came to the part about not having an opinion, I interrupted myself to say, "I did not have an opinion then, but I do have one now."

Mr. Keller stumbled and broke the cardinal trial lawyer's rule—"Never ask a witness a question you don't already know the answer to."

"Mr. English, what has happened that you suddenly have an opinion?"

"Well, since I've had time to think about it, and now seeing the slides showing all that scarring, I put two and two together." I spoke confidently. "So, Mr. Keller, here's what I think: that because of the double process I performed on Clara Binge, her scalp was sensitive. So when she, for whatever reason, decided to set her hair right away, leaving hot plastic curlers for some minutes against her tender scalp, which had been previously scarred by plastic surgery, the heat probably did cause a blister, which then was exacerbated by her rubbing Vitamin E oil on it."

"Thank you, Mr. English," he finally interrupted me. "That is all."

Her attorney's closing argument was long and laborious. In essence, he was accusing me of being the best actor ever, who sells beauty for a multi-million dollar cosmetic industry. Listening to Mr. Keller accuse me of being a professional actor and lying about what I had done, prompted me to self-reflect. *Hmm … how ironic. I have been an actor—I have been putting on an act for most of my life, pretending to be someone I wasn't, even to my own parents. But today, I am an actor telling the truth.* My confidence grew, even with that revelation. I knew that everything I had said in court was the solid truth.

"He never wavered once," her attorney was loudly announcing. "Not even one time did he stray from his lines, did he? Just look at him," pointing at me. "It shows he is a real salesman, a salesman that was well-rehearsed!"

He stood before the jury, pointing at me—as he no doubt had rehearsed—and elaborating on my great acting job. It was a challenge to keep stone-faced, as my mind raced. *We didn't sit here for four days watching me on* Merv Griffin. *No, we had to listen to testimony that went on and on, like her friend who used to be on TV on the show* Green Acres, *tell how depressed Clara was, dealing with being single, and how she was afraid that "one of her dates might run his fingers through her hair and feel the bald spot." Which bald spot? She had quite a few! And each one of them was from her own doing, not mine.*

I was hoping the jurors were having similar reactions, and could see through the grandstanding and overreaching, as well as the misrepresentations.

Fortunately, enough of them did. When the verdict came in, we were triumphant. However, it was very close, Mr. Ware told me. He had interviewed the jurors and found out that the foreman was against me, and he had held sway for a little while. "We were lucky, Don. It was a good thing you told me about the face-lifts when you did."

"Congratulations," Mr. Ware said to me as we parted.

Yeah, that's right—Congratulations, Don, I said to myself as I roamed the court's parking lot looking for my car. It was hard to believe that I had outsmarted the psychic's lawyer with only an eighth-grade education.

When I found my car, there was Clara Binge standing by it, talking to her attorney; for a second I was worried. It just turned out that, coincidently, Mr. Keller had parked next to me.

I couldn't help smiling and nodding at them when they saw me approaching.

They had lost the case and she had to pay all my court costs. I felt my smile turn into what my mother used to call "a shit-eating grin," as I realized that I had actually won through intelligence and honesty.

Not bad with only an eighth-grade education, I mused. *Not bad at all.*

Flying high on that victory only lasted three months. By then a much more dangerous tempest was heading my way. It hit the shore hard. When Dorian Grey's phone rang just as I was about to walk out the door of my hair salon. I was the only one left and it had been a long day, so I decided to let the answering machine get it.

"Hello," a deep male voice echoed across the empty room. Something about his tone—somber and stiff—kept me from walking out. "I usually don't like leaving a message," the man continued, "but this is Jerry Sanders from the Humboldt County Public Defender's office in Eureka." He paused, just as if he knew I was standing there deciding whether to pick up ...

CHAPTER TWENTY EIGHT

In the Devil's Arms   1981-1983, Los Altos, California

It was now six months since Michael's murder, escape and conviction. Even though I knew he was behind bars for life, he continued to haunt me. I sat alone at my desk in a small room behind the stylist chairs in my salon. The many before-and-after pictures I had of my clients lay on my desk, ready to be put into a scrapbook I had been given for my 27th birthday. As I looked through them, I wondered what these people—some of whom who had become friends— would say if they ever found out who I really was.

During my trial, I sat in terror of being found out. I was sure the stacks and stacks of lies I had built my life upon were going to crumble and bury me. I would lose everything and have to start over. Each day when the court doors opened, I watched the stream of people taking their seats and prayed that none of my clients would walk through the door. When that fear was not realized, I believed I had escaped the humiliation of my past.

I thought it would be easy to go back and live under the umbrella of facades I had carefully constructed to protect me from my embarrassing past. I lived in the world I had been creating in my mind since the day Michael locked me in the rickety shed with the rusty nail. And from the day I found out my brother committed murder, I attempted to deny that reality, outwardly pretending it never happened, just as I had done while he was heaping abuse upon me. The only person I had told was Diane, and I knew she would keep my secret. All I wanted was to step back on the stage and continue to act out the part of an educated straight man, born into a well-to-do family with a silver spoon in my mouth. I liked that world.

When people asked if I had siblings, my immediate response had always been, "Oh, no. Not me." Michael had been dead to me for the last ten years. This aura of success and normalcy was one I had worked extremely hard to create. But as I sat there at my desk looking at the pictures of all my clients who believed my lies—believed in me—I understood the truth. I had draped pretty layers of lies all around me, while the heavy veil of self-hatred and disgust still remained, leaving me feeling dirty inside.

For months now, Michael was alive again in my mind. I had no choice but to think about him, about the horrendous murder, about the potential impacts of a high-profile trial. That focus had a powerful affect on me. I was plummeted into the cave of memories and feelings my protective psyche had buried over. They had virtually no conspicuous existence in my mind. Nevertheless, like the little shaft of light Michael allowed to reach me between the plywood boards, a narrow shaft of light still shone on those caves. At moments when my guard was down, or at other times when I did want to explore, I slid down that shaft. I was Alice in Wonderland sliding down the rabbit hole, confronting many locked doors, and then finding the keys that fit.

I was sixteen years old the last time I saw my brother, barely approaching manhood. Now, at 27, I was starting to come to grips with the fact that I had deep feelings of self-hatred, which were rooted in what my brother had done to me when I was young. He robbed me of the precious jewel of innocence that is sewn into the lining of our newborn souls. When that is stolen, there is a void, an empty space that refills itself with bizarre scenarios of distrust and confusion.

It is a rape of the worst kind.

What happened to me made me feel like an object, an object to be used for sex.

Michael had stolen my innocence and, in the void, planted a seed of confusion. Even when he stopped the sexual abuse, he further mastered the psychological and physical abuse—he nurtured that seed very well. It grew into adulthood along with me. It caused me to seek out malignant environments, places where other tormented souls gathered.

Tears ran down my face as I sat at my desk, coming to grips with the reality that I was one of those cursed and tormented souls whose experience of abuse re-circuited the brain, and therefore the body. Psychically and physiologically, I was so used to abnormal sex—as an object to be used—that regular sex with someone who did love me would rarely excite me. On the occasions that it did excite me, it would not be long before some part of my personality, the part that was disgusted and shamed by my past, took over. At those times, I would experience life as that personality, or identity. His name was David, and he needed to feel the fear and humiliation we felt as a child, still believing that was all we deserved.

I locked the door to the salon in a daze—knowing where I had to go. It was an establishment in San Francisco where the walking wounded appeared at night, like zombies ... *dead inside long before they ever get there.*

It is hard to describe a club like that. First of all, it was dark, dark in every way. The walls were painted black and the glow of red was the only source of light, causing everyone's skin to look devilish, by intention. The club's black corners were usually occupied, each filled with a mesh of clothed bodies intertwined, faces indistinguishable.

Two men approached me as I entered and mentioned they had seen me there before. "David. My name is *David*," was my response when one asked.

"Well, David, this is John, and I'm Steve."

Steve smelled of beer breath and pungent sweat-soaked leather from the vest that he wore shirtless. We exchanged the usual friendly handshakes. He was tall and burly and dressed in black. He wore leather chaps so when he turned around his butt was exposed where the seat of his pants was missing. I noticed that when he smiled, something wasn't quite right. His dark eyes looked dim; there was no life to them.

"Let me get you a beer, David," he said, adjusting his cap. He reached over and squeezed the top of my shoulder and then walked towards the bar.

John leaned into to me and whispered loudly into my ear, "You have beautiful skin." He was a few years older than Steve, and wasn't as handsome. They might have been in their thirties, but the red lighting made it hard to tell. John's hair was light brown and cut short like a policeman's. He kept whispering into my ear and then I felt his tongue take a long slurp over the entire side of my face. Startled, I pulled away with a disgusted grunt and then reached up to wipe away his salvia.

"It's OK," he smiled with the same soulless smile as Steve. "I'd sure like to do that to your whole body. You quiet ones are always the best fucks."

"Here's your beer, David," Steve returned, interrupting John's lewd comments.

The bottle of beer was ice cold and felt good in my hand.

"Here's to a fucking good night!" Steve said, clicking our bottles together.

"You plan to see the show?" John asked, starting to lean into me again. Now forewarned, I turned and moved back to avoid more tongue-lashing.

The show he was talking about started at midnight in the back section of the bar. The room was called "The Dungeon." I peeked in once, years before, and couldn't believe what I saw. Men were tied up, naked, and engaging in unimaginable sexual acts.

John continued to glare at me, waiting for an answer. "Well, maybe," I said, knowing I wouldn't.

"Steve is part of the show tonight," he announced with a sense of pride. "So now you'll have to come and watch."

I nervously gulped down more of my beer trying to figure out how I would get out of this one.

"Doesn't David have great skin?" John declared, brushing the back of his hand against my cheek, nudging me closer to Steve.

It might have just been my imagination, but it sounded like the music was getting louder and it definitely felt like the space was getting hotter.

"Let's see that pretty chest of yours," I heard one of them say, but I couldn't make out which one. I looked down and saw a hand begin to unbutton the top of my Pendleton shirt. I had a low cut tank top underneath and suddenly felt a hand slip inside it. One of them was stroking my hairless chest. I tried to move away, but their hard muscular physiques became one wall; there wasn't anywhere to move. The music was blaring even louder and I began to feel dizzy. Then I felt my shirt come off and the top of my jeans being unbuttoned.

"Hey, stop!" I managed to shout, hardly able to hear my own voice through what felt like cotton stuffed in my head.

"What's wrong, David? We just want to have a little fun with you," Steve growled rubbing his crotch up against me.

"I need some air!" I managed to say, "I don't feel so good."

"You know what, David, now that you mention it … you don't look so good either. Why don't we take you in the back room and lie you down?"

"No!" I exclaimed. "I think I just need to go outside for a minute."

"OK, David," John whispered calmly, and then ordered Steve to go along outside with me.

"No. I can go by myself," I argued. I was pushing at their chests, trying to get past them.

I knew I needed to get away from these guys, but the room was spinning around in circles and my mouth had the same cotton-filled feeling as my head.

"Here, drink some of your beer," one of them said, putting the bottle up to my mouth, as if he had read my mind. I gladly took a sip. Then the bottle was yanked away and the rest of the beer poured down my neck, drenching my entire front.

"Oh, let's not let that beer go to waste!" John cried, bending down to lick the foam off my chest.

I couldn't believe how light-headed I was feeling after just a few sips of beer. The people in the bar were beginning to move in fast motion and the lights were getting brighter. Suddenly, the dizziness began to dissipate. I felt my body start to get warm and a very pleasant full body sensation took over. I had never felt like that before. Then it dawned on me, *they must have put something in my drink*. I wanted to panic, but I couldn't. I just felt good all over. I noticed John and Steve were standing in front of me, smiling and staring. I don't know why, but all of a sudden I wasn't afraid anymore and I asked Steve for a sip of his beer.

"Sure, David. *Anything* you want."

After I took a sip, Steve brought his face next to mine and planted soft kisses across my lips, and then all at once forced his tongue deep into my mouth. I felt another tongue licking the back of my neck and was amazed how sensual the feeling was. Each sexual nerve in my body was experiencing an ecstatic response, beyond anything I had ever felt before.

That was only the beginning. I didn't know it at that moment, but I was to be the star of the sex show and Steve had been assigned as my partner. The whole ordeal still remains a misty nightmare. I can only remember bits and pieces—more like stop-action photos.

When the show was over, most of my body was lathered with Crisco and body fluids. My head was pounding from the poppers (amyl nitrate) that had been shoved up my nose. I remember removing the leather straps from my wrists and then finding a corner in the room where I could lie down. I passed out.

It must have been about five o'clock in the morning when I woke up. My clothes and shoes were lying beside me, along with a big black bath towel. When my eyes finally began to focus, I could see two guys passed out on the floor directly across from me. The stench of cigarettes, poppers and sex filled my nostrils—I thought I was going to throw up. I shakily struggled to put my clothes back on. My socks were missing, so I had to force my bare feet into my boots. I headed towards the rear exit, none too steady.

"Hi, there," I heard a voice say as I was about to open one of the two metal doors that led to the alley. I turned around and recognized a guy I'd had a conversation with earlier that evening. I remembered him because his plaid Pendleton shirt was similar to mine.

"You look like you had a rough night," he said with a friendly smile. When I had first looked back, I wasn't sure if he, too, was on his way out the back door. I nodded and smiled, holding the door open for him anyway. When I tried to focus enough to see if he was coming out, my vision blurred, I wobbled, and felt as if I was going to faint.

"Hey!" I could hear him say, "You alright?"

I stepped back inside and found the closest wall to hold onto.

"Yeah, I'm alright," I said, putting my hand up to stop him from reaching out to me. "I'm just a little dizzy," I mumbled. "I'm OK. Really."

"Let me get you some water." Before I could answer, he was moving. I watched his blurry image walk to the bar.

The cup of water he brought back to me that dreadful morning led to one of the most important connections of my life. A spiritual connection, one that fortunately appeared in my life at a time when I needed it the most.

His name was Ricardo. When he brought me the cup of water, he probably saved my life. I don't know if I believe in angels, but if there is such a thing, then definitely Ricardo was one. When we left the bar that morning, we decided to go and get a bite to eat. I suggested the 24-hour coffee shop around the corner. We both ordered blueberry pancakes and I lost count of the times the waitress refilled our coffee.

I learned Ricardo was in town on a vacation from Hawaii. Hawaii was my favorite place to vacation. I think he said he was younger than I was, but I remember thinking he looked a little older. I was sure he was Hispanic because of his black hair and dark olive skin, but he never mentioned it, and I had no reason to ask.

I don't recall how we got on the subject of spirituality, but we discovered we were studying the same metaphysical material. Listening to the way Ricardo talked so casually about "the law of cause and effect," I noticed he was using the word "law" instead of "karma," to describe why taking responsibility for our own actions was common sense.

"We all have beautiful souls," he said, confidently. "We just find it hard to believe that sometimes."

Here we were talking about beautiful souls and taking responsibility for our actions when I–David had been drugged and raped just a few hours earlier. I was not excusing the violations, but I had to acknowledge in my mind that the awful experience had been a risk David had been willing to take. We both knew exactly what kinds of things happened in that bar. David was the side of me, or the identity, that was seeking out such humiliation.

Ricardo then surprised me with an unexpected question. "There's something I don't quite understand about you, David." Of course, he was using the name I had automatically given. "It sounds like you have been on a fairly spiritual path for quite a long time, a lot longer than I, actually. So I can't stop wondering, why on earth you were hanging out in The Dungeon?"

The server came by, lifting the glass coffee pot, the wordless gesture for, "Wanna a refill?"

We shook our heads simultaneously.

"Wow," was all I could say, shocked by his question. I stared down into my coffee cup.

"I'm sorry, David. I don't mean to—"

"No, that's OK. Actually, it's a good question—one I have asked myself many times before. I haven't really talked to anyone about why I do the things I do, but what you said about the possibility of my soul ... well, being beautiful. I'm not sure that can be true."

"David, please believe me. I can see what a special spiritual being you are ... it is all right there—right inside of you."

Why he believed in me, believed that there was something special about me, I had no idea. Nonetheless, I replayed that conversation with Ricardo over and over in the car as I sleepily drove home. The idea that somewhere deep inside me, I might have a beautiful soul—even with all that I had done, and all that had happened to me—gave me hope.

I got home as people were leaving for work, and I slept all day. In that deep, exhausted slumber, the memory of confused sexual feelings from when Michael abused me resurfaced from their burial ground. Like the ghouls my older brother threatened me with, they began to haunt me. I didn't know that the wounded four year old was too damaged and trapped to get out. I had spent my life lying—I had not told my parents or anyone else about the abuse—so there was no one to tell little Donnie, "It is not your fault. What was done to you—was not your fault!"

Since that first call from Mr. Sanders, I had been wishing that Michael could be locked up for good, so that both my mother and I would be free from him forever. With his capture, plea, and life sentence, it was quite likely he *would* be locked up for good. The big question, however, remained: "Will that make us free?" Sadly, the basic premise—the premise my lies were built upon—was turning out to be faulty.

Just being aware of where my brother was, even locked up—made it difficult *not* to feel his presence, his influence, on our lives. In fact, his reappearance in our lives reminded us that we needed something else to believe in, something that could help relieve the painful memories and the fear we had been harboring for longer than we ever imagined.

My mother and I had been researching and investigating different spiritual practices since Michael's arrest. We kept digging deeper, hoping maybe a spiritual answer would appear. Each weekend, we spent most of our time on the phone, discussing the philosophy of metaphysics and the many facets of what people called "karma." Mom had given me several books to study. Some made sense, some didn't, and some were so far out, I could not begin to comprehend them.

But we would discuss them just the same.

Those weekend calls were special to me. Having found something we could share meant a lot. We would discuss everything, from the twelve steps of AA to what happened to our souls after we died. We had come so far since those bitter days when Michael's darkness and her alcoholism were contaminating our lives.

Of course, the part my mother had no idea about, was that I also had been hoping my spiritual studies over that year would take away the desire and compulsion to be degraded and used for sexual pleasure. Obviously, if the night before was any indication, it had not worked yet.

To be free was going to take inner transformation. But maybe this new notion, "It's all there, right inside of you," was the starting point for building up the strength I would need.

When I woke up that evening, I decided to call my mother. I wanted to talk to her about what Ricardo had said.

The conversation started easily as I told her about meeting Ricardo and his ideas about karma. Then, steeling myself for the worst, but trying to hope that my mother would understand, I took a deep breath, "You see, Mom, when I began to contemplate that I might a have a beautiful soul, I gave it some thought. And I realized my soul was gay."

"What did you say?" she asked, probably thinking she had not heard me right.

"Mom, I'm gay."

"Oh … that's what I thought you said," she said, sounding relieved. "You know I think your father had an affair with a man just before he died."

That was it? I was flabbergasted. *Here I am baring my soul, revealing the secret I have been so afraid would send her back to the bottle, or alienate us, or both. And there are no fireworks? No crying? All she does is toss in an offhand shocker that just maybe my father had an affair, a homosexual affair?* I was astonished by her calm reaction, and incredibly relieved at the same time. And it all came about because I might have a *beautiful* soul.

Thank you, Ricardo, I mused, and hung up the phone. *Thank you very much!*

CHAPTER TWENTY NINE

The Law of the Universe

1985, Los Altos, California

Two years had passed since I had told my mother I was gay. We had received no more news of Michael, so the murder was safely under lock and key somewhere in my subconscious. I was in the first healthy, loving relationship of my life—it seemed that everything was following the formula of success that Richard had taught me. Jason knew of my obsession to hide my troubled past, but never questioned me much about it. One of the great things I loved about him was his sincere interest in spirituality. Happily—and not surprisingly—when I introduced him to mom they immediately hit it off and he became very fond of her. I still reserved most Sunday afternoons for my mother. This particular Sunday was Mother's Day. I had made reservations at the very sophisticated Yacht Harbor restaurant in Oakland's famous Jack London Square. I had reserved a table that overlooked the water and made sure we were all dressed to the nines, so that our entrance would, of course, turn heads.

Whenever I went to a high-end restaurant, which was quite often, I would slip the maître d' $20 so we would be sure to receive special attention. Making an entrance was new to Jason, but he caught on quickly and actually became quite good at it. We were lucky that afternoon, because the maître d' was obviously gay; I am sure he could tell Jason and I were a couple. After he seated us, I asked Mom and Jason, "Did you notice we have the best table in the restaurant?"

They both nodded with approving smiles.

After we sat down, we all exhaled at the same time as we drank in the exquisite view. The stark white tablecloth mimicked the billowing white sails atop the variety of primary-colored boats jetting through the sparkling calm waters.

As usual, God, love and happiness weaved in and out of the different topics we discussed. Mom mentioned she had heard something about the virus they were calling AIDS, and wondered what we knew about it.

Jason and I looked at each other.

"You know, Mom," I started to say, after what seemed like a long uncomfortable pause. Before I could finish, Jason interrupted me and began to talk in his predictable relaxed manner.

"Elizabeth," he began, after taking a sip of his wine. "From what I have heard, they don't really know very much about it. I'm sure they are going to find a cure and we will all wonder why we allowed ourselves to get into such a panic."

His words of optimism lingered until the waiter appeared with our entrees. We had all ordered lobster and the three plates glistened with the orange glossy shells.

"Mom," I said, looking at Jason while addressing her, before I began to speak. "Jason and I are going to Hawaii over the Fourth of July holiday."

"Oh that's wonderful!" she said exultingly. "You know Donnie took me to Hawaii a couple of years ago and I just loved it."

"Well, this time, I got reservations at a five-star resort on the Big Island. It's the Rockefeller resort," I announced, talking a little louder in case anyone from the next table might be listening. "It's where a lot of my clients go. It's outrageously expensive."

Jason broke in, "I told him we did not have to go to such an expensive place. I would be fine staying in Honolulu the whole time."

"Don't bother arguing with him, Jason. You know Don, he has to go and do all the things his rich clients do."

"Come on you two!" I defended myself. "I don't always do that."

"Well, almost always," Mom said with a reticent smile.

To justify to myself that I was not turning into a complete snob, I started to give examples. Then I told them I wanted to make this trip different. "You know something? I want this trip to be a spiritual trip."

They both stopped eating and stared at me.

"I know what you're thinking, but I mean it. I have been busy studying some of my books on spirituality that talk about how the different vibrations are associated with cause and effect. Especially the ones about colors, and how they have different levels of vibrations. You know, 'auras.' I feel like I'm going to discover something in Hawaii this time." I reached for my wine and noticed they were still staring.

"Stop it! Don't look at me like that!" I exclaimed again with a chuckle. "I mean it, I really do!"

At that moment the waiter walked up to the table and asked if everything was to our satisfaction.

"Yes," I answered, still chuckling. "Everything is perfect."

As soon as we got up to leave, I asked Mom and Jason to wait out in front, while I went to find a restroom. When I entered, I noticed the man standing at the urinal looked familiar, but I couldn't place him. I went and stood on the other side of him and as I began to urinate, I went into shock, realizing how I knew him. It was Steve from the S&M bar. I stared straight ahead and was glad the urinal was in front of me or I might have wet myself.

"Hi," he casually said.

"Hi," I replied with a gulp.

He said nothing more.

I stayed at the urinal and waited until he finished washing his hands. After he left, I stepped away and looked around, realizing there was no one else in the restroom.

The experience of seeing Steve affected me in a strange way. Sexual memories flooded my mind and a sexual charge began to pulse through my body.

I turned the faucet on to wash my hands. What happened next is hard to describe. When I glanced up at myself in the mirror … the reflection was not of me. I mean, it was me, but it was me as *David*, my wounded self from The Dungeon, a few years before.

"David?" I whispered to the mirror, looking around to check the restroom again.

David had not been back since I was raped at the S&M bar. Even though he had disappeared, I still entertained thoughts of loveless, manipulated sex. Since I had met Jason, I had been able to fight off any urge to act on them by focusing on my spiritual development.

"Don!" I heard my name called, snapping me out of my trance. I looked and saw Jason through the steam-filled mirror. I guess I had left the hot water running, so half of the mirror was fogged up.

"What's going on? Are you OK?"

"Yeah, I'm OK. Why?" I asked, nonchalantly turning off the water.

"You've been in here for awhile, so your mom—"

"Oh," I said, quickly interrupting him. "My stomach was acting up, probably all the rich food. But I'm OK now."

"Good." He tenderly patted my shoulder. "Are you sure? I can drive home if you want."

"No really, I'm fine," I insisted.

The next two months passed quickly as Jason and I prepared for our trip to Hawaii. It was the second of July, 1985, and we had just arrived in Hawaii making record time from San Francisco to the Honolulu airport. Beating the clock was a game we liked to play because of the three-hour time change. If our 9 a.m. flight left on time from SFO, we could be on the beach, swishing the little pink umbrellas in our Piña Coladas by 11:30 a.m. Royal Hawaiian time.

The Royal Hawaiian was also known as "The Grand Dame of Hawaii" because of her age. I think the hotel was one of the first hotels built in Hawaii, if not the first!

Bordering on offensive, her pink flamingo-colored stucco exterior and royal purple trim screamed *gauche* from the moment any guest approached the circular driveway. Like seeing an old lady with too much make-up, you smile graciously and forgive her thinking, "Well, that's just what happens when you get old."

Upon exiting our limo we were immediately welcomed with vibrant smiles from each and every employee. The moist warm air, scented with exotic floral perfumes, enveloped us. A lovely lei of plumeria flowers was placed around each of our necks, as if to say, "Yes, you are in Hawaii! Aloha!"

Entering the lobby, a huge columned archway framed the most beautiful view I had ever seen—white-capped waves rolling atop the clearest of clear aquamarine sea.

It demanded an immediate exhale.

The young woman at the desk was doing her best to explain why the hotel was overbooked—"A Buddhist Convention," giving me a look, like I should know what she was talking about.

"I don't understand," I responded, with a tinge of indignity, "What does a Buddhist Convention have to do with me not getting the room I reserved?" "It has something to do with a World Peace Buddhist organization." She was giving it her best shot, maybe hoping that when I heard "world peace," I would be less irritated. "They're putting on a parade for the Fourth of July. Oahu has been taken over by them ... 20,000," she added, starting to roll her eyes. "I am very sorry, Mr. English," she apologized, for the third time. "I hope you understand."

No, I don't understand, I wanted to say. But then she told me that because the hotel had made the mistake, she was able to upgrade us to a suite in the Tower.

"I hope that is OK," she asked, with a pleasant smirk on her face.

"Oh no ... that's great," I said graciously. "Thank you." Jason was standing behind me. I turned and glanced back at him to see if he had heard the good news.

The happy smile on his handsome face told me he had.

We heard later that most of the hotels were full, due to the invasion of the *Patriotic Buddhists*. When the desk clerk mentioned there were 20,000 Buddhists in town, I immediately scoured the lobby looking for people with shaved heads and dressed in red robes. I did not see one shaved head in the bunch, only groups of people dressed in white shirts and pants, almost like a casual uniform. It looked like they had their choice of white pants, but they all had the same polo shirt, with an emblem on the pocket that said something about World Peace.

I had to say, contrary to my stereotypical impression of hordes of religious people, they looked "normal." What was conspicuous, however, was that, unlike groups from one American church or another, they seemed to come in all colors. That diversity seemed to fit with their choosing to put on a parade in celebration of America's independence.

Oh, the parade ... it finally clicked why some folks were calling them "the Patriotic Buddhists."

A group of them exited the elevator we were riding in, so I had a moment to whisper to Jason, "What do you think this is all about?" He shrugged his shoulders and said in an undertone, "There are so many of them we're sure to find out, whether we want to or not." The elevator door reopened and, sure enough, there stood five more white uniforms.

I glanced over at Jason and I could tell we were thinking the same thing: *Surrounded once again!*

And that was how our trip began. The next day we gloried in the beauty of Hawaii—the beach, the views, the sunset.

On the third day of our trip, before the much-awaited Buddhist Fourth of July parade made its way down Waikiki's main street, Kalakaua Avenue, we were sitting on our hotel room's lanai, enjoying our favorite breakfast, the exquisite Royal Hawaiian's signature French toast with macadamia nuts and fresh coconut syrup. We debated whether to attend the parade, thinking that perhaps a day on the beach, free of all the other Buddhist hotel guests, might be peaceful in itself. But in the end, our curiosity won out. The over-the-top flower-covered floats, the sensational live music, and the diversity among the thousands of members could lead one to believe maybe there was hope for world peace after all—it did for me, at least. I was stunned by each bright shining face I saw marching energetically by, even in the midday heat—the temperature was in the high 80's. I felt *something* and found myself emotionally wiping tears from my eyes.

When I saw the SGI banner boldly stating: "*World Peace through Individual Happiness*," I told Jason that they must have paid dearly for that good of a slogan. It made sense when I thought about it. *Who would care if there was peace in the world if your own personal world sucked?*

After the parade, I decided to go down to the beach and catch up on some of my reading. Jason opted to go and do some last minute shopping.

I was about fifteen minutes into my book, *Auras and their Meaning*, when two women that looked about my age, one with platinum blond hair and the other with bright red hair, both wearing—what else?—those white uniforms, interrupted to ask about my book.

"*H-i-ya-a,*" One of them greeted me in a strong Southern accent. I looked up and then answered their question about my "Aura" book. Before I knew it, they sat down in the sand beside me, and began telling me about their Buddhist practice. They were both from Georgia and had been Buddhists for about three years. I shared with them how colors have a vibration of their own, saying that was what my spiritual practice was. I actually made that up because I felt like I needed to validate what I was doing, even though it was not really an "official" spiritual practice. They informed me, excitedly, that they too believed in and worked with, vibrations. "We chant!"

Oh, boy! I thought. *Wait 'til Jason hears about this!* And the more they shared about their Buddhist practice, the more I realized how much we had in common.

The mantra they chanted, they said, had something to do with the Mystic Law of Cause and Effect.

"By chanting, the Mystic Law's vibration somehow puts you in rhythm with the Universe. Ya just try it, and ya see for yourself. It places ya in the present moment like nothin' you've ever experienced."

Their accents were so cute, I couldn't help myself. There I was on the beach, repeating their Buddhist chant.

"Here." The one with bright red hair pulled out a card from her bag. Her friend moved over to my towel and sat down beside me. I looked up from the card she held in her hand as a toddler screeched and ran over the corner of my towel. I reached out to direct the little person away to avoid a towel full of sand. Ignoring the child's intrusion, the redhead spoke without hesitation. "The chant goes like this, 'NAM-MYOHO-RENGE-KYO.'"

They encouraged me to chant for whatever I wanted. "Why y'all can chant for anything. Just anything yer little heart desires, a new car … a girlfriend." The redhead said "girlfriend" after looking to see if I was wearing a wedding band. "The most important thing is that y'all chant. Chant - chant - chant!"

It all sounded a bit materialistic and worldly for a spiritual organization—whoever heard of chanting for anything you wanted, even a car? Nevertheless, I made a deal with myself: *I will chant to have and enjoy the best Hawaiian vacation … ever!* Knowing that in the past I had had some great vacations here, I figured that would really put "chanting" to the test.

As they got up to leave, they pointed to the card they left me and simultaneously said, "Now, don't forget how to say it."

Oh my God! I thought, panicking. *They are gonna start chanting again right here in front of everybody!* But they didn't, thankfully. They just waved and said goodbye. As soon as they left, I gathered up my stuff and went up to the hotel room. I set the Buddhist card on the dresser just before going in to take a shower. I looked at the black bold lettering and said the mantra out loud. *"Nam-myoho-renge-kyo. Nam-myoho-renge-kyo … Nam-myoho-renge-kyo."* I was pretty sure that was how they said it.

I don't know why I did what I did next … but I started chanting on my way into the shower. I must have figured it would sound better with the water running, and, of course, no one else could hear me. Then, just as I was getting the hang of it, I wanted to make sure I was saying it correctly, so I got out of the shower, dripping wet, and went back to the dresser to look at the card.

"Nam-myoho-renge-kyo" the card said. Hah! Just what I thought … I was forgetting the *"kyo!"* When I turned to dash back, I heard the door open and saw it was Jason.

"Are you *OK*?" he asked, obviously concerned, seeing me standing naked and dripping wet.

"I'm fine. I'll be out in a minute!" I yelled, disappearing back into the bathroom. I gave the chant another try while I did my final rinse.

"Jason, you won't believe the conversation I had while I was down at the beach a little while ago." I said slipping my t-shirt over my head as I picked up the chanting card off the dresser.

"See this? This is what all these Buddhists here do—they chant."

"Chant?" he responded, surprised. "They're not like those religious nuts that hang out at the airports and pin flowers on you, are they?"

"No … I don't think so," I replied, not as sure as I wanted to be. "Actually these two women came up to me while I was down at the beach. They were pretty normal looking … other than those white uniforms."

Jason shot me one of his looks and I knew what he was thinking. "Yes, Jason, they are part of the Buddhist Convention."

"You mean they all do some kind of crazy chanting?"

"Yes … but it doesn't seem so crazy," I said, surprised that I was defending them. "It was weird how I started talking with them. They just came up to me and asked me about the book I was reading. It was the one about auras and vibrations. When I mentioned vibrations, that's when they began talking about chanting, and one thing led to another and before I knew it, I was saying their Buddhist chant."

"Wait!" Jason exclaimed. "Back up! You were doing what? Chanting on the beach with everyone watching?"

"No! I mean … yes. But it wasn't really out loud. It's sort of a quiet chant."

"A quiet chant?"

"Yeah, it goes like this, *Nam-myoho-renge-kyo … Nam-myoho-renge-kyo.*"

I whispered it softly a few times without looking at the card, impressed that I had not forgotten it.

"That sort of sounds cool," Jason said, calming down and then motioning to me to show him the card.

"Are you sure that's how you pronounce it?"

"Yeah. They went over it with me."

We turned towards the bed and sat down.

"*Nam-myoho-renge-kyo … Nam-myoho-renge-kyo*" I chanted, underlining each syllable with my forefinger for him.

We began to say it together, almost as if we were singing a song. After what must have been a minute, Jason stopped and asked if I knew what it meant.

"Oh. There is a translation on the back. See, it means "Devotion to the Mystic Law of the simultaneity of cause and effect through teaching or sound."

"Those words mean all that?"

"Yes, that's what they said. It has something to do with the sound and vibration that puts you in the *now*. And then something about 'the rhythm of the universe,' that was how they phrased it at least."

We glanced at each other, and with a slight, almost simultaneous nod, we sat for a few more minutes chanting the Buddhist mantra. A faint breeze blew in from the open shutters off the balcony, joining the sounds of waves softly lapping across the white sandy shore below us. *Could this really be the Mystic Law of the Universe?* I wondered; then I remembered what I had agreed to chant for, the most outstanding Hawaii vacation. *We'll see*, I thought to myself.

257

We'll just wait and see.

Our early morning island hopper flight the next day allowed us to arrive at the Mauna Kea Resort on the Big Island in less than an hour. The limo let us out right in front of the most spectacular lush gardens. The largest ferns I had ever seen framed the hotel's entrance. There, I came face to face with a large statue of the historical Shakyamuni Buddha, six feet high and made of solid brass; this was no simple statue. The serene look on his face was mesmerizing. I thought of the serenity prayer my mother said repeatedly, and then decided it was almost like chanting:

God grant me the serenity to accept the things I cannot change, courage to change the things I can, and the wisdom to know the difference.

I found out that the organization holding this convention was the Soka Gakkai International-USA and from what I had learned so far about this Buddhism, Buddha was a human being, a teacher who never claimed to be a deity. He taught that serenity and wisdom resided within all human beings. The Buddha's goal was to teach all human beings how to manifest that serenity and wisdom, to be able to deal with any challenge and become undeniably happy.

Just as my mother practiced her Serenity Prayer, my *Nam-myoho-renge-kyo* chant quickly became my prayer for finding the endless compassion Buddha said was within me already. I recalled what my father told me in the dream after he died—that within the shell of our body was a spirit that went on after death, and that spirit was love. To me, that was exactly what the Buddha taught. The idea that I did not need to worship anyone or anything to manifest the *God-like* or *Buddha-like* nature within me made sense, so I continued on my chanting journey.

CHAPTER THIRTY

A Sea of Change

1985, Los Altos, California

It was the very best vacation I had ever had in Hawaii. When Jason and I returned home from Hawaii, we both became SGI-USA Buddhists. This was a huge step for me—the saying "Never say never" comes to mind, when I think about joining SGI. After my Jehovah's Witness experience, I preached that, "Organized religions were not for me." I would never belong to one. Never!

However, unlike my teenage experience with Sally and Mary, the Jehovah's Witness ladies, who had dictated extreme rules I would have to follow if I wanted to rise up on the final day, I was assured that Nichiren Daishonin's Buddhism, as practiced by folks in this organization, SGI-USA, did not have a list of requirements. Equality was a guiding principle—there were very clear teachings; that everyone has a Buddha nature, or the inner capacity to become enlightened, "just as you are." So being gay was not an issue; Jason and I felt at home.

The only concept I struggled with was that of karma. I spent hours wondering what I could have done in a past life to deserve the kind of torment Michael showered upon me. Often I attended group chanting and study sessions where different concepts were discussed, and where I easily could have asked any number of questions. In fact, that was encouraged, but I was afraid to ask about karma.

My Buddhist practice was too precious and vital for my survival and healing to have it tarnished in any way. I was afraid that if my interpretation of karma was correct, then it would follow that I had done something terrible in a past life, which caused me to pay a huge price in this life. Since this idea made me have even darker thoughts about myself, I chose to focus on the part of my practice that made me feel good.

One of the parts that really I enjoyed was when we got together to chant for world peace. After participating a few times, I discovered that in order for me to chant for world peace, I had to find a way to be happy and find peace within myself first—otherwise I could not honestly care for and help others along the way to peace.

However, after hours of meditating on how to find happiness and peace within, I was led down an unexpected path. When I chanted for my own happiness and began to think about what that might mean in my life, I realized that many of my sufferings came from having sex with men. I was still with Jason and still in love with him, so although I understood that my relationship with him had not caused me any suffering, I was well aware that Michael, Darren, the men at the S&M bar, and others had caused me great suffering. I even began to believe that I was creating new bad karma in this life by having sex with men and that I would have to pay for it in my next life. I felt like I had done enough paying for bad karma, and with the AIDS epidemic looming, I made the decision that I no longer wanted to be gay. I did not want to be a homosexual.

Part of me started to think that it might have been Michael's abuse that made me gay in the first place. Hadn't my first sexual experiences been with a man—really a boy, but a male in any case? Hadn't my need for abusive sexual encounters in the past years proven that my sexual identity was screwed up from the beginning? So, I pondered, *How would I know, if I am really gay—if I don't experience anything different?* I put the heartbreak I would feel over not having Jason in my life aside and concentrated on how I was going to become straight.

Had I not been told early on that I could chant for anything? That by chanting *Nam-myoho-renge-kyo* my life would move in the direction of my happiness? I wanted to be happy and that meant being normal. So, why couldn't I chant to be normal? I began to strategize how I was going to live the rest of my life. I determined that I was going to be straight, not just act straight, as I had done before.

The news reports about the AIDS virus were becoming more frightening, so I figured it was as good a time as any to begin my new heterosexual lifestyle. Chanting was moving my life in the right direction, and soon I thought, I would be just like everyone else, maybe I would even get married and have a family. I was on a quest to leave everything of my past behind once and for all.

Unfortunately, and obviously, the decision to chant for a sexual identity change did not bode well for my relationship with Jason. We went out for what he thought was going to be a romantic dinner. After we ordered, I totally shocked him when I told I wanted to date women.

"What did you say?" he exclaimed.

"I have gone over and over how to tell you this. I don't want to be gay anymore."

"Just like that?" he said, raising his voice. "You don't love me anymore?"

I looked around and noticed the people at the table next to us had stopped eating, presumably to hear our conversation better.

"Lower your voice," I whispered. I glanced at the eavesdroppers and leaned closer over the table to softly say, "No, it isn't that, Jason, at all. I don't *not* love you … I just don't want to be gay anymore."

"You think you can change, just like that?" he cynically asked.

"No. I don't know. But I am going to use the chanting and try. They say you can chant for whatever you want, and I want to be straight and to live a normal life."

"I think you're crazy."

I dropped my head and rearranged the silverware on the sides of my plate.

"Is that why you introduced Madelyn to our Buddhist practice?"

"Why do you ask?" I replied, picking up the napkin from my lap, and then putting it back again, just to avoid his eyes. Madelyn was my chiropractor and I had asked her on a date later in the week, but I wanted to get this conversation over with first, so I wouldn't feel guilty. When I did look up at Jason, I saw tears on his cheeks. Before I could say anything, he threw his napkin on his plate, got up, and walked away.

I nervously looked over at the nosy people next to me and smiled, as they pretended not to have heard.

Over the next few months, Jason and I tried to live together as friends. He still did not believe in what I was trying to do. So, after many heart to heart talks, and a whole lot of tears, we decided to go our separate ways.

Breaking up with Jason was my first step into the world I was determined to create. Pretend or not, I had a goal. I wanted to be normal and I would do just about anything to make it happen.

I chanted for hours, which turned into months, trying to dissolve all my homosexual tendencies. I chanted to forget how I felt when I looked at an attractive man. I chanted for Madelyn to fall in love with me, even though somehow I knew I probably would not be able to get an erection when it came time for us to have sex. No matter how much I chanted, my attraction to women was nonexistent. And although Madelyn may have fallen in love with me, I felt nothing but friendship towards her.

I then tried to date other women, thinking maybe Madelyn wasn't my type. But what was my type? Since I was new to the heterosexual world, I made the decision to play the field and find out. After my break-up with Jason, I started flirting with some of the women in the Buddhist organization because it seemed the easiest place to meet my dates. First I dated brunettes. I liked dark-haired men, so I thought that might work—but nothing. There was no sexual energy. I tried a small petite blond, but she reminded me of little boy, and that was a real turn-off.

I lost count of how many talks I had with my penis. Why couldn't I be attracted to a woman's body? It didn't make sense. I had known gay guys who could do it with women. I chanted with images of naked women in mind, works of great artists, such as Rubens and DaVinci, trying to internalize the beauty of breasts. I wanted so badly to understand what was wrong with me. Why couldn't I just be straight?

The first woman I dated after Madelyn was a larger-boned woman, brunette and rather masculine looking. I thought maybe I could pretend she was a guy, pretend she had a penis. She was so aggressive—she might as well have been a man. I had to push her off me while we were in the car talking. She slid her hand in my shirt and started playing with my nipples. I hadn't even kissed her yet. I didn't know women knew some guys had sensitive nipples. I pulled back, taking her hand off my chest and nervously asked her to stop. She didn't.

"You know what?' I finally said. "I'm not that *kind* of guy. I like to take things slow." She laughed and scooted closer.

What in the world was happening to me? I thought to myself, as I told her I was serious. *I can't believe this—I never had a guy come on to me this!*

I only dated a few more times. I realized during this dating process that I was also trying on personalities at will. None of them felt like they were really me—but I wasn't sure who I was. I was going against my internal feelings and acting like I was supposed to act, pretending to be straight, pretending to enjoy kissing a woman, pretending to do whatever I needed to in order to get my desired result. At this point I understood that letting the woman assault my nipples in order to be accepted as normal, was not much different than performing oral sex on Michael so I could have the pair of pegged leg pants I wanted so badly.

Pretending was not working and dating was not producing my desired results, so I decided to put women on hold and became more involved volunteering my time with the SGI organization. After chanting daily for six months to be straight with no positive results, I started to believe that chanting might not work. Giving it one last try, I decided to attend a New Year's Eve World Peace chanting session at the Buddhist community center in San Jose. I was about to greet the New Year as a practicing Buddhist—or perhaps I should say, a skeptical Buddhist with a whole lot of questions.

I met someone that night who helped me to release some of the bitter fetters of my past. I like to think of this person as another one of those angels who show up in your life just at the right time.

There was a buffet with a variety of foods set up in one of the back rooms of the Community Center; tables and chairs were randomly placed about the room. We began our conversation with the usual introductions. Her name was Kaaren; she was married and had two young boys. She looked young, except for her short prematurely gray hair, which I eventually dyed to match the soft brown of her eyes. When she told me she had been practicing Buddhism for ten years, I was impressed, and thought she was someone I would like to get to know. We found a table and sat down, hitting it off right away. She told me she considered herself a "Ju-Bu" because her family was Jewish and now she was a Buddhist.

"That's one of my favorite things about this sect of Buddhism," I mentioned enthusiastically, "You don't have to give up your religion or philosophy—you just add Buddhism to it."

"Exactly!" Kaaren agreed, nodding her head.

The more we talked, the more comfortable I became. I don't remember how the subject came up, but she began telling me how she and her husband had held Buddhist meetings in the county jail. "You see, Don, we don't discriminate against anyone, even people in jail."

"You go into jail and teach Buddhism?"

"Yes! And you've met Larry Kline, one of the SGI leaders for the San Jose area, right? Larry was introduced to Buddhism while spending time in prison. He has a very compelling story, and I am sure he would be glad to tell you about it sometime."

When she mentioned Larry and prison in the same sentence, I almost choked on the egg roll I had just popped into my mouth. "Argh!" Embarrassed, I coughed, not wanting to spit up.

I don't know why I felt compelled to tell her about my brother; I had never told anyone before, but I decided to tell her. "I have a brother in prison, for murder," I began. "His sentence is thirty years to life."

"Do you go and visit him?" Without hesitation, she put it right out there, probably expecting me to say, "Of course."

"What?" I exclaimed, looking around the room and realizing I had raised my voice. "You don't understand. My brother is evil."

Kaaren sat across from me and remained quiet for a moment. Her facial expression had not changed one bit when I told her Michael was a murderer. I was waiting for her to ask about all the gory details, but she didn't.

"There are no coincidences in Buddhism. Michael is in *your* life for a reason. He is *your* brother, Don, not some Joe Smith!"

I listened to her for the next few minutes as she explained, "Michael is your brother, so you need to pray and chant for him to become happy. What he did is in the past, and there is nothing anyone can do to change that. The only way you can release the past is to chant for him to become happy."

I stopped eating and looked at her like she was crazy. All I could think was, *She cannot be serious!*

"Someone explained it to me like this, Don, 'Having resentment for another person is like taking poison yourself, and then waiting for the other person to die. You are the only one that really suffers.'"

I scoured my mind for something to debate, for a way to disagree with what she said. But her next question surprised me even more than her first.

"Do you think anyone prays for your brother's happiness?"

"What?" I snapped back right away. "I think more people are praying for him to die."

"That is my point!" she said, excitedly. "You are his brother ... so if you can chant for him to find a way to create happiness for himself, even though he is in prison, then the other people around him will benefit by his kindness."

In my heart, I did not believe Michael deserved happiness, not after all the pain he had caused me and so many others. I did want very badly to be the good, peace-chanting Buddhist, but inside there were moments when I was glad Michael was in a prison box now, buried in his own pit. The child in me wanted to stomp across that pit and pour pincer bugs in to bite him— and then listen to him cry out while I walked away. There were moments when no part of me was willing to forgive him. The idea of having hope for him and saying prayers for his happiness? That seemed impossible—I just did not believe that I had that kind of compassion in me.

She offered a suggestion:"If you can pray and chant for five minutes a day for him to improve his life, I guarantee the chains of resentment that bind you will disappear. Do you think you can try that?"

"I'm not sure, but I'll think about it."

After our conversation I joined the rest of the New Years Eve chanters, and then at midnight I meditated about the suggestions Kaaren made about praying for my brother.

I'll try it, I decided while driving home from the center. *But only for five minutes a day, that was what she had said. OK ... five, I agreed to myself. Five out of my forty-five minutes of chanting—that was all!*

Kaaren thought that this spiritual path could clear my mind of past pain, but I was still confused in so many areas of my life. I still wished I could be straight, still had bouts of wanting the sexual humiliation I found at the S&M club, still hoped that I could stop pretending, stop the illusion and lies and start being myself—whoever that person was. If this chanting for Michael might release me from the prison he created inside me, I would try.

For the next six weeks, I sat in front of my Buddhist altar and chanted exactly five minutes each day for my brother's happiness. It was after the sixth week of trying to chant five minutes for my brother that the discussion topic of a Buddhist meeting was how to "turn poison into medicine." Someone laid it out: "If you want to rid yourself of the hurt and heartaches you have experienced in the past, you can chant to change poison *into medicine*. Once you take the experiences that poisoned you and turn them into healing, then you will be able to attack life in a more positive way from that moment on!"

265

This became my new catchphrase— I would turn poison into medicine. Michael was my poison and I would turn him into my medicine. The next time I chanted for my brother, I decided to write him a letter that was meant to heal me.

I started by telling him that my search for my own happiness was the reason I was contacting him. I wrote, "I have come to the conclusion, Michael, that what has happened in our past, I have to let go of—I cannot harbor my hatred for you anymore. I forgive you, and I would like to come to the prison and visit you."

I did not mention my new Buddhist practice, only that I had been on a spiritual journey, and had come to the realization that we were brothers in this life for a reason.

When I received his reply, I sat in front of my Buddhist alter as I read it:

I have been on a spiritual journey also, Donnie, and have been praying to Jesus to repair the damage I've done to you. When I received your letter it proved to me God was listening and I was going in the right direction accepting Jesus into my life. I've included the visitor forms with this letter and will continue to pray more than ever I can see you soon.

I was shocked at the coincidence of our simultaneous spiritual quest. It did hurt that he had not asked for forgiveness, but rather gave a blanket statement about repairing the damage, almost like there were some dents in the car door that could be pounded out and fixed. He had no idea he had totaled my life.

Still I saw this as a positive response and believed that the time I spent chanting had really paid off. The massive virtual bricks I had been carrying on my shoulders were beginning to lift. But I still had my doubts. My ability to go back and forth, from one persona to the next when needed, came into play again. One day I felt like I was growing in my spiritual practice, and the next I thought I was crazy for writing the letter, crazy for opening the door for Michael to walk back into my life, crazy for thinking forgiveness might heal me. Those doubts multiplied when I told my mother about my plans to go see him. She said she was through with him, and had no intentions to ever see him again, and did not want to talk anymore about it.

I added her to my chanting list.

CHAPTER THIRTY ONE

The Family Stain

1986, Los Altos, California

After numerous phone calls to Folsom Prison to find out about visiting hours and regulations, and a few brief letters back and forth with Michael, the day of the visit finally arrived. I decided to do my chanting for the entire two-hour drive. Halfway there, I contemplated turning around, wanting to forget the whole thing. My fear of meeting Michael face to face after all these years haunted me more intensely, the closer I got. When I saw the large green and white sign sitting in a barren field that read FOLSOM STATE PRISON, it sent shivers through me. *Nam-myoho-renge-kyo,* I repeated as I turned to drive through the gothic black iron gates and followed the signs to the prison's parking lot.

"What d'ya you think you're doing?" An old toothless man asked, as I got out of my car. He stood before me with his bony chest pushed out. "Get out of here! I'm saving this parking space for my daughter!"

"Excuse me?" I looked around and noticed other spaces were obviously available.

"Move your car or I'm gonna pop you in the nose!"

"*Oh fine,*" I moaned, thinking, *I am not off to a very good start.*

I got back into my car and shut the door as fast as I could. As I backed out, the old man was furiously shaking his raised fist.

I locked my door.

I wondered what the next obstacle would be. Signs that read "Visitor Check-In" were pointing to a small building that sat on top of a shallow hill. I walked towards the building, sure that I was making a mistake in coming. Twice I turned and walked a few steps back towards my car. When I was within a few steps of the front door, I decided, *Well, I might as well get this over with.* I didn't realize it at the time, but I had gotten there just as the doors opened, so I was one of the first visitors in line. As I approached the front desk, I was clueless about what I was supposed to do. It was similar to a doctor's office waiting room, except a dour-looking guard sat behind the Plexiglas reception area instead of a smiling receptionist.

The first question threw me off. "Who are you here to see?" the guard asked.

Remembering what Mr. Sanders had said about his crime being described as sensational, I wondered if my brother might be one of the famous prisoners.

"Michael English," I responded, handing him my driver's license.

I looked at the other visitors beginning to pile in as the guard recorded my information into a book. I remember arrogantly thinking, *Wow, I'm not dressed up, but my casual clothes may as well be a tuxedo, compared to the way the other people are dressed.* I turned and saw a large room off to my right filled with maybe thirty black hard plastic chairs; a few people were already seated. I self-consciously noticed several were staring at me. Like my father, I occasionally was asked if I was an actor and today, leaving my designer movie star-style sunglasses on probably only helped give the impression that I was—or at least was trying to look like—a celebrity.

I sat down to wait for someone to call our bus group. Minutes later, I was walking through the metal detectors and listening to the guard drone on, in a flat monotone, the visitors' protocols. No this … no that … no the other thing. By the time they were finished with what we could not bring in, I was surprised we were allowed to even wear clothes inside.

Once everyone in the waiting room cleared the metal detectors, we were put on a small bus that then took us to the visiting facility. I stepped onto the bus and took a seat halfway back. A woman that looked like a bag lady plopped down in the seat next to mine. It looked like she hadn't washed her dingy gray hair for days, and her foul body odor won the battle with the diesel fumes circulating through the open windows. I turned my head away and sank my nose into my shirt, inhaling my favorite Polo cologne, relieved that I had remembered to splash some on.

As we rode, I wondered: *What am I going to say to Michael? What should I do when we are standing face to face?* More anxiety-ridden thoughts ran through my mind: *Should I shake his hand? Give him a hug?* I hoped my belief in the Buddhist philosophy about acceptance would kick in when I eventually saw him. I kept reminding myself of my goal to turn poison into medicine.

The woman stood up when it was time to get off the bus and asked me who I was there to see.

"My brother." I tried to hold my breath as I spoke.

"I'm here to see my husband," she volunteered, standing in the aisle, keeping me from getting out. The other passengers turned sideways to get by her, some giving her dirty looks for blocking their way.

Oh no! Those people must think I'm with her! I panicked, worrying, as usual, about what everyone around me was thinking. I could tell she was a bit deranged by the way she continued talking. It was like she was in a trance.

"My husband's innocent! He was framed. No way he should be here," she moaned, not moving an inch.

"I'm sure he is." I looked past her, trying to gauge if I could manage to step around.

"Come on!" The bus driver roared at us from the front of the bus.

"You believe me, don't you?"

"Of course I do. But we have to get off the bus now."

"Come on! I have to get back!" The bus driver continued to yell.

She grimaced, looked down at her feet and finally stepped aside, letting me slip by. I leapt down the bus stairs, and trotted to catch up with the other passengers.

We had to go through another pat-down and metal detector when we got into the visitor building. Nobody said a word to me; it was as if I was an outsider to them. And yet I couldn't help thinking, *I am one of you. I have a brother who is a murderer.*

They all seemed to know what to do. While they were taking off their shoes and belts, I noticed everyone had a small plastic bag filled with coins. Michael hadn't said anything about bringing money.

As I put my shoes back on, after I passed through the detector, it hit me. *In just a couple of minutes, I will be in the company of my brother. It's been fifteen years. Fifteen years, almost half my life.*

The guards directed us to line up and wait until we saw the last prisoner exit the door on the other side of a large recreational room full of vending machines. We were each given a number and told to sit down at that numbered table. The prisoner would be given the same number. I felt a shiver go all through me as I stood waiting. I was not sure if it was from the cold sterile environment, or from the freezing air blowing noisily from the air conditioning vents above us. I folded my arms to send the chill away.

The first prisoner to walk out was African-American. He sat at his table, and then from behind me, people shifted around as a woman stepped forward, holding the same number. I felt relieved not to be the first visitor to walk across the room.

Michael was the fourth man out.

I moved briskly towards Michael, chancing only a few brief glances his way. His looks had not changed much. The prison's standard-issue blue long-sleeved shirt fit snug, accentuating every inch of his upper body. His hair was on the long side and he sported a meticulously trimmed mustache. When I reached the table, our eyes locked right away and we each put out a hand—that was an automatic reflex. My knees felt weak. But after we shook hands, I consciously decided to go ahead and hug him. I reached my free arm around his shoulder and his body went stiff; it was as if I were hugging a statue. His body felt hard and muscular; he smelled heavily of cigarettes.

I bumped into the chair and it made a loud squeak as it scratched over the cracked linoleum floor.

"Let's sit down," Michael said, nodding to the four chairs around the table.

There were windows in the room, but they were closed and barred. I could smell body odor mixed with fumes of cleaning solvent. It turned my stomach.

"You really look good, Donnie. I guess we can thank Mom and Dad for those good genes."

Our father, hearing him mention our dad … I hadn't thought about him for such a long time. Yet the sudden pain I felt emerged from deep in my heart. I wondered if Michael felt the same way.

"You look good too," I said, my eyes dropping to look at his muscle-bound chest.

"Yeah. And hey, it doesn't look like either of us have any gray hair yet."

"I don't know, Michael. I see a few there at your temples."

He laughed, running his hand back along the side of his hair, his Elvis Presley gesture. The sound of his laugh, almost like a giggle, made me relax for a moment. Then my stomach tightened into a knot when Michael leaned into me and whispered, "Hey, Donnie, see that guy right over there? The one sitting with the blond girl at the table next to us?" His eyes lit up with a sense of pride. "That's the Hillside Strangler; he's sort of a celebrity here."

I casually glanced in their direction and then back to Michael. I was shocked. He looked like a regular guy, not like the demonic image I had in mind.

"He and I work out in the yard," Michael commented, acknowledging him with a nod after he caught us looking his way.

"You work in the garden together?" I asked, thinking maybe that was where they grew their food.

Michael laughed, "No, brother! It's where we lift weights and work out!" He grabbed my hand and put it on his flexed bicep. "What do you think about that?"

The way he grabbed my hand without any warning, placing it on the muscle, had me flashing back to all the times he took my hand and put it where he wanted it. I wanted to pull my hand away and run from the room, but I silently chanted, then squeezed his muscle, and gave a nervous laugh. "Wow. You must really be working hard." He mumbled something about there not being much else to do, and then asked about Mom.

"Mom?" I repeated. "She's still sober; AA has really worked for her. She's never had a slip."

He froze for a second, focusing his dark eyes on mine. His brows arched together, creating a frown, before he asked, "You think she'd come here?"

I thought about his being friends with the Hillside Strangler. "I don't know. I mean, I know why she doesn't," and then I stopped in mid-sentence, realizing what I was about to say would hurt his feelings. The "old me" wouldn't have cared about how he felt, believing he deserved every minute behind bars, but the "new me" believed I could forgive Michael. My mother, on the other hand, would need more time to deal with her understandable resentments.

271

"I know," he quickly intervened, "it's going to take time—a lot of time—for her to forgive me." He paused, appearing to contemplate what to say next. "You know, Don, the Bible talks a lot about forgiveness, and I have a lot of begging for forgiveness to do before I ever reach salvation."

I thought of the few times, the very few times, that my older brother said he was sorry for what he had done to me, such as when he picked me up off the floor of the shed after I stepped on the nail and he saw the trail of blood. Even then, it may have been a phony apology, coming more from his fear of getting caught than any sense of responsibility.

But it never mattered how many apologies he gave me, because the next day he would inevitably do something else to hurt me.

I still wasn't sure about God's forgiveness. Was forgiveness even possible—even appropriate—if the person keeps committing the sin? My new belief system was all about cause and effect. I guess that was why I was sitting there. I knew I had to see him if I wanted to alleviate the excruciatingly painful effect he continued to have on me.

Probably because of the shocked look on my face, he immediately added, "Don't get me wrong, Donnie, I'm not one of those "Born Agains" that wears the Lord on his sleeve. I have been studying the Bible, and yes, I've accepted Jesus as my Savior, but I'm not a fanatic. Really."

"What made you … I mean, what was it that caused you to believe in Jesus?"

It is hard to put into words the charm that still oozed from Michael. His face had an honest, transformed, sparkle to it. I wanted to believe it was possible that he had become the kind of man I could trust and that—for once in our lives—we might be friends.

Michael sat back against his chair and crossed his arms, intensely focusing on me. He then looked up, as if to wait for a voice to talk to him before he began to speak.

He uncrossed his arms and leaned closer to me. "I don't how to say this, but He came and talked to me."

"He?"

"Yes, He! Our Lord Jesus. He came to me while I was praying."

Hearing him mention Jesus coming to him, I instantly thought of Grandma and the visit from Jesus that she talked about. I almost felt like I was the only one *He* hadn't come to visit. It was hard to follow what else Michael was saying. He started quoting Bible verses and said he had a small following in his cellblock; the men asked him to give sermons.

"I really do understand that I am just a conduit for Jesus," he proclaimed, albeit with a hint of modesty. Then, to my surprise, he changed the tone of his voice, as if he were a minister.

My brother, a minister? Someone other prisoners asked to give sermons? This was hard to fathom. I wondered if this was truly Michael, or just some made-up version of him that worked to get whatever he wanted. Had he fooled these guys, just as he had fooled our parents for all those years?

"The most important thing," he raised his forefinger up, "is for people to find Jesus for themselves."

He then reached over, placed his hand on my shoulder, and squeezed. "It sure is good to see you, brother. You don't—"

"Uh, Michael," I interrupted to ask where the restroom was.

I needed a break from this *new* Michael, so I got up and went towards the direction he pointed. When I returned, he was sitting with his arms crossed, sporting a big grin, and looking at me up and down.

"You look in pretty good shape. Do you work out?"

I told him that I had joined a gym and we began to share details of our weight-lifting routines. I was glad we had found something we both had in common: our vanity, the inherited family trait. Before I knew it, a buzzer went off, letting us know we had only had five minutes left.

"Wow, Donnie, I can't tell you what your coming here today means to me," he said, with what seemed like truly heartfelt emotion. All the men, including Michael, stood at the same time. We both looked around the room and watched awkwardly as couples kissed passionately, fathers hugged their children, and grandmothers cried. I wasn't sure what to say or do, so I lifted my hand from my side and patted his shoulder, and then decided to try another hug. This time, his body was more relaxed.

"Well, goodbye, Michael," I announced, grasping his hand. We shook with equal strength now. I could feel his hand was crisp with calluses, probably from all of his weight lifting. I was no longer a boy, but a man, standing eye to eye with his big brother. After I let go, I turned and began to follow behind the other visitors. The guards were commanding the couples that were still clinging together to separate and say their goodbyes. I started to chuckle because it was like hearing parents scold their kids for misbehaving.

"Come on! Break it up!" a guard brusquely ordered from somewhere behind me. "Unlock those lips and get going!"

Then another, "Keep your hands to yourself. There are children in the room and you know the rules!"

A mother carrying a newborn cried into her baby's blanket in front of me. I flashed her a gentle smile while we waited together for the elevator to arrive.

I was relieved that leaving Folsom was a whole lot easier than coming in. No pat-downs or metal detector machines to navigate, and you got to keep your shoes on. When the guards opened the front doors to let us out, the outside light streamed in. After walking through windowless hallways, it felt like a camera flash.

Two buses were waiting outside. I scanned the people standing on the sidewalk, looking for the bag lady. "Whew," I sighed. She was nowhere in sight.

People seemed to be friendlier to me, exchanging smiles as we formed a line to get on the bus. Or maybe it was my perspective that had changed. I realized that when it came right down to it, I really wasn't any different from them. My family had been stained, just like theirs.

I was there to try to forgive Michael, but I wondered about those seated around me. The bag lady had nothing to forgive, since her husband was innocent. The man at the next table sounded worried, lamenting about what would happen once his brother got out. I overheard the mother with her baby talk about going on welfare. All I could think about was how my life was so different from everyone else I had observed. Or, that is, *at least by appearances*, the circumstances of my daily life were much better.

All that was irrelevant, though, to the one thing we definitely all had in common: we were here at Folsom Prison visiting a convicted felon. Someone we loved was locked up behind these ugly walls, maybe forever.

After weeks of sleepless nights, running through every scenario in my mind of what that moment would be like—that first glimpse of Michael, and every subsequent moment in his presence—I was thrilled at how victorious and relieved I felt. *I did it! I stood before him, and faced the fears.* I realized that I had enveloped those fears in the harbored resentments that I had fought to keep hidden in the back of my mind.

The lady sitting next to me on the bus turned and smiled, interrupting my thoughts. "I saw you sitting with Angelo's friend," she commented, just as the bus came to a stop. "Oh?" I stalled, momentarily perplexed. But then I recognized her—she was the woman who was visiting with the Hillside Strangler. She was acting like she was very high on drugs; I couldn't believe the guards had even let her in. She slowly inched her way closer to me.

We both stood up and walked off the bus together. I turned and headed in the opposite direction, without looking back.

When I got to my brand new BMW, my stomach let out a loud growl. I was famished and could not wait to find a place to eat.

About an hour from Folsom, I saw a billboard off the freeway that read: "Murder Burger - The world's best burger! Next Exit!" I chuckled. *How could I resist? What a hoot!* I thought, as I took the off-ramp. The road took me into Davis, a bustling college town with maniacal students riding bicycles. The hamburger stand was a drive-through, but it had a small semi-open patio off to the side, with thick yellowing plastic windows and a few picnic tables placed on the center of a concrete floor. I scanned the menu and ordered the burger with bacon and avocado. After I took the first bite of my Murder Burger, I had to agree. It was the best hamburger I'd ever had. The fries held a close second to McDonald's crispy ones, and the fruit shakes were made with the richest tasting ice cream.

How ironic, I ruminated, as I sat alone at one of the tables. *Here I am at Murder Burger after visiting a murderer. I have spent fifteen years hiding from Michael, terrified that he would find me and hurt me again. Now, actually seeing him locked away from the world, I finally feel safe.*

CHAPTER THIRTY TWO

Confusion Abides 1986, Los Altos, California

All the things I had prophesied for so long, including the effects of following Richard's formula for success, seemed to have worked out. I was living the life of my dreams. Between that comfort and ever-increasing courage from my Buddhist practice, I felt it was time to redesign the warped and twisted inner world that was the foundation of my childhood. In the midst of everything, I felt it was important for both my mother and my brother for her to forgive him and to finally be willing to visit him in Folsom. The defining moment came when I told Mom that I believed Michael had turned the corner and there was a chance he could really change.

"I don't know what else I can say to convince you," I said, almost with a whine in my voice. "I think if you went and saw him you would be able to see what I see. He is really different."

When I was pleading with her, I realize now, I was attempting to cover up my own carefully controlled doubts. I held tightly onto my hope that Michael had actually learned his lesson this time.

"You really think so?" Mom sighed, her eyes filling with tears.

"Yes, Mom. I really think he's going to change this time."

She agreed to go with me, but was still filled with trepidation. This would be my third visit, so I was less nervous. She was still in a state of agitation when we arrived at the prison on the designated day. I was not confident that she was going to go through with it. Sensing her apprehension as we walked across the prison's parking lot, I avoided telling her about all the security precautions. I hoped that once we were inside the doors of the visitors' entrance, she would not turn and run.

Yet, just as we were about to walk in, Mom tugged at my arm and cried, "Don, I don't think I can do this."

"Mom, it's going to be OK. Really it is," I reassured her, hoping we hadn't come all that way for nothing.

She secured her birthday gift, a Gucci clutch, under her arm and pushed out her chest. "OK, son. Let's go. I sure hope I don't regret this later."

Now that it was all happening, the anxiety and anticipation of seeing Mom and Michael come together mounted for me. We had no problems going through security, fortunately. When Michael walked out from the prisoners' door, I heard Mom gasp with amazement, "I don't believe it. He still looks good!"

Michael began to walk to his table. Just before he spotted his number, he saw Mom and me walking towards him. He knew she intended to come, but probably did not believe she would actually follow through. You could see his smile clear across the room. By the time we got to his table, Mom's arms were already open. I watched them fall into a long embrace; their tears conveyed that all that had transpired in the past had evaporated in that powerful moment.

As they reconnected, my mind wandered to the times of our lives when they were getting along. One of those memories was of the day Michael beat me and the two of them banded together against me. But now, Mom was sober, so I knew that would change everything. My determined prayer for this day was that some of the deep-seated wounds would have a chance to heal. It appeared by the way Mom's eyes danced and sparkled with love, as she gripped the hands of her first-born, that I was seeing some tremendous actual proof. We were off to a very good start.

"You still look as handsome as ever," Mom sighed, staring intently at Michael's face. She glanced at me and asked, "Don't you think he looks good, Don?" I nodded as he modestly responded, "Oh come on now, stop it." He ran his hand through his hair, giving us his signature Elvis Presley look.

I recalled the many times, when I was around seven, that Mom and Dad would tell Michael that he was as handsome as Elvis and how they let him dress and style his hair in imitation of "The King." They were proud of their then-thirteen-year-old's good looks. Twenty-five years later, sitting in a prison visiting room, my mother's praise of her son, a convicted murderer, was right in sync with my memories of growing up in a family as much concerned with vanity as almost any other trait.

I sat back in my chair and observed Mom and Michael, amazed how easy it was for them to fall into a conversation, even after fifteen years since last seeing each other, and knowing what Michael had done to be in this place. It struck me that there must be a profound mother-child connection which, only a mother knows, that is able to transcend virtually any heartache and pain.

I began to worry that when they ran out of things to talk about, the topic of who I was dating would come up, and Mom would reveal that I was gay. I just wasn't ready for Michael to know that, and maybe I never would be. Mom didn't know I had tried dating women, but if the topic came up, I was prepared to casually say something to the effect that really, I was into women. Of course, that would have been a lie; I still had zero attraction to a woman's body. I wondered if my mom would go along with my fraud, or if she would laugh and side with Michael, cajoling me to tell the truth. But they kept talking about things like the food in the prison, Mom's dogs, and other mundane topics. I was relieved they never meandered to the "subject of me."

The vision of them happily being together that day still remains emotionally etched in my mind.

The renewal of their relationship continued. Michael wrote her letters filled with kind and loving thoughts. I started to believe that the family stain was finally beginning to fade.

My mother was on a high for weeks after that visit, but I was still struggling with my lack of interest in women. I had thought that forgiving Michael would be the linchpin to my straightening out the bizarre sexual feelings I'd experienced with him. I had hoped the confusion would just go away. Then I began to wonder once again, if how my brother messed with me sexually as a child might be the reason I had sexual feelings for men. *Maybe ..., I thought, spending time at Folsom and forgiving him might have "broken the spell."*

So, armed with this new notion that the spell might finally be broken and having some degree of hope that I could be "fixed," I decided to take action. I had a very honest discussion with a woman friend, sharing everything— my desire to be normal, my chanting to be straight, and how much I wanted to want a woman. I also mentioned my conundrum: since I had never been with a woman, how could I really know? When I finally asked if she would be willing to sleep with me, she generously agreed.

The time arrived and we went through the motions of having sex. If I wasn't sure I was gay before, then the disastrous experience I had with her confirmed it. Fortunately, after our sexual rendezvous failed, the whole issue fell to the side of our friendship and we never mentioned it again.

Once I experienced a woman's body, it was clear that becoming heterosexual wasn't ever going to happen for me. Looking back at all I did—psyching myself up to ask the favor and then to have sex with my friend—proves how desperate I was to change. I so fiercely wanted to desire a woman, to enjoy making love to a woman. But even when I watched straight porn, I always found myself looking at the guys and not the women. The frustration I had with myself was indescribable.

But I finally did decide that it was no longer necessary to chant to change my sexual identity; I began to chant to be happy just as I am. Yet I still wasn't ready to admit to the world that I was homosexual. Some of my friends that "knew," both gay and straight, did question why I did not want to come out. I would respond, "My sexuality isn't anyone's business but my own," and then quickly change the subject. I had worked so hard to create the image of a straight man dating women that I couldn't imagine admitting it was a "front," that I was a fraud. Looking back, I think that by then, I was more ashamed of the lie itself than the truth of being gay. So, as the saying goes, "I remained in the closet."

During this turbulent time, I thought about Debra, and how much I missed her. I had just turned 31 and remembered fondly the surprise birthday party she threw for me on my 26th birthday—I really was surprised. Debra was such a good friend and was one of the few people that understood my sexual struggles. I appreciated that if it had not been for our great relationship, I wouldn't have had my successful business. Yet I couldn't even remember why we had lost touch. I decided to give her a call and find out how she was getting along in Eureka with her new salon and with her goal of having a family.

The beginning of the conversation felt a bit strained. I hadn't talked with Debra for almost four years, and it sounded like I caught her at a bad time. "I hope I haven't interrupted something," I interjected, upon hearing her say something to someone else.

"No, Don, it's fine, I'm just facilitating a play date for my son."

"You have a son?" My voice rose at least two octaves. I couldn't believe it—Debra had gotten married and her son was already three years old.

"Just a second," she said. It sounded like she was putting the receiver down. A moment later, she returned to our conversation.

"Yeah, I got married," she sighed. "He's not the man of my dreams. But we have a lovely son."

Debra paused, giving me time to read between the lines of what she had just said. *At least she sounds relatively happy,* I mused.

"Actually, Don, I'm so glad you called," she went on to say, quickly changing the subject. "You won't believe who is living here in Eureka!"

"You mean I know someone who moved up there and didn't tell me?" I chuckled. Suddenly, I realized the irony of my comment and felt the tension build, thinking about my brother's horrendous history in Eureka.

"Well, I don't know if you really know her. She's your brother's ex-wife."

"Sheila?" I blurted out, almost dropping the phone.

"You know her? When I mentioned you to her she sounded like she'd never met you."

"That's a long story." I didn't want to venture back into the past.

"Then you know you have a niece?"

"Yes," I answered. "Her name is Michaela, right?

She confirmed that, and before our conversation ended, she told me she was Sheila's hairstylist now and had even cut my niece's hair.

"My God, it's a small, small world," I responded, shocked that Sheila, the Carmelite debutante, had wound up in the same city where her ex-husband had committed murder; I couldn't help wondering if she knew.

Before I hung up, we reminisced about how we put the salon together, not knowing what the hell we were doing.

"It was barely short of a miracle," Debra agreed. "How's it doing now?"

"Very well, actually. And, let's see, I did some remodeling so I could hire more stylists. Oh, and I got rid of that wallpaper you never liked."

"I never said I didn't like it," she chortled. "I'm just not a fan of floral prints."

"Well, it's been completely painted over and the reviews seem to agree with you," I laughed. "You know, Debra, a lot of your clients still ask about you."

"Be sure to tell them I said 'Hi.'"

"I sure will."

After we said goodbye, I reflected on the crazy coincidence I had just discovered—my old partner is now styling my ex-sister-in-law's and my long-lost niece's hair. *What were the odds that would ever happen?*

I couldn't wait to tell Mom the story. I knew Tuesday was her weekly AA meeting night, so I would have to wait until nine. She had called me every night since we each received a large manila envelope with the prison return address containing a surprise from Michael. He had been able to book an overnight family visit for the three of us. The prison had what they called a Visiting Tower. It was a three-story structure with a studio apartment on the top that was generally used for conjugal visits. If a prisoner was not married, he could have family members come. Mom was excited to go. I, on the other hand, was not so thrilled. Spending a few hours with Michael in a large, relatively open prison visiting room was one thing, but having to be locked up with him overnight, and in what likely would be no more than one room, was not appealing. Not terribly appealing at all. But I would do it for my mother, and, hopefully, to have some kind of positive impact on him.

Based on Mom's first and only visit with Michael, she said, "This will be like old times when we all lived together in the apartment in Seaside, before he left for good." I left unspoken my reaction: *I can't understand how you could forget how traumatic those times were, Mom.*

I guess I had done a better job strategizing how to get them back together than I had thought possible; maybe even better than I had hoped.

I pondered the unimaginable: *Soon the three of us would be a family again.*

Mom, Me and Michael

1987, Los Altos, California

We arrived on a Saturday afternoon. On the bus ride to the Visiting Tower, my mother and I sat next to a woman who told us her husband was innocent. *Of course*, I thought, *aren't they all?* She went on to explain how a girl he had picked up hitchhiking accused him of raping her, "but what really happened," she assured us, "was that she had raped him. But the damn jury believed her story instead of his." She began to give us details, but luckily, the bus came to the stop where she was to get off. The visiting area where she would stay with her husband was a less secure building than the one where we would stay with Michael. As she stood up, she began waving frantically at a tall, strongly built, very good-looking man peering from behind a chain link fence.

"That's him!" She was pointing wildly. I heard Mom snicker to herself when she saw him. We both knew, just looking at him, that a woman wouldn't have a chance in hell to hold him down, let alone rape him. We managed to hold it together until she stepped off the bus. Then we simultaneously burst into hysterical laughter at her bizarre story.

"Wait 'til Michael hears this one," Mom chuckled, turning around to get another look at the guy.

Our visiting unit was about four short blocks further down the road. We could see the three-story tower as we approached. The bus driver hollered to us that this was where we were to get off. We were only allowed to bring our overnight bags, a small cooler and a carton of food, which was all we would have to eat. The driver stepped off the bus, went around to the back, and unloaded everything. We had already been cleared through security; the only thing they rejected was my bottle of cologne. They said something about the amount of alcohol content, so I told them it was fine to throw it away.

The three stories of metal mesh stairs leading to the front door of the apartment clanged and echoed with each step we took. The eerie thing was that once we went in, we would not be allowed to come out until the next evening. I wondered how Michael was able to get this kind of privilege, but then reminded myself that Michael, with his "special powers," somehow seemed to get whatever he wanted. I did find out later that it was not magic; he had met the requirement of maintaining a flawless behavioral record for some lengthy period of time. Because of Michael's crime, though, he still had to be locked in the most secure building.

After they brought him from his unit and delivered him to us, finally releasing his shackles, two guards were posted outside the solid steel front door. Michael complained about how difficult it had been to climb the stairs all locked up.

Bars covered every window. A slot with a tiny door was built into the front door. Michael was required to speak to the guards through that slot every two hours, to assure them he had not escaped.

It truly was a studio apartment; everything was in one large room, very dank and drab. The only place for privacy was in the closet-like bathroom. Michael joked, "This is so small you have to step outside to change your mind." Hearing him make a joke helped relieve some of the tension I was already feeling, being together in such close quarters. The linoleum-tiled floor reeked of bleach, no doubt the standard cleaning supply. The whole apartment was infused with a disinfectant odor. Although I could barely breathe, I felt relieved, since I could only imagine what had gone on between the previous night's inhabitants.

Scanning the room with its minimalist furnishings, I was shocked when I figured out where I was supposed to sleep. There was a small couch and only one double bed, placed at the far end of the room. I looked down what I thought was a hallway, searching for another bed, but it was only an alcove. *Nam-myoho-renge-kyo*, my mind rang out automatically. This was a much worse situation than I had expected. I had assumed that at least I would have my own bed. Then I realized Michael had never spent a night here, so I was sure he was as surprised as I was that there was only one way to accommodate the three of us—Mom would have the couch, of course, and I would have to sleep in the double bed with *him*.

As I was having my own private anxiety attack, Mom and Michael were unpacking and discussing all the food we had brought and what Mom would cook. I began to unpack my bag. I overheard Mom telling Michael about my Buddhist practice and how involved I had become. I had already shared that with Michael in an earlier visit. He had told me then that he was surprised, because when I had mentioned in my initial letter that I was on a spiritual journey, he assumed I was a Christian. From that time on, he never talked about Jesus to me again.

"Maybe you can teach me that chant you were talking about," Michael said, walking across the worn linoleum floor to where I was standing.

"Sure, I have a card right here." I pulled a card out from the side of my bag and motioned to the couch for us to take a seat. We both sank into the stained olive green cushions, falling into each other. The springs were shot, so it was a challenge to sit up straight. "OK," I began, pointing to the black letters on the card.

"Is this Japanese?" he questioned, immediately trying to pronounce the words. "N-a-a-m—m-i-o-o-h-o- ..."

"It's actually a combination of Indian and ancient Chinese, using Japanese pronunciation."

"Oh," he said, staring at the card. I could tell by his response that it was already too much information for him.

However, he caught on rather easily, and we sat and chanted for maybe ten minutes, filling the room with the ancient melodic mantra, creating a sense of peace—exactly what the chant was all about. I was thrilled.

The aroma of Mom's good cooking wafted by us as we completed our last chant. "Mmm ... something smells good!" We both sang out simultaneously.

I was surprised by how relaxed we were within such a short amount of time.

Mom announced with a giggle, "After I read the form telling us what we could bring into the prison, I thought we might as well be having an outside picnic." Watching her unpack the cooler, Michael and I agreed. She was right; the only difference was that rather than the sounds of birds chirping, we had a small refrigerator that periodically made gurgling sounds, followed with a loud vibrating noise that settled right into the floor.

"Whooh ... what was that?" Mom's eyes grew wide the first time we heard it.

"It sounds like the refrigerator is possessed with evil spirits," Michael chuckled.

In order to fit into the cramped space, the small round table, covered in stained yellow Formica, was stuck so close to the cabinets Michael could barely pull a chair out. He placed his hands on the table, causing it to wobble, revealing how the table legs were lopsided.

"I'll fix it." I tore off a piece of cardboard from a box and then bent down to even out the shorter leg, allowing me the small victory of stabilizing the table.

Mom began to set the table, multitasking; she was also cooking the spaghetti she had emptied out from cans. Everything we brought had to be in cans, but Mom had brought her special spices, turning what would have been a completely bland spaghetti dinner into an Italian feast, even including a loaf of San Francisco's famous Boudin sourdough bread. My mind stepped back to visualize the scene. I marveled, *Mom, me and Michael, sitting together at a table, having a meal. Miraculous—never in a million, no, a billion years, would I have ever thought this possible.*

As we began to eat, there was a long pause of silence. Not having a clue what to talk about, I decided to bring up the woman on the bus who said her husband had been raped by a girl.

"You won't believe the story we heard on the bus coming here, Michael." Mom put down her glass of Coke and began to laugh as I told the story.

"I know who you're talking about," Michael interrupted. "He's in my cellblock."

"Yeah, his wife pointed him out when she got off the bus. He was huge, at least 250 pounds," I interjected, trying to finish recounting how absurd it was to believe he could have ever been raped by a woman.

"I know it sounds crazy," Michael said, interrupting me again, "but the woman really did rape him. He told us all about it. He said that he felt the jury had been tainted somehow. They gave him twenty years," Michael huffed, twirling his spaghetti around his fork.

Mom snuck a glance my way as she wiped the corners of her mouth with her napkin and pushed her chair back to stand up.

"Oh … I forgot, I have some Parmesan cheese."

I watched her rummaging through the groceries, finally finding the can.

Good one, Mom, I thought, as she gracefully changed the subject. The rest of our conversation was more about Mom's work and her adventures in finally learning to drive a car. Michael had always given her a hard time about not driving.

After we finished our meal, Mom began to clear the table.

"No, let me do that," Michael said, getting up from his chair. She put the plate down and smiled graciously, agreeing to Michael's proposal.

After he cleared the table, Mom and Michael's conversation harkened back to all that happened after Dad passed away. I got up and went to my bag to get the book I had brought to read and then sat down on the couch. After a few minutes, I overheard Mom ask Michael if I had told him about not going to high school all those years. He must have shaken his head, because she went on to tell the whole story. She finished by expressing how amazed she was that I had come so far with only an eighth-grade education. Michael did not comment. Instead, he began describing how well he was doing in his cellblock and about all the privileges he had been given.

The small rays of sunshine that had been streaming through the barred windows began to disappear as the afternoon sun slipped away. The room's light faded to gray, so I reached over and switched on the avocado green glass lamp on the side table so I could continue to read. I did my best to ignore their chatting. I could feel exhaustion catching up with me; I kept fighting off yawns, but they were winning.

It was so odd, everything about this togetherness. Michael talking with our mother at the table, as if we weren't all locked inside a prison together, me sitting on the couch feeling mentally, and even physically, exhausted by it all.

Around 8 p.m., Michael said it was time for him to check in with the guard at the door. This was protocol and they were very strict. I have no idea where they thought he would go; after all, we were three stories up and all the windows had bars. But then I remembered that Michael's nickname was still "Houdini"—making him report was probably the reasonable thing to do.

Shortly thereafter, Mom went to the only closet and brought out the bedding for the couch. The double bed, already made, was pushed up against the wall in the corner of the room, allowing only one way to get in. Michael didn't come to bed right away, so I made my way between the cold sheets.

I had forgotten my pajamas, so I had to sleep in my underwear. I wasn't sure if the sheets were just cold, or if my shivering came from how awkwardly anxious I felt. Within a few minutes, my brother's body would be next to me. Unexplainably, the thought of sex and the past experiences I'd had with him caused a disgusting wave of arousal to pulse through me. I did my best to extinguish those confused thoughts. Nonetheless, I was still aroused.

Mom had already changed into her nightgown and I watched her as she finished tucking in her bedding, struggling a bit with the lopsided cushions. She crawled into her masterpiece of sheets and blankets, and then sighed. Shutting her eyes, she mumbled something about it having been a very long day and that she looked forward to getting some sleep.

I heard Michael check in with the guard at the door. I kept telling myself I had to quit shaking. I turned on my side, facing the wall, and pulled the covers all the way up to my neck. I breathed deep into the pillow, feeling a mix of frustration and consternation by the hardness of my erection.

Michael switched off the lights, so I turned back to see him walk towards the window by the bed. He lit a cigarette and stood looking out through the glass and the iron bars.

"You know, Mom," he said in a loud whisper, "it's great you came here."

"What, son?" Mom sounded as though she had been on the verge of dozing off, but was struggling to be responsive.

"I am so glad I'm here with you and Don. I've been looking forward to this, especially to being somewhere that's quiet."

Mom didn't respond, so I thought she probably had not been able to stay awake. I couldn't tell whether Michael even noticed. He went on, commenting that he had to deal with constant commotion 24 hours a day, and how great it was to not hear any noise for once. I squinted through my half-closed eyes to see his silhouette standing off to the side of the bed. He was shirtless. Suddenly a flash of light swept through the room. It was the searchlight, a guard making rounds. As the light flooded the room, I could make out his exhalation of smoke as he glanced over towards the bed.

"You asleep, Don?" Again, Michael whispered, more gently this time.

I remained silent.

He went on murmuring, probably assuming I was asleep. "It's so damn quiet. I don't know if I can sleep."

A cloud of smoke from his cigarette passed over my face while he talked as if no one was listening. "Hmm," I heard him softly lament, "how did I ever end up …?" His voice trailed off. Then I heard him say, in a low guttural whisper, "It is what it is, I guess."

The light came back through the room once again. I could barely see Michael through the half-opened slits of my eyes as he walked towards the bed. He began to undress; I first heard his belt unbuckle and then the sound of his pants dropping to the floor. I cleared my throat, breaking the silence, and then cleared it again, to make it obvious I wasn't asleep.

"Well, are you ready to sleep with me tonight?"

I froze. Furiously, but silently, I screamed to myself, *Stop trembling!*

As Michael slid into the bed, I felt the covers lift up, sending cool air between the sheets. I scooted over and turned to face the wall.

"It's so quiet. I sure hope I can get some shut-eye, Donnie boy.… Ha, get a load of that … it's too quiet to sleep. Now that's a good one!"

"Yeah," I responded, letting the covers loosen around me so he could have his share.

"Goodnight, Donnie," he said, and then I felt his hand softly pat the top of my head, like our father used to do.

My eyes widened, staring into the dark. His hand fell and rested alongside my pillow, making contact with my hair. A chill coursed through my body along with the cursed unwelcome and unexpected sexual feelings. In the darkness, the truth—that this man, my own brother, used me for his pernicious pleasure throughout my childhood—rushed over me like a giant waterfall, extinguishing my erection. I was relieved. I finally felt those sexually charged chains loosening their grip on me, letting me breathe more easily. I felt his power over me beginning to slip away. He patted my head again and turned over, mumbling something I couldn't make out.

I tossed and turned, still alert to every movement Michael made. It was a very long night.

Prison Love

1987, Los Altos, California

A month had passed since the Tower visit with Michael. Mom and I still continued to reminisce about our 24 hours with him. She was surprised how little food there was to bring back. Michael ate just about everything we brought, which was a lot. I don't think either of us could imagine the steady diet of what he called "slop" day after day. Mom's face lit up after each meal that Michael scarfed down as he virtually bellowed out, with a sigh of satisfaction, "I forgot what a great cook you are, Mom." Leaning back in his chair, he would pat his protruding stomach with one hand and pick his teeth with the other.

I could tell those 24 hours had a profound effect on her. She would speak of her older son with a sense of hope and contemplate what kind of future he might have.

"Don," she would say with bright optimism in her voice, "I don't know about you—but *I* think Michael has changed. I think his stint in prison has really done him some good. He just might be able to pull his life together after all."

Whenever she would talk about him that way, I would listen, but I never said anything to encourage the idea that Michael might be cured of his demons.

I tried to share with her my theory, "Mom, I'm not sure Michael can change without *help*."

"Help?" she asked, confused.

"I've talked to a few doctors. I gave them Michael's history and they told me he might be suffering from bipolar disorder."

Every time I brought up my theory, she made her position clear. "I don't think your brother is mentally ill. He has a habit of getting mixed up with the wrong people. That's been his problem since he was a teenager." And then she would say she didn't want to hear about *the polar bear* thing anymore.

I wanted to explode. I wanted to describe all the things he had done to me on his own, all the horrific torture he invented. I wanted to yell at her, "None of that had anything to do with 'getting mixed up with the wrong people.'"

I needed something to be seriously, chemically, mentally wrong with him in order to understand why he did what he did to me, his little brother. It seemed to me that my mother should be searching for something like that too, something to help her understand all that had happened to the family at Michael's hands. But, as I had done so many times since I was four years old, I kept my pain cooped up inside. As a child, that was about protecting my father's physical safety from my brother's threats. Now, as an adult, it was about protecting my mother's emotional health from the pain of the truth. I never could bring myself to tell her about all the sadistic things Michael had done to me when I was young. I knew that she already had enough guilt on her plate from her falling-down drunk days.

Without revealing Michael's long-standing malicious tendencies, I tried different ways to help her understand and accept the possibility that Michael might have a chemical imbalance in his brain. But she vehemently resisted. Her denial only became stronger over time and I finally gave up. She was probably, consciously or not, trying to cover her own sense of shame. I definitely could relate to that.

After the overnight stay, I began visiting my brother once a month. As I shared with my clients the tale of how I was chanting with the determination to change poison into medicine, and how I had forgiven Michael, many of them decided to follow my lead and began practicing Nichiren Buddhism. Of course, I did not share with my clients or fellow Buddhists what Michael had done to me personally. Rather, I chose to describe all the pain he had inflicted on others. This allowed me to keep up the illusion that I had always had a happy, successful life. The positive response and encouragement from everyone helped me to believe that working on my relationship with my convicted murderer-brother was the right thing, even during the times when I felt confused inside.

Driving two hours to Folsom and two hours back gave me a lot of time to review and reflect on my life with Michael. My purpose in continuing to visit him was twofold. First, I knew the only way I could release myself from the fetters from our past was by forgiving Michael. I had come to realize that, regardless of how legitimate my anger was, it was the linchpin of the virtual chains he had bound me in. As long as I remained in that state of life where anger predominates, I felt powerless and victimized. Michael didn't suffer from my continued anger; I did. I was beginning to understand what Kaaren had told me from the beginning: *It is like drinking from a goblet of poison and expecting someone else to die.*

My second purpose was to help my brother recognize he needed psychiatric treatment. I was hoping all the effort I was putting forth would someday allow him to trust me enough so that I could help him see he had a substantial mental problem.

Even though I was feeling pretty good about how I was doing on the *forgiveness* front, I feared I would not be able to get my brother any psychological help until he was released from prison. And Michael getting out of prison before receiving professional treatment? That was an idea I did not even want to contemplate. I also had considered the possibility of having him live with me, but soon decided that was definitely not an option.

When I first started visiting my brother, I made sure to arrive as the doors opened, which meant I had to leave home at 6 a.m. Spending four hours with him behind the stone walls of Folsom began to take a toll. I kept trying to believe that spending this time with Michael would allow me to get closer to him, and that the forgiveness I offered would be the foundation of a new trusting relationship. But each time I got back in my car, I felt empty, alone and confused.

After a few months of this routine, I began to leave at eight in the morning.

For this one visit, I did not get out of the house until nine. When I finally made it through the security routine, we had barely an hour to visit. The first thing Michael did when he greeted me was to look at the wall where the prison's clock was hung.

"You're so late, Don. Looks like we'll have to talk fast," he said, with a slightly forced chuckle, still studying the clock.

"I'm sorry for being so late, Michael. I had to finish up some bookwork for the salon," I explained. I did feel a bit guilty about the lie, but went on anyway. "Coming here really puts a dent in my day, so time gets away from me sometimes."

Michael pensively nodded his head in agreement.

"But I guess if the salon wasn't making money, I wouldn't have bookkeeping to do," I added, with a slight laugh, "so I shouldn't complain."

"Yeah," Michael agreed, looking down at the table. When he looked up, a frown had overtaken his face. The inflection in his voice was more serious than usual when he all but whispered, "I have a big favor to ask."

"Before you start, Michael, I brought some coins so you can get something to eat." I pulled out the small plastic bag filled with quarters from my jacket pocket. I was allowed to bring five dollars in quarters for the vending machines. This was a major treat for him. He looked at the clock again, and then at the bag of coins, and mumbled, "I don't care for anything."

He neglected to ask if I was hungry, and went right into his request. "Do you know someone, a lawyer maybe … that could do something for me?"

"Yes, actually, I do," I replied, as he glanced again at the clock. "She's a friend of mine. She is a Buddhist also."

"She's a lawyer?"

"Yes, she has her own law practice in Monterey." I was wondering what legal help he needed.

"Do you know if she handles divorces?"

I looked across the table at him after I set down the bag of quarters, which I had forgotten I was even holding, and repeated his word, "Divorce?" The last I knew, his divorce from Sheila was finalized years ago.

"Yeah, uh, I married this girl Teri, and she sort of helped me out while I was in the Eureka jail. She was real young," he muttered under his breath.

I was staring inquisitively at Michael's face and trying to take in all that he was saying. There had been many opportunities for him to tell Mom and me this news, like during 24 hours in a tower.

I was jolted back from my thoughts when he asked, "Anyway, what's your friend's name?"

"Her name is Rose."

"Do you think she'll help me?"

"I don't know. All I can do is ask her. Actually, I'll be seeing her tonight at one of our Buddhist meetings."

"Good," he happily sighed, and then acknowledged the prisoner who had just approached our table. "Hey, Angelo!" Michael jovially greeted him and rose up from his chair. I recognized the Hillside Strangler from Michael's pointing him out in the past. I remained seated.

"Don, this is my friend Angelo."

I slid the chair back so I could stand up. A woman came over and handed Angelo a soda just as I got to my feet. She looked familiar; I then remembered her from a previous visit. Later, I found out she was Angelo's fiancée. Michael hurried through the introductions and sat back down before they finished with their small talk. Taking the hint that Michael wanted privacy, they walked back to their table. He motioned me to sit back down.

"You know what, Michael? I need something to eat. You want anything?" His eyes went directly to the clock ... we only had twenty more minutes left to visit.

"No," he tensely uttered.

I could almost feel Michael's eyes on my back. I got the feeling if he had the power to make me move more quickly, he probably would have turned it on. I returned with two bags of Cheetos and put one down on the table for him. Before I could even sit down, Michael was tearing open the bag and rushing to tell me, one more time, that he needed to get out of his marriage. As I listened, my mind began to wander, *Why is he so adamant about not being legally married anymore?*

"Are you going to tell me what happened with the marriage?" I asked, curious about how a marriage works behind prison walls.

"I met her a few days after I was arrested. Her name is Teri, and she had a job as a babysitter. Anyway, that's a long story. Last I heard, she was living in New Mexico." He avoided my question. Staring into my eyes with that old familiar intense focus, he only stated, "I need an attorney to file some sort of petition there. This means a lot to me, bro, I really need this divorce."

I was surprised at his optimism. His sentence was 28 years to life, so I couldn't help wondering, *What are the chances he could meet someone to marry while in prison?*

"I'll see what I can do," I assured him.

As usual, Michael did not ask a thing about what was going on in my life. Instead, he just went on about his reasons for wanting a divorce. "My cellmate is married and his wife showed my picture to a friend of hers."

I nodded, now sensing what was coming next. I had seen his picture. It was of him working out in the yard, where the inmates lifted weights. He was shirtless, exposing his tanned, muscle-bound, tattooed chest. It was a very sexy picture.

"I started falling in love with her just through the letters she wrote to me. She's such a beautiful writer," he moaned, with a lovesick look on his face.

Her name was Josephine and they had been writing for two months.

"I didn't say anything the last time you were here, because I wasn't sure if she was for real." He slid up to the edge of his chair and leaned into me. "She *is* for real, Don. She came to visit me already!"

Now I really had to fight to keep from breaking out in laughter as I remembered the women I had passed in the waiting room that morning. There were a group of midgets dressed like hookers, waiting together to visit their boyfriends and husbands. The little women were dressed in brocade corset tops, accentuating their cleavage, which seemed odd, since they looked like little girls pretending to be streetwalkers. I felt like I had just stepped into a Fellini movie. They each had on a pound of make-up, ratted hair, and wore hip-hugging short skirts with black fishnet stockings. Two of them had ridden the elevator with me earlier. I couldn't help but eavesdrop; they talked loud and chomped on their chewing gum, not caring who was listening to their tons of drama. It was apparent they had come to meet "lifers,"—guys with life sentences, who weren't going anywhere—in hopes of marrying them so they could have conjugal visits.

Michael began to describe Josephine. He mentioned everything about her except her height. "She has beautiful dark brown hair and, uh …," he paused, his eyes looking off, as he tried to regain a mental picture of her. "And brownish blue, no, I mean dark blue eyes." He stopped until the picture fully came into his mind's eye. "Yeah, dark blue eyes and soft milky white skin."

Great, Michael, you don't even know what color her eyes are. What about her height? Come on, Michael, how tall is she? I wanted to say. I nonchalantly snuck a glance at one of the midgets who sat holding a big tattooed man's hand two tables over.

"When do I get to meet her?" I interrupted excitedly.

After he made me squirm for a minute, he blurted out, "She's five-foot-seven! What'd you think, Donnie? That she was one of those "whore dolls" you see in here?"

"No! No, I didn't," I protested, trying not to laugh. But then my brother cracked a smile, and we both broke up. We laughed so hard together we almost fell off our chairs.

On my drive home, I automatically began chanting my mantra, reviewing all that Michael had shared and had asked of me. It was the only way to calm down. The stress of visiting him was becoming more intense.

I was beginning to wonder if he even appreciated all that I had done for him. I had ordered a small color TV, and had it sent to the prison. He said how much he liked it, but never uttered an actual "Thank you."

He would bring up how lucky I was to be living in the "free world." Of course, my first thought was, *It wasn't luck, Michael. I didn't go out and murder someone.*

What I really wanted to do was to confront my brother about all he had done to me. I wanted to ask him the question that had been plaguing me over all these years: *Why in the world would you do such awful things to me?* But it just never seemed to be the right time.

I couldn't question Michael, but I began to deeply question my own actions and motivations: *Why am I being so generous with him? Why do I keep expecting him to change? And more importantly, is my being happy reliant on how Michael treats me, or rather on how I treat him?* I had been struggling mightily for years to understand, and to make the right decisions, about my relationship with my brother. Over time, I had sought professional help and the support and guidance of trusted friends. But I knew that, bottom line, I would have to find the answers from within, from a spiritual perspective.

From both my study and practice of Nichiren Buddhism, I was learning to accept a basic tenet of Buddhist philosophy—that our lives exist within the reality, the absoluteness, of the law of cause and effect. I could try to deny or ignore the strictness of that universal law, but that would be about as effective as deciding I could step off a precipice and not fall.

Sometimes the strictness of cause and effect seemed frustrating, but more often I was finding it quite freeing to discover how much power I really have over my own life. And I loved the Buddhist principle that my effort to live with a compassionate heart toward others was itself a cause to unleash my own unlimited potential for happiness. Even that I have such potential amazed me.

Yet, in dealing with Michael, I was still perplexed. The cause my brother had made, taking the life of a human being, was clearly the antithesis of Buddhist, or humanistic, values. It had to be the worse cause another human could make. And yet Kaaren and others were supporting my being with him and chanting for him to have a good life.

I got it that practicing Buddhism is about treating each person with dignity and respect. Conversely, besides committing murder, Michael had caused most of the bad effects in my life, the things I was still struggling to grasp, like my own sexuality. I wondered, *Since he made so many bad causes, how could he deserve the effect of being treated with dignity and respect? Am I being a person of compassion or just a codependent family member?* Each time I left Folsom, I felt like I had a lot more meditating and studying to do before I could feel truly clear and confident about our reconciliation.

A month after the Josephine discussion with Michael, I was enjoying with my mother her traditional Thanksgiving dinner at her new apartment in San Leandro. Ever since she claimed her sobriety twenty years before, Mom went out of her way to make Thanksgiving and Christmas extra special for me, since she knew that most of my childhood holiday memories were tainted by her drinking. She was determined to create new memories to replace the bad ones. It was odd, though, that no matter whatever we would discuss, or how I tried to steer our conversations to things going on in my life and hers, we always tended to veer back to saying something about Michael.

"You know, Don," she hesitantly broached a surprising subject, "since there's just the three of us now, what do you think about going to Folsom on Christmas Day, to spend it with your brother?"

I had just finished stuffing my face with delicious smoked turkey with apple dressing and my absolute favorite, candied yams with marshmallows baked on top. I was stunned by her suggestion. "Are you serious?" I exclaimed. "You want to spend Christmas in Folsom Prison, Mom? I don't know …"

She reached across the table and patted my hand. "Donnie," she began, with calm seriousness, "I've been thinking; we are all the family we have, and it might be nice to spend it together. And, just like you've been saying, he's really different, so much so, I can hardly believe it. My prayers have been answered."

This was actual proof of my efforts and dreams coming to fruition. Mom was accepting Michael. As her hopes for him to change were becoming reality, she of course wanted to see him more. Ironically, though, this was just as I was deciding I needed to see him less. So now I wasn't certain that I wanted Michael and Folsom Prison to be included in the creation of our new holiday memories.

"Sure then," I agreed with false alacrity, "If that's what you want, we can spend Christmas at Folsom."

"Good! Then it's all set," Mom beamed, getting up from her chair to get the pumpkin pie she had made with a new recipe.

When she turned around, she began talking about an idea for our Christmas with Michael. "I think I'll put together a breakfast and pack it so we can eat it on the way."

"Oh, that's great, Mom." I wanted to change the subject.

I knew it was selfish of me, but I really did not want to spend Christmas with Michael in a prison visiting room. Yet the truth of the matter was, I had no one to blame but myself for Mom's renewed expectations and hopes for my brother. So we let Michael know we were coming.

December 25th 1987 was sure to be a Christmas I would never forget.

CHAPTER THIRTY FIVE

A Christmas ... Interrupted

1987, Los Altos, California

It was 6 a.m. on Christmas morning.

"How exciting is this, Mom?" I was trying to summon up my own excitement as I picked up the picnic basket she had packed for our breakfast stop on our way to Folsom Prison.

"We have fried egg sandwiches, and I filled the thermos with fresh squeezed orange juice. Oh!" Mom interrupted herself, and rushed back inside the apartment. She came out tapping her forehead and sighing that she had almost forgotten the chocolate chip cookies. "Now that would've been a shame," she lamented as she walked to the car, "especially after I got up so early to bake them."

"Can I have one now?" I asked, eyeing the foil wrapping.

"OK," Mom conceded. "Just one"

I had three.

We stopped for our breakfast right outside of Sacramento. When we drove into the parking lot of the rest stop, Mom spotted a picnic table under a huge heritage oak tree.

"This is perfect!" she exclaimed, mentioning how lucky we were to have such a warm winter day.

My creative mother had thought of everything. We had wine glasses for our orange juice and she spread out our makeshift tablecloth, the set of yellow and white checkered cloth napkins.

It wasn't a smoked turkey, but I could tell she was doing her best to make my Christmas a good one. I watched her set everything up and was glad to see the elation emanating from her face. Everything was going fine that Christmas morning until we arrived at the prison.

A few minutes after we signed in, I heard my name called over the loudspeaker: "Don English to the warden's office."

I went to the reception desk and told the officer that I had just heard my name called. He simply said, "This way," and coded a number into the door, motioning me to enter as it swung open. The door closed behind me and I assumed I was to continue down the white-painted hallway to the only open doorway at the end.

When I walked into that office, a rather burly gray-haired man, apparently the warden, glanced up. I don't know if he could tell that I was as much concerned as I was confused. Without standing up, he pointed to the chair facing his desk, and stated rather brusquely, "Please take a seat." As I sat down, he asked, "So you're here with your mother?"

"Yes. Is there something wrong? Should I go and get her, sir?"

"Yes ... I mean, no, you don't need to get her, but there *is* something wrong. Your brother got caught this morning trafficking marijuana."

"Oh," I muttered, looking past him, not wanting to make eye contact.

I did not want to believe this was happening. Here I had I put so much faith in Michael, and I had believed him when he bragged about how well he was doing. I felt embarrassed for some reason and went on trying to defend him.

"Excuse me, sir, but I thought my brother had a good record. At least that is what he told me."

"Yes, that's right, he did," he replied, looking down at the folder I assumed was my brother's.

"But this," he began, with emphasis on the second word. "With this charge, he's been sent to the Segregation Unit. You and your mother will not be able to see him today. In fact, he won't be allowed visitors at least until he's released from there, maybe longer."

I sat and stared at him for a moment and then stood up, not knowing what else to say. I was dreading having to tell Mom. I reached out to shake his hand and knocked over a container of pencils.

"I'm sorry," I apologized, scrambling to pick them up.

"That's OK," the warden assured me with a slight laugh. "It's not the first time someone's done that."

The walk back down the hall was a long one. *How am I going to break this to Mom? She is going to be absolutely livid!* I opened the door into the waiting room and immediately spotted Mom sitting amongst a family with three or four toddlers swarming around her. She stood up when she saw me and snaked her way through the obstacle course of children. She chewed at her candy apple red lipstick as I began to tell her about Michael's marijuana escapade.

"What!" she yelped.

"Calm down, Mom," I whispered, noticing people were staring. "Michael just got into a little trouble—"

"Trouble, my ass!" she protested loudly. "Trafficking drugs? When he knew we were coming all the way up here, today, *on Christmas Day*? That son of a bitch! I knew he couldn't change!"

I gently grabbed her trembling arm, knowing she was on the verge of tears.

"Come on, Mom. Let's go.... We'll go home now."

Other visitors gawked when we left the building. I am sure it was partly because of the scene Mom made, and partly because we were both overdressed. Mom had on her brilliantly red Christmas dress, and I wore a black velvet sport coat with a white shirt tucked into pressed jeans. We had been styling, and we gave those who observed us a lot to talk about, given that our costumed entrance was followed by our noisy, escape-like exit.

The trip home was extra hard on Mom, or more accurately, I should say that I was extra hard on her. Feeling frustrated, I began strategizing about how to make excuses for my wayward brother. This was my unconscious reaction to the guilt I felt about her tremendous disappointment, since I had been the one who so doggedly pushed her to re-enter Michael's life.

As soon as we got outside the prison gates, I stepped on the gas. How fast I drove was one of our ongoing arguments; I usually remembered to slow down when she was in the car. At this point, I was too disheartened. I could not think of one decent reason that could explain Michael's actions.

"Have you lost your mind?" Mom yelled, pressing both her hands to the dashboard while dramatically slamming her right foot against the floorboard, as if there were a passenger's brake.

"What?" I exclaimed. Her sudden outburst startled me. Then I realized how fast I was going. I had forgotten she expected me to drive slowly, like the stereotypical "old lady."

Slapping the top of the steering wheel, I defended myself, "I am not reckless. I'm driving like everyone else on the road."

"No, you're not!" she hollered back, still firmly pressing down on her imaginary brake.

I knew it wasn't my driving we were arguing about, but something much deeper. We were both so horribly frustrated and saddened about Michael that we were screaming at each other, just to get it out of our systems. I did slow down, and by the time I made it to the freeway, she had calmed down and settled into her seat. It was half an hour before either of us was able to talk again.

"*M-o-m,*" I began, infusing my apology within each letter.

She of course recognized the tone, and before I could continue, said she was sorry for yelling at me.

"I'm just so upset, Don. I had such hopes for your brother and now he's gone and disappointed me again."

"He's probably never going to change into the son you want him to be, Mom. We just have to try and love him for who he is."

My mind flashed back to that time in Seaside when Michael and Mom ganged up on me, and she let him beat me up. I looked down at how fast I was going and eased my foot off the gas.

I had forgiven her, and even Michael, even though at the time I never believed either action would be possible. So now, I felt, it was her turn to forgive Michael.

Pompously, I added, "That's what I'm doing. After all, he is *my* brother, like he's *your* son. Can't you just accept him, like I am, and make the best of it?"

She sat up straight in her seat and clasped her hands firmly in her lap.

"That's fine," she said, speaking through her clenched teeth. "If you want to accept him, then do it! But I'm not! I absolutely refuse to go through this again!"

"Mom, I don't think you understand—"

"No, son!" She drew out her words with utter conviction. "*You* don't understand. Like I've said before, I can't help but love him as my son, but I hate him as a person! Michael's dead to me now."

After a moment, I turned my head to make another point, but saw Mom was facing the car window. She was crying.

I remained quiet for the rest of the way home. So did she.

When we arrived at her apartment, we exited the car at the same time and walked in together. I went over to her silver-tinseled Christmas tree standing in the corner of the living room and plugged it in.

"Hey, Mom," I called from where I was kneeling and reached for the plug. The tree lit up with a rainbow of colors from the many strands of lights she had strung. I crawled backwards from the wall, admiring it, "I think this might be the prettiest tree you have ever done."

"What, honey?" she endearingly answered, while picking up her toy poodle. "Cindy, Cindy, Cindy," she cooed in baby talk. Cradling her, my mother came over and sat down on the brown velour couch and snuggled her face into Cindy's topknot. "What am I going to do with you, little girl?" Mom continued to coo, tightening the green and red bow.

I turned and sat down cross-legged on the carpet, saying my *oohs* and *ahhs* about what a lovely job she had done on the tree. And then I began to recall the infamous Christmas in Moss Landing when Dad was about to put the angel on top of the tree, but slipped off the stool after having one too many drinks, and fell face forward, taking the entire tree down with him.

"Wasn't that awful?" she softly chuckled, gazing up at the angel that sat regally on top of the tree.

I joined in and we gazed at the tree together.

Mom broke the silence: "That poor little angel. It's incredible she survived all of that."

"I don't know how you have managed to keep her protected all these years, Mom. She has to be older than me."

"I don't know either, son. I guess she's just a *toughie.*"

The lights warmed up and began twinkling on and off, reflecting bright colors against the barrage of silver tinsel Mom had meticulously draped over the artificial tree's branches.

The angel's porcelain face and golden blond hair glowed; she still looked virtually brand new. Her survival through the myriad of moves over the years may have been a minor miracle.

I decided to get up and join her on the couch. I was still feeling badly about our argument in the car. I started to apologize again, "Mom, I want to tell you how sorry I am about—"

"No," she interrupted once again. "I'm the one who should apologize."

Cindy began to squirm in my mother's arms, and then true to a poodle's nature she jumped to the floor and gave her body a thorough shake, sending the holiday bow flying. It landed right at Mom's feet. We both knew there was no way that bow was going back on Cindy's head this night.

Mom bent toward the floor, scooped the bow up and set it down on the coffee table. When she looked back at me, her eyes were brimming with tears.

"I want to tell you something, Don, so please just listen. This is very hard for me to say."

I reached for a Kleenex from the end table and handed it to her.

"What happened today, with Michael? When I heard how he had ruined our Christmas, well, it affected me. I can't even find the words for how much it hurt."

"I know, Mom," I interrupted, to give her a moment to pull it together. "It was awful, what he did, knowing we were coming today."

She wiped her nose and then placed her hands together in her lap.

"I can't do it anymore, son. I mean it, there's no way."

I quietly listened to her tell me that what Michael had done to her, to us, was threatening her sobriety. "I'm craving a drink, and that hasn't happened for so long," she cried.

The pain was too much for her to handle. She loved her first-born and would have done anything in the world, if it only could make him change. But there was nothing more to do, nothing more to give. And this betrayal was the last straw.

"I can't let him back in my heart, Donnie … I just can't."

I reached over and embraced my dear mother, tearfully whispering, "Don't worry, Mom. It's OK. You never have to see him again."

It had seemed to be the most disastrous Christmas Day ever. But as I was driving home, I unexpectedly encountered news that altered my life for good. I was halfway home from my mother's when I happened to turn on the car radio; the topic seemed to be recent scientific news. A famous doctor was explaining that neurologists were now able to prove that at least some homosexuals were born with something in their brains that *determines* their sexual orientation.

I immediately turned up the volume.

It was hard for me to follow his medical explanation of exactly what it was that caused this, but when I heard that studies proved that sexual orientation was not a choice, but rather something that was set within the brain at birth, I paid attention.

Listeners called in with questions, the exact questions that were running through my mind.

"So what you're saying," a caller paused in disbelief, "is that it might be scientifically impossible for someone to change from being a homosexual to a heterosexual?"

"That's right," the doctor confirmed. "There is a section in the brain that dictates whether someone will be physically attracted to the opposite sex, or for that matter, to the same sex."

I slammed on my brakes, almost hitting someone crossing in front of me. It was dusk and a light rain was falling. After stopping and mouthing, "I'm so sorry," to the startled pedestrian, I pulled over to the side of the road. I collapsed over the steering wheel, overcome by an explosion of emotions.

"I knew I couldn't change.... *I knew it! I knew it!*" I cried. I raised my face from the rim of the steering wheel and gazed at the windshield wipers melodically swishing from side to side. My sexual attraction to men, a part of me ever since I could remember, finally made sense.

The days that followed this revelation were awash with joy and sadness both. I was not sure who I really was. I had spent my life feeling both guilty and undeserving of any true love, due to what our culture had labeled "abnormal" and "sinful." Those judgments certainly played into the reasons I had tried so hard to be straight. I had pushed Jason out of my life, tried dating women, and went against everything I felt inside, just to prove I was "normal."

The message on the radio that day would take awhile for me to fully absorb—*I am actually normal ... just the way I am.*

CHAPTER THIRTY SIX

A Full Seven Years

1987, Los Altos, California—1994, Los Altos, California

Soon after the failed Christmas visit to Michael and my revelation while listening to the radio that day, I fell in love again. This time I was able to embrace my sexual identity without feeling like I was a defect of nature.

Ronald is Filipino and is one of the most genuinely good people I have ever met. He didn't appear gay at all, so when I introduced him as my roommate, it was not that obvious that we were a couple. It still would take me a few more years to come out to my clients, but in my private life, I was at peace with who I was becoming, or rather, with allowing my true self to emerge. Ronald and I lived together for seven years and he has remained one of my best friends.

During those seven years, I sold my salon, Dorian Grey, and moved my business from Los Altos to Downtown Palo Alto. I created what I like to call "a boutique salon." The location was perfect for business and it was just a few blocks away from where I was having a home built. The move allowed me to invite only my preferred clients to be part of my new enterprise. I then hired an assistant who worked closely with me and was well suited to catering to my select clientele. I was fully booked and no longer accepted new clients. My boutique salon was a success.

My mother remained active in AA, but for many years, she also had been bouncing around New Age and psychic groups. At first, I had thought this spiritual journey of hers was too weird, but then I saw her confidence and joy grow, as she learned more and more about herself and opened up to other people. I was experiencing very similar effects from my Buddhist practice, so we grew to appreciate and respect each other's different paths, and to enjoy the considerable common ground.

Mom occasionally travelled to Arizona to participate in seminars, particularly in the town of Sedona, often called the "Metaphysical Capital of the United States." Yet it was still a shock when one day she decided to pack up and move to Arizona. Her fear of earthquakes may have been one factor, but the most significant was her sentiment: "I think I have found my people."

I told her I would miss her, especially our Sunday evening dinners, but that I was thrilled that at age 77, she had the courage and the energy to follow her dreams.

I spent much of my free time during these years working on Soka Gakkai International-sponsored world peace cultural festivals and local discussion and study activities. I even started a SGI gay and lesbian group in Silicon Valley.

Following our aborted Christmas visit, my mother remained true to her word. She never saw Michael again.

I, on the other hand, continued to communicate with my brother, mostly by letter. My help with finding him an attorney did lead to his getting a divorce from Teri. Now he was planning to marry Josephine. It was going to be a prison *double* wedding ceremony, but that was not even the most surprising part. In another of the amazing and convoluted coincidences abounding in both of our lives, Teri—out of the blue—had written Michael to tell him she might see him in the visiting room. Her fiancé had just received a life sentence after his third felony conviction, and, of all places, he was going to be housed at Folsom.

Michael's letter went into great detail about how Teri's boyfriend had been assigned to *his* cellblock, and how they had become friends. So the upcoming double nuptials were for Michael and his wife-to-be, Josephine, and for Teri, his wife-of-old, and her intended. I had no idea life behind bars could be like this!

Once he was married, Michael requested a transfer, in order to live closer to his wife, and it was granted. He was moved to Vacaville State Prison, and with Josephine in his life now, I was able to cut back on my visits with little guilt.

My energies were pouring into a new direction in my life.

In the summer of 1994, I purchased my first home. The house had been in foreclosure for two years, resulting in serious cosmetic deterioration. During the months I was in negotiations with the banks, I worked on plans for the interior design, even though I didn't have a signed contract. In my heart, I knew this 50's ranch style house was meant to be mine, and fortunately, I was right. Because I had taken action, doing much of the design work prior to the sale, renovations were able to start immediately.

On a whim, anticipating how dramatic the improvements might be, I had a professional photographer take pictures before construction began. At that time, a friend suggested I enter my remodeling project in the annual *Better Homes and Gardens* amateurs-only home improvement contest. My remodel was simple; it involved no major architectural changes. I replaced an eight-foot sliding glass door that led out to a private patio with a set of French doors, and had a six-foot bay window installed with a built-in curved bench that served as seating for the generously sized breakfast nook. Then I updated the galley kitchen, adding emerald green granite counter tops, walnut-stained hardwood floors, and walls painted with light and dark shades of cappuccino. This created what everyone said was a stunning transformation.

Unlike the horror stories I had heard from clients about their never-ending remodels, mine took only four months. That was definitely a benefit of working on the plans before I even owned the house.

After my childhood of constant moving in and moving out of apartments, and then living in a series of rentals as an adult, I was elated to move into my own home–truly an "American Dream" moment. To discover I had a natural talent for interior design was icing on the cake.

I was at the salon when the call came in. Out of the more than 7000 entries nationwide, I had placed first in the *Better Homes and Gardens* contest! I was proud to have a six-page layout in a national magazine and reveled in the honor. Something I had enjoyed since childhood—design, color, and space—had become realized and recognized.

When I received the call about my design award from the magazine, the familiar rush of beating out the competition returned from my skating days: *First place—I had won first place!*

I celebrated by inviting all my clients and friends to an open house party in my award-winning home. Fortunately, the beautiful late autumn day stayed warm into the evening, allowing me to take full advantage of the large wraparound patio.

Excited about the success of my first renovation, I decided to try again on another property. After only ten months of ownership, and in the midst of rising home prices of the mid-90's, the sale of that first home cleared a profit of one hundred thousand dollars. The planets must have been aligned for me because, a few years later, the sale of my next purchase produced eight times what I made on the first. I was like a snowball rolling down a hill, gaining energy and excitement with each twist and turn.

I realize now that during all of my newfound success, I was unconsciously trying to leave my brother behind.

The open house was wildly successful and the next day, I must admit, I was floating in a sea of self-acceptance and approbation. I was sitting in my family room enjoying a roaring fire in the state-of-the-art fireplace I had designed. I had just opened one of my favorite bottles of Cabernet when the phone rang. I looked at the clock. It was 6 p.m., too late in the evening for the call I was expecting from the *Better Homes and Gardens* coordinator about the logistics of the upcoming photo shoot.

"Hello," I answered.

"Can I speak to Donnie?" a young woman asked apprehensively.

"This is Donnie ..." I was perplexed; the only people still using my childhood name were my mother and Michael.

"I'm so happy you're home, and that I have the right number," she said, her tone becoming more relaxed. She paused for an instant before announcing, "I'm Michaela, your brother's daughter."

This was the most unexpected person I could ever imagine calling.

I immediately recalled the last time I had seen her. She was a six-month-old baby cradled in her mother's arms and I was afraid to hold her. Hearing her voice as an adult sent a chill up my spine.

She told me she was nervous, but that she had made a determination to connect with her Uncle Donnie. She had the maturity to add, "I know this might be awkward for you."

"No, no, I'm very glad you are calling, Michaela. It's just that I am surprised you were able to get my number."

"Yeah, it wasn't easy," she sighed.

She went on, but didn't offer an explanation, so I decided not to pursue it.

Very soon the sound of her voice reminded me of someone. And then it came to me—it was her grandmother. And the more we talked, the more I detected similar personality traits. Just like her grandmother Elizabeth, she possessed great clarity and went straight to the point.

I had sketchy recollections of Michael talking about his daughter and trying to get her to come to the prison to meet him. I realized, though, that when I asked about her on other occasions, Michael managed to change the subject.

Once, when I asked him about the murder he and Mona had committed, he immediately went on the defensive. "You know, Donnie, we were so strung out on drugs, I don't really remember any of it." He did not elaborate, and, in fact, asked me not to talk about it anymore. When I later inquired about Michaela, he responded the same way.

I was not sure where this conversation with Michaela was going, but I offered, "You were a baby the last time I saw you. Your mom and Michael visited our San Leandro apartment. Mom and I were both shocked because we had no idea Michael had even gotten married, to say nothing of having a baby."

"They separated before I knew I had a dad, so I have no memories of him."

Lucky for you, I thought.

"Your mom pretty much disappeared," I commented. I was saddened, listening now to Michaela's grownup voice. I couldn't help but think, *All my life I had had a niece, some semblance of an extended family, but again, because of Michael, our lives were stripped of these relationships.*

I thought about the night Sheila called to let my mother know that Michael had been arrested, and that she was going to get a divorce and move away. My mother had stunned me when she selflessly ordered Sheila to take her baby and to never tell us, nor anyone else, where she and Michaela were living.

Michaela picked up the family story. "When I was six months old, we moved from Carmel to Los Angeles. Mom met a Navy man and fell in love. When I was small, they told me they were my adoptive parents and that there was no history of my biological parents, so of course that's what I grew up believing.

"Was that man a good father to you?" I inquired, adding in my head, *He had to be a hell of a lot better than Michael could ever have been.*

"He was OK. And it wasn't until after the … uh … the murder was in the news here in Eureka that I found out that I was not adopted."

"I'm sorry, Michaela, but I don't understand. You thought you were adopted by *both* your parents?"

I was trying to fathom this. *Why would Sheila decide to lie about being her biological mother? Did she think she was somehow protecting her daughter from finding out about her criminal father, or maybe from Michael eventually finding her?* I just couldn't figure it out.

"It's a long story. Do you have time?"

"Of course I do. But why don't you give me your number so I can call you back, since this is long distance."

"Thanks, I'd appreciate that."

"Give me about fifteen minutes," I said.

I went to the kitchen and filled my wine glass to the top. *I have to call Mom*, I thought, already dialing her number.

"Pick up!" I whispered into the phone on what must have been the tenth ring. *Damn, she's not home.* Her new life in Arizona, with all her spiritual and social activities, kept her so busy that I no longer could keep track of her schedule.

Still, I could not believe my mother wasn't home when I needed to talk to someone, to share this unbelievable moment. I sat and watched the clock, waiting for exactly fifteen minutes to go by, thinking through everything Michaela had just told me and writing down a few notes so I could relay them to Mom later.

I dialed Michaela's number. I found myself entranced by what now seemed to be a mutual inquiry. I truly was happy to hear from her, but I was also a little reluctant to hear "the long story," especially if it involved any of my brother's unscrupulous escapades.

"Hello," she answered.

I was right. Even the way she says "hello" is just like Mom.

We resumed our conversation: "So why did you all move to Eureka from L.A.?"

"I'm not sure. I was five years old, so I never asked them."

"Did they ever have any idea Michael was living there also?"

"Not at all. We didn't know until the murder."

What an unbelievable coincidence: Michael and Sheila both ended up living in the same small town after all those years. It was downright crazy. I raised my wine glass and took a long sip; it was close to being empty again.

"Actually," I said, "I heard part of the story of how Michael and your mom both ended up in Eureka from the lady who does your mother's hair."

"Debra? You know Debra?" she asked excitedly. I remembered Debra had said she also cut Michaela's hair every once in awhile.

"How do you know her?"

"Debra and I go way back. We were partners in a salon together, forever ago."

"I'm not sure, Uncle Donnie, if even Debra knows the whole story. It's not something Mom shares with many people because it sounds like a movie script, and nobody believes her."

"I can see why!"

"Actually, you have no idea how strange it got."

"OK, but let me just say that I know my brother, so I could believe anything."

Suddenly, my African Grey parrot Zorra, whom I had purchased after buying the house, began squawking loudly. I grabbed a blanket off the couch and hung it over her cage. "Sorry for the noise; I have a very jealous bird."

"Oh, that's OK," she assured me and continued on. "So, as I said, I had been told by my parents that they had adopted me. Then one morning at breakfast, when I was ten years old, it was Mom, me, and my babysitter. She'd been my sitter for almost a year by then, and had sort of become part of the family," Michaela explained.

"We were about done with breakfast when my mother dropped the news section of the paper on her plate and gasped, 'Oh my God! I can't believe this!' I couldn't tell if she was frightened or what, but before I could even ask what was wrong, she told me to go outside and play."

"Mmm ..." I muttered into the phone, guessing what was coming next.

"And I guess you know, Uncle Donnie, that my father's murder case was front page news, at least up here. Later, I found out why Mom was positive it was him; the paper had printed his full name—Michael Ray English."

"Um, Michaela, you said that your parents had told you that you were adopted ..." With some trepidation, I plunged on, "So, with the shock of the news, is that when your mother told you that Michael was your father and she was your real mother?"

"No," she responded abruptly. "Actually, I heard it from Teri. I mean my babysitter."

When she said "Teri," my mind raced to the woman Michael had divorced, with my help. I recalled that he had said something about her being a babysitter.

Unintentionally, my voice rose a good octave or more. "Teri told you Michael was your father? How did she know?"

At that moment I heard "Cr-a-a-c-k!" A burning log was splitting up in the fireplace, sending out sparks. I was irritated to be interrupted, but went over to move the metal screen closer to the hearth, and just stood there as I listened to her response.

"Well, when my mother realized it was my father in the newspaper that morning, she did something I know she regretted later. But I guess at the time, she really needed someone to talk to and assumed she could trust Teri, even though she was only like maybe nineteen. Mom admitted the whole truth: that she was once married to Michael and that he was my father. And of course that also meant that I was not adopted."

"Oh my," I nearly swooned back into my seat.

"Exactly," Michaela agreed with my solemn sigh.

"But, Uncle Donnie, you haven't heard anything yet. What Teri did after she found out who Michael was, you won't believe."

She was right.

"I still didn't know about my father, but soon after my mother told her, Teri made a beeline to the jail to make arrangements to visit him, behind my mom's back, of course. I'll never know why she felt so compelled to meet him."

While Michaela shared this craziness, I was thinking, *Michael, you must have figured God was on your side. Or, more likely, that you were one of the luckiest people on the planet. Not only was there a young woman wanting to visit you, it was the young woman who babysits your "long-lost" daughter!* Knowing Michael, he wouldn't have had any problem drawing Teri into his web. With his good looks and hypnotic charm, this girl never stood a chance. One of Michael's specialties was to manipulate the truth, to make himself out to be the victim. No doubt he convinced Teri that Sheila had wronged him by taking off and hiding his little girl from him for almost ten years.

Michaela was going on, "It didn't take long before Teri told Michael everything, about babysitting for me, and how mom raised me as if I were adopted. By her third visit, Michael proposed marriage and Teri was thrilled to accept."

With this new information, I was more than speechless; I was flabbergasted. Although of course I knew about Michael's now ex-wife Teri, I had no idea of her history with Sheila and Michaela. Nor did I know of the whirlwind courtship. Three weeks. It took my brother only three weeks, to convince an innocent girl to marry him, an accused murderer, dressed in a jump suit, and locked behind bars. He still had his special powers. The magical powers I believed in as a child were still present in some invisible way.

"Are you there, Uncle Donnie?" Michaela asked.

"Yes, yes, I am. And I'm sorry, Michaela, but forgive me. I just want to make sure that I'm getting this right. First, I did know that Michael had married a woman named Teri. But are you telling me that she was your babysitter, and that when she found out that your mother had been married to an accused killer, and that he was your father, she just went to the jail and fell in love with him, and basically spilled the beans about you and your life?"

"Yes," she answered firmly, adding, "Unbelievable, huh? Obviously, she and my mom became instant enemies. But Teri went ahead and told me

317

everything, and once he was sentenced and in prison, she even tried to get me to go visit him."

"Actually," I interjected, "Michael mentioned once when I was visiting him a while back that you had written him, but that you never came to see him. Are you still in touch?" I asked.

"He told you we had connected?" She sounded distressed.

"Well, yes … kind of. He said you needed some time to figure things out."

"That's an understatement," she harrumphed. "How much has he told you about my mom and me?"

Contemplating what I should say, I went over to the fireplace again and, reaching over the screen, jabbed at the crumbling fire logs with an iron poker. I could think of no reason not to be completely honest.

"Well, actually … hardly anything," I answered, simultaneously watching the fire die out.

"Well, he was right about that—I have taken some time, a long time." I heard her exhale deeply into the phone before stating, "I've pretty much come to the decision to never to contact him again."

I felt a sense of relief at hearing this. The last thing she needed was someone like Michael in her life—father or not.

"Maybe it's none of my business …" I left my comment hanging as a question. I knew she was 21 or a little older. I could not tell by the tone of her voice whether she was simply apprising me of her decision, or if she wanted my feedback. At the same time, I was feeling guilty because so much time had passed and I had never attempted to try to meet her, even after Michael knew where she was.

"No," she interrupted, "I wanted to talk to you. From what my father told me about you, you really have your life together. He's the one who gave me your phone number and encouraged me to connect with you."

The more I listened to all she had been through with her mom and stepfather, it was clear that my niece was certainly on her way to getting her own life together. "Michaela, it seems to me, from all you have described, you already know best how to deal with my brother."

"Thank you so much, Uncle Donnie. I'm not going to let him add me to the list of gullible women he has so cleverly manipulated," she boasted. "You don't have to worry about me, because I've definitely got *his* number!"

I gulped down the rest of my wine, totally engaged in what she was saying. It turned out that having a conversation with someone you are related to, but have no shared life experiences with, was exhilarating, and also a challenge.

My mind had been spinning the whole time she was telling me the story of Sheila and Teri; it had been useless to try to slow it down. "So you think it was Teri who helped him escape?" I asked, still struggling to weave all the loose ends into one coherent story.

"Well, of course, I don't know for a fact. It did strike me though, that my father did get married. And I can't imagine that Teri would want to be married to someone on Death Row ..." Her voice pointedly trailed off.

"So, maybe he's not Houdini after all," I muttered into the phone, without thinking.

"What?"

"Everyone called Michael a Houdini because he seemed to escape every situation."

"Not this time," Michaela said brightly. "Twenty-eight years to life, if they can keep him behind bars." With a definitive tone, she added, "And I've decided his sentence will be life without me."

She really did have his number, I concluded as we said our goodbyes. *And maybe,* I pondered, getting up to refill my glass of wine, *I would just have to find within myself that same resolve—to cut him out of my life.*

CHAPTER THIRTY SEVEN

My Father 1994, Mountain View, California

I spent many days thinking about Michaela's words, especially about how she was refusing to be drawn into Michael's web. My Buddhist practice taught me that *acceptance* was the path. I struggled and chanted with Michaela's words in my heart. I had accepted, and maybe even forgiven Michael, but did that mean he had to remain part of my life?

I struggled daily with my growing fear that Michael was not capable of changing. In the reverse of my past encouragement to believe that Michael was changing, I now preached to Mom that he was not going to change, that she had to accept Michael as he was. Nonetheless, I still harbored hope in my heart that one day he could be, he would be, a normal person. I wanted so much for him to sit down with me and say with all sincerity, "I'm sorry, brother, please forgive me."

But now, every time I visited him, he seemed to be even more focused on himself, his needs, and his life. I would do my best to tell him what was going on in my life, but he soon would bring the conversation back to what he needed and wanted from me. My dream of a changed brother became more and more unlikely.

For the first time, I entertained the idea of stepping back and having minimal contact with him. I bounced back and forth, one day wanting a life free of Michael and the next day feeling guilty, conscious that I was all the blood family he had left, since both Mom and Michaela had refused to contact him ever again.

I reasoned that unlike me, Michaela never knew her dad, and that since she was still young, it was easy for her to erase him from her life. But for me, my spiritual journey had led me to reconnect with Michael with the intent— or at least the hope—of reaching forgiveness and acceptance. How could I walk away now? What would that say about me and the spiritual practice I professed? Was I giving up?

Sometimes I was able to sit back and laugh at the way I had lied about my own life, telling everyone I was someone I wasn't. Yet, that determination—to leave the reality of my past behind—was actually what had allowed me to visualize and then create the life I now had.

Was my life better before Michael walked back in, via his defense attorney, bringing with him the feeling of dread, guilt and pity that littered my early days? Even though publicity around his case had never reached me, he once again had become an emotional presence in my life. Subconsciously ignoring the effects of his abuse had no longer been possible.

Making the connection with Michaela, and considering all the information she had given me, led me to reevaluate my future plans with Michael. I had no regrets about reuniting with my brother; that process had allowed me to peel away a few of those toxic layers of hatred. In a way, those were critical steps on the path toward my goal of being free from Michael's past torments. Although I had not reached total forgiveness or total freedom from him, I was a definitely closer than I had been before my first visit.

Now I was wrestling with how much more effort I was willing to invest in an unimaginably complicated relationship. I seriously contemplated that maybe, just maybe, I had already invested enough of myself. It had been almost two months since I had visited Michael. Over time I became more honest with myself about my ability to accept him for what he was—a person with deep psychological problems.

I knew I needed to take a break from Michael, but I wasn't sure how to put that desire into action.

I thought about the many times I had wanted to tell him the truth—to scream out and confront him for all he had done to me. But I could never make the words leave my mouth.

At times, I fantasized about writing him a letter to let him know the truth—how much he hurt me, ruined me in a way that nothing else in life could. To make him hear "You were my big brother. I was a little kid. I trusted you. But you abused me, beat me and terrorized me for years!" It felt good to think about putting the words on paper, but I still believed that even after he received my words, nothing would change, that somehow Michael, literally, could not "feel." My pain and my shame would be exposed, and I would be at risk for being humiliated by him once again.

Yet, as my feelings revealed themselves, I found I could not sit across from my brother pretending that all he did was in the past, dead and gone, when the memories and the effects were still alive inside me. In the end, I decided that at my next visit, I would tell him face-to-face how I felt, no matter how difficult it was.

The drive to Folsom Prison that morning was the hardest ever. All my thoughts were about Michaela's dramatic revelation about her father's manipulative marriage to Teri. That was what had caused me to begin doubting if Michael could ever change.

The Saturday morning traffic was light as usual. I arrived late, which was probably a subconscious message that I really did not want to be there. The run through the metal detectors, the pat downs and intermingling with the other visitors was second nature to me by now. I peered through the large front window of the bus. I had gotten a seat right behind the driver. Given the state of my nerves, it was probably a good thing that no one sat beside me.

Soon the row of three cement housing units came into view. Each one had a large block letter painted on the outside: A, B and C. Michael was in building A. He had explained to me that Building A had the highest security; it was where the prisoners considered the most dangerous were housed, sometimes for their own protection. Some had committed famous crimes like his friend Angelo, the Hillside Strangler; some had molested children, which he added, with great disdain, was considered by all the other prisoners to be the worse offense. As he was describing this, I couldn't help but think: *Michael, you don't even realize that you are talking about yourself, do you? What would your good friend the serial killer think about that?*

Michael also explained the bizarre circle of prison life and how you gained membership into a special society, really a gang, that was run by a group of men who were in for life. Your ticket into this society was to murder a "special" prisoner—child molesters and snitches topped the list. Once a prospective member killed the assigned target, he was accepted into the club, which meant access to rewards like drugs and sex. Michael then said that the best thing about becoming a member was that you never had to worry about your name showing up on the list. Building A was heavily staffed with guards, but murders were still committed. I didn't ask—I didn't want to know—if he had become a member. At times, he would point out some of the "targets" and talk about them, and then predict how long they would be staying alive.

I noticed that this visit was becoming more strained as we ran out of things to talk about. I looked at the large prison clock that hung directly behind where Michael was sitting. We were allowed about twenty minutes more, and I still had not found the courage to say what I had practiced. There was a long moment of silence when I could have started talking, but still, I did not.

Just then, Michael leaned back in his chair and crossed his arms. "You know, Don … I'm not sure if you know something about me."

"Know what?" I asked, surprised at this comment, which seemed to come out of nowhere.

He uncrossed his arms and then leaned forward. "Well, I don't know if you know this, but … well, I'm not a stranger to the gay world."

Hearing Michael mention the word "gay," I immediately became uncomfortable. I didn't feel right talking about it; I stiffened in my chair. I'm not sure why, but I never wanted to talk with him about being gay. Maybe I was afraid he would make fun of me. After all, the whole time we were growing up together, he constantly called me a sissy, which I was sure these days would translate into *"queer."*

I tried to change the subject. I wanted to stay in my closet, lock the door and move on to another topic. "Donnie," he interjected with a frustrated tone; his eyes held mine in a long stare. Then he slid his chair closer while reaching his hand over to rest on my forearm. He mildly squeezed my arm. "I want you to know …" he began again, but then hesitated, glanced around and lowered his voice to a whisper. "As I said, I'm not a stranger to that world and," he paused again, shifting his eyes to look past mine, "I even have someone here to, you know … help me out whenever I get horny."

I moved my arm so it slipped away from his hand and reached for my Coke. The soda quenched the parched feeling in my throat. I am sure now as I think back to our conversation that he had scripted every word and knew how exactly how uncomfortable I would be. The two people at the table next to us got up and accidentally bumped Michael's chair. Since he was sitting on the edge of his seat, he fell into me. I caught him by the arm so he wouldn't fall.

"Thanks, bro," he said, and once again, his eyes locked onto mine. "I'm not sure how to ask you this, but I'm going to ask you anyway."

"What is it, Michael?" I whispered, parroting his quiet tone.

"I've always wondered something, uh … if you knew about our dad?"

"Dad?"

"Yeah," he said, deepening his tone as he looked around the room. And then he leaned closer, so that we were almost eyeball-to-eyeball. "Did you know he had his own gay thing going on?"

I reached for the can of Coke, but could feel it was empty. I held on to it anyway. I felt awkward having this conversation with him. My eyes dropped down as I searched the table for something to say. I was desperate to avoid the memory of Dad and Michael's fight about the kiss.

Michael filled in for my absent response, "If you don't want to talk about it …"

"No … it's not that … I'm just not sure I know what you mean?"

"So you don't remember that time when we were in the bathtub together, and I …" he paused, "you know, *we* were fooling around … and Dad walked in?"

I looked up, trying to remember anything like what he was describing. I did remember there were baths when Michael sexually messed with me; I could not recall Dad ever catching him. But I figured it must have happened or he wouldn't be bringing it up.

"Not really," I said, slowly shaking my head.

"Well, you were only seven then, so you might not recall. I can't believe you don't, though. You don't remember that Dad came into our room, after we got out of the tub? And that he was naked?"

"Really?" I almost yelped. I looked past him, not wanting to look him in the eye. I was shocked that I could not remember any of this, but I listened intently, hoping something he said might jar my memory.

"Yeah, he was naked, and he made us sit on the bed with him—you next to him, and then me next to you."

"Were we still naked?"

"Yes. And that was the crazy part … he told me to show him what I was doing to you in the tub."

Michael's eyes gripped mine in an endless moment. It felt like he was trying to bore into my mind, and then he confided, "I looked at him and shook my head and told him, 'I wasn't doing nothing, Daddy. Really, I wasn't.' That was when he insisted that I show him exactly what I had been doing to you in the bath. You still don't remember this, Donnie?" Seeing the confusion on my face, he reached out to grasp my arm again.

I squeezed the empty Coke can, feeling it collapse in my hand. At that moment, the five-minute warning buzzer went off. Trembling, I hurriedly pushed my chair back and stood up. My mind was racing as fast as my heart. I looked around the room, wanting to find someplace to go and throw up. I was nauseated, hearing Michael tell his disgusting story of what our father tried to do to us.

"Are you OK, Donnie?" Michael asked, patting the outside of my shoulder.

What I said and how I exited the prison that day is another blurred memory. All I wanted to do was erase all that Michael had just told me.

The days that followed were the most turbulent of my life. I did recollect that during an earlier visit, my brother talked about an episode on the *Oprah Winfrey* show in which some expert reported that many child molesters were themselves molested as kids, creating a chain reaction. And at that time, Michael shared that he had been "fooled with" when he was only five years old. He had insinuated then that it was our father—my hero.

Three days later, I was still reeling from Michael's story, and was still trying to recall that one incident. I could not. But that night I had a dream in which Michael and I were in the visiting room talking about that same *Oprah* show. But instead of talking about someone on the show, he was talking about our father and how he heard about a father molesting his sons. I confronted him in the dream, saying that I knew he had made everything up about our dad messing with us. As soon as I began yelling at him, I woke up with tears running down my face.

I sat up in bed and I knew in the depths of my heart that what he had said about Dad was all a vicious lie.

It all made sense now.

Michael had been looking at my face, trying to gauge my response to his horrific bathtub tale, fishing to find out how much I remembered from my childhood. He was still working on his original plan, the one that kept me from ever telling my father what Michael was doing to me. When I was a child, he threatened to physically remove my father from my life. Now he was trying to destroy my memory of him. I was sure that he had created this lie just for that evil purpose. Because I had not confronted him, Michael did not know that I had been through hell to remember every abuse I had suffered at his hand, starting at age four. I was absolutely certain there was no way I could have kept buried a memory like that, involving him and Dad.

What Michael accused our father of doing never happened. I turned over in my bed and sobbed into the pillow, *knowing* my father was a good father. He would never have done anything to hurt me.

CHAPTER THIRTY EIGHT

Prayers Are Answered

1994, Tucson, Arizona

After three months of no contact after that horrific last visit, I received a letter from Michael saying that he had "Big News." His wife Josephine was moving to Los Angeles, so he had put in a request for a transfer to a prison in Bakersfield, about two hours outside of L.A., and wanted me to help Josephine with her move down south. I laughed, crumpled the paper into a ball and threw it away. With a feeling of relief, knowing I did not want to be connected to his drama anymore, I responded out loud to my empty kitchen, "No, brother, I will not. Just like your daughter, I've finally got your number!" Then I opened a bottle of wine and celebrated my newfound freedom.

The next morning I awoke, not from my alarm, but from a phone call. I caught it on the third ring. Still asleep, I slurred, "Hello?" into the receiver, trying make out the woman's voice. "Mr. English?" she asked, sounding professionally crisp.

"Yes," I answered; squinting at the alarm clock, which read 6 a.m.

"I'm sorry no one called you last night. I'm calling from Tucson Medical Hospital. We have your mother here."

"What!" My heart jumped to my throat. "What did you say?"

"Your mother had a heart attack last night and she is in the Intensive Care Unit, waiting for test results to come back. The doctor suggests you get here as soon as possible."

I hung up the phone and made arrangements to fly to Tucson on an afternoon flight. The doctor called soon after and told me the bad news; my mother was going to need open heart surgery. She had a defective valve and three severely clogged arteries.

From the Tucson airport, I went directly to Mom's apartment. Her friend Alice had also called and asked me to swing by there first to pick up some things she had forgotten to bring to the hospital. Alice lived at the retirement complex, and also had a poodle, just like Mom's. On some previous visits, there would be not one, but two hyper toy poodles for me to tolerate. It had been about a month since Mom's latest "Cindy" passed away. She had called me then, devastated. At least she had Alice's poodle as a surrogate.

I stepped into her apartment and immediately felt the emptiness of there being no Cindy to greet me. Mom's poodles were such a part of who she was. In the next moment, I felt the more profound emptiness of my mother's absence. Normally by now, I would have been wrapping my arms around her slim body and giving her a loving hug and a tender kiss on the cheek.

Shaking those sensations off, I shifted gears into the practical world. I looked at the list of incidentals I was to gather for her. Along with the special tortoise shell brush I had bought her years ago, I threw in her favorite deck of Tarot cards; I knew when she felt better, she would be doing readings for the staff. After I dropped these things into her tote bag, I sat upright in her living room recliner and began meditating and chanting to prepare myself for seeing my mother in what must be a weakened condition.

I realized I simply was not prepared for the worst. I did know, though, that I needed to be strong for her. I couldn't let her know how worried I was. With my final repetition of *Nam-myoho-renge-kyo*, I mentally determined, *"I must do it; I can do it!*

When I arrived at the hospital, the doctors and nurses could not have been nicer. The heart surgeon personally met with me and assured me that if this were his mother, he would want her to have the surgery, because her chances of living with only one working heart valve were slim. Still, he was honest with me; the heart attack had been rough on her, so the chances of surviving the operation were not good either. He then said I could go see her.

Three different people gave me directions to her room and all three were wrong. Or maybe I was so worried, I simply could not remember moments later what they had just said.

When I finally found her room and peeked through the half-closed door, I could see Mom was asleep.

A nurse saw me and motioned for me not to go in. I presumed she wanted to talk about my mother's condition; I was incorrect. She actually wanted to tell me what an incredible mother I had. I guess the two of them had gotten onto the topic of spirituality. Ever since my mother moved to Arizona, she had become a regular at mystical energy field conferences and she sought out every spiritual center Sedona had to offer. She definitely had synthesized her AA spiritual higher power with the secrets of the universe and morphed into someone I liked to call my New Aged Mother.

And later, on my way out, a male nurse stopped to introduce himself. He turned out to be another of her fans. He wanted to bring his wife in so that she could receive some spiritual guidance from my mother. I couldn't believe it—Elizabeth English was becoming everyone's Motherly Guru.

After the chat with the first nurse, I entered Mom's room. I was glad to see she had a private room so we could be alone. Sitting by her bed and holding her hand, I mentally rehearsed my lines for my "strong, courageous son" performance. After about twenty minutes, her eyes opened. She blinked a few times, adjusting to the bright glow from the row of florescent lights above her bed.

"Hi, Mom." I was stroking her arm and gazing at her pale face.

"Son, is that you?"

It took her a minute to fully wake up. When she started speaking with more energy than I had heard in a long time, I reminded myself that my mother was most likely on her deathbed, and that I should not get my hopes up. With my Buddhist practice, I tended more toward the positive, but still had to subdue the effects of repeated disappointments and failures. I had learned well the lesson of diminished expectations.

"How are you, Donnie? You're probably worried sick about me."

"No, no, Mom," I replied, dutifully, but without confidence. I quickly realized I wasn't going to win an award with this performance. I was finding it difficult, and then impossible, to fight back my tears. I fell into my mother's arms, whimpering how much I loved her. She patted my back, assuring me she was going to be alright.

Thank goodness, the nurse brought in lunch, interrupting my flood of emotions. As she sparingly ate, Mom described the connections she was already forming with a couple of her nurses. I sat and listened, wondering if her spiritual generosity was responsible for her unexpected vibrancy. I assumed it was.

"Oh, Elizabeth," the nurse exclaimed, picking up the tote bag I had placed on the end of her bed. "You like Christian Dior, too. Why am I not surprised? That's just one more thing we have in common."

For years my mother had been adamant about my not buying her expensive gifts. Whenever I took her shopping and tried to get her to try on something from the finer clothing aisles, she resisted. I would be patient through her familiar litany—that I had sacrificed enough for her when I was young and she was a drunk, and so she did not want me doing anything for her now. But still I wanted her to have the best of everything. However, once I got her into the Gucci store, she was entranced. I am not exactly sure why, but after that, she did not have a problem with my buying her designer handbags and other leather accessories. And since she obviously didn't have to try them on and therefore would not see a price tag, I could really splurge on the latest classics. I was proud when the nurse noticed her bag.

The morning of her operation arrived. Again the surgeon warned me that my mother might not make it and gave me more bad news. They had treated her for a serious infection, but would not know if it was gone until they opened her up. And if it had persisted, he said, Mom would likely die, almost instantly.

I walked into her room with the most positive expression I could muster up. I was surprised to see so many people already present. The male nurse was there with his wife and whispered to me that it was his normal day off, but he picked up this shift.

I stood back in awe, watching the impressive orchestration of this life or death struggle. I gazed over the shoulder of one of the doctors and observed the anesthesiologist getting ready to put Mom under. He asked her a question and then chuckled at her response.

All I could think was, *How remarkable! Mom is in a surprisingly good mood, for what sounds like an enormously complicated operation.* Then it occurred to me that maybe the surgeon had not told her how serious it was. When nurses passed by me to leave the room, they would pat me on the back and tell me how much they were praying for her to make it.

I did my best to fight back my tears.

Just as the anesthesiologist was finishing, my mother raised herself up slightly and quietly said she had an announcement to make.

Noticing no one was paying any attention, she boldly pronounced, "Excuse me, everyone! Excuse me! I have an announcement to make." Mom waited until every person looked at her, and then she sat straight up, waving her forefinger in the air. "I want you all to listen. I have something to say!" I glanced at the startled faces of the medical professionals all around me and felt embarrassed. It was obvious she was feeling the effects of the anesthesia.

"Everyone! E-ver-y-one! I want you to expect a miracle! EXPECT A MIRACLE TODAY!" she shouted. Then she fell back against the pillow and closed her eyes.

And that is exactly what happened.

After the surgeon finished the operation, he came out to the waiting room and told me, "You know, Mr. English, I was only able to do so much. The rest was up to your mom and God. I have to admit, she was right! We did have a miracle today."

Mom recuperated in record time. She was lucky she had been so dedicated to her health, always looking for the latest recipe from the fountain of youth. I never knew the health of a heart had such an effect on a person's energy level. Six weeks later, when she was back on her feet, there was nothing she couldn't do. But it wouldn't be until a couple of years later that she would have an opportunity to take full advantage of this revitalization and newfound health.

I remember it was right after Veteran's Day when Mom called with a huge surprise. I thought she was having a hallucinogenic reaction to her heart medication, because what she was talking about seemed impossible.

Her voice bursting with excitement, my mother exclaimed, "Don, I have sensational news!"

"Ooh," I muttered, hoping it wasn't going to take too long. I was about to walk out the door to leave for the salon. My first client was due in thirty minutes.

"I'm moving to Washington DC!"

Yup. She must be hallucinating.

"One of the veterans at the Senior Center here knew I served in World War II. She asked if I had a picture of my Army troop to place on the Center's bulletin board for the Veteran's Day celebration."

"Oh, that's right," I interjected, realizing she was actually very serious, "you were in the Army. I almost forgot."

"When my friend saw the picture, and the date it was taken, she told me that since I was in the Women's Army Corps in 1943—you know, I was part of the first group of women soldiers—I qualify for the Soldiers Home. I already checked, and for just one-third of my income, all my expenses will be paid." Her enthusiasm was overwhelming. "On top of all that, I'll have access to the famous Walter Reed Medical Center. Can you believe it?"

"Please, Mom," I broke in again. "Hold on a sec." I walked into the kitchen and sat my briefcase down on the kitchen countertop. "OK," I said, taking a seat on the bench near the kitchenette's bay window. Checking my watch, I noted I only had a few minutes to take all this in.

"Don, I want you to know," she hesitated, sounding as if she was about to cry, "ever since my heart attack, I've worried about having another one, and how I might end up disabled. The last thing I want is to be a burden to you."

"Mom, don't think like that."

"Son, listen to me," she quickly forged ahead. "I can't tell you how relieved I am. Now I will never be a burden to you. The benefits from my military service will take care of everything, and you will never have to worry about paying to take care of me."

"Mom, you know I wouldn't mind." Tears were beginning to roll down my cheeks as I listened to her admit her fears for the first time, her fears of the worst that could possibly come.

"I am so sorry for all I put you through when I was drinking, when you were a child. I don't have to worry any more about you sacrificing your life for me, as an adult. When I had my heart attack, I knew I couldn't die; you would have been devastated. So that's why I prayed for a miracle. I knew I couldn't leave you then, and now you'll never have to spend any of your hard-earned money on me ever again. My prayer has been answered, son."

Hearing Mom's prayer about not wanting to be a burden helped me understand how important it was for her to make amends to me for the suffering she'd caused early in my life. I never once resented her for what she had done in the past, at least, not since she stopped drinking. Back when I was twelve, having a mother that didn't drink was more than I ever could have hoped for. Back then, the notion of her maintaining sobriety for decades seemed impossible. And for the rest of her life? Absolutely inconceivable. But she had amazingly transformed the impossible to the possible—how could I resent that?

Mom quickly followed through with her plans. In saying her farewells to her friends in Arizona, she proudly detailed the great history of what would be her next, and as far as she was concerned, her final residence. She had it down pat: "It was first established by Congress in 1851. Later it was called the U.S. Soldiers' and Airmen's Home, and several United States presidents, including Mr. Abraham Lincoln, spent their summers there." And then she would finish with, "Can you believe it? I'm one of the luckiest women in the world!"

Mom's move to DC went smoothly. Actually, as I think back to the multitude of moves we did together, this one was by far the easiest.

Lost and Found

2004, Palo Alto, California

I had been seeing a wonderful man, Jim. Our relationship had begun as a friendship, but was now slowing deepening and evolving, and soon he would become my life partner. Together with a couple of my clients and a few of my fellow Buddhists, we were celebrating my latest purchase, an oceanside property in a beach community just outside the town of Santa Cruz. They joined us at my favorite restaurant overlooking the beach of Capitola by the Sea. I reserved the restaurant's banquet room with its glassed-in terrace and the most unbelievable view of the Monterey Bay. After everyone arrived, we stood and beheld a dramatic bank of fog beginning to roll in.

"Well, it's the will of the mist," I announced, remembering that adage from my beach days in Southern California. I looked around the room at my dear friends and reflected on my turbulent past. *So many years have passed.* Like the fog, an immense wave of appreciation began to roll over me for all the incredibly good fortune that had come my way since my forlorn teenage years.

I had just turned 50. I caught my reflection in the shell-framed mirror hanging across from me. I knew I didn't look my age, both because of good genes and because I religiously used my mother's compendium of lotions and potions for combating those pesky signs of aging.

Seven years had flown by since my mother had moved to DC, and I still received packages containing her most recently discovered recipes for keeping youthful. Mom had been thoroughly enjoying her status as one of the few women at the Soldiers' Home who was relatively healthy, mobile, and still interested in men. Never failing to have her makeup and dress "just so" before leaving her room, she had received plenty of attention. Recently, she had more heart trouble, resulting in surgery, and she had to move to the LaGarde Building, the long-term care unit of the Home. But by then, Mom, too, was seeing a wonderful man, a resident named Mickey. She was happy and we were both falling in love. Life was good.

Just as we sat down to dinner, I noticed a missed call, identified as "urgent," on my cell phone. The waiter was about to open the second bottle of Dom Perignon champagne when I heard the *beep* and saw DC's area code flash across the screen. I thought quickly, *it's got to be about Mom.*

"Jim," I whispered directly into my partner's ear to drown out the volume of celebratory chatting. "I have an urgent call; I'll be right back." He patted my leg and asked if he should go with me. I said I was fine, excused myself, and dashed outside.

Standing with the ocean mist dusting my cheeks, I listened with shock to the voice message. I then rapidly entered the callback number, impatiently counting each ring. "Good evening, LaGarde Unit," the operator answered. "How may I direct your call?"

"I'm not sure," I replied. "My mother, Elizabeth English, is living there, and I just received a message that she and her boyfriend have been reported missing."

A moment of silence ended with the receptionist returning to the phone, obviously only half-listening to me.

"I'm sorry, sir. You said your mother is missing something here?"

"What? No, no, she's not missing *something*," I answered, nervously clearing my throat. "I got an urgent phone message about my mother and her boyfriend, saying that they are missing from the Home. And I'm 3,000 miles away."

"It's midnight here, sir. Do you know who left you the message?"

"No, I don't. Please connect me with the doctor in charge."

"That would be Doctor Elliott," she hesitated, "but I'm not sure he's available right now."

"What?" I exclaimed. "You don't seem to understand. I just received a message that my mother and her senile boyfriend, *your residents,* have been reported missing. They could be somewhere on the streets of DC, and yeah, that's my point—it is midnight! No one knows if they are dead or alive, and you're telling me you can't connect me to a person who can help me?"

"Sir!" she responded immediately. "Take a deep breath and calm down."

I was indignant. "I don't need to breathe!" Taking a deep breath anyway,

I asserted as calmly as my fear would allow, "I just need for you to connect me to the doctor."

"Yes, sir, I'll put you through to the nurses' station."

"No!" I protested. And then she took her revenge.

Click.

When your 87-year-old mother has moved clear across the United States and has fallen in love with the man of her dreams, it can be a terrific thing for them both—as long as they can remember their way back to the retirement home. The news I finally received was good. Mom and Mickey had indeed gone missing, but were both found sound asleep in his car, stopped alongside a road about two miles from the Home. The police officers described them as being visibly upset, although apparently more with each other than about being stranded.

Mickey's encroaching senility seemed to produce increasingly aggressive behavior. The week before, Mother had told me that Mickey had accused her of sleeping with one of his friends, and then tried to hit her with his car. Shocked and extremely concerned, I immediately notified the staff about Mickey's behavior. It wasn't until a few days after the disappearance that anyone responded, and by then, it was to also tell me that Mickey had just passed away.

The Armed Forces Retirement Home was occupied by nine hundred men and a mere one hundred women. Although she never expressed it, I'm sure that for the prim and trim Elizabeth English, this was like living in the Playgirl Mansion. But falling in love? That was definitely not something she had contemplated.

But fall she did, and she believed she could live happily ever after. Naturally, I was curious to meet him. But there were conditions. Just as I had lied to everyone about my past, Mom had made up a personal history to present to her Prince Charming, and I was ordered to keep all her secrets. He never was to know that she'd had a drinking problem, or that one of her sons was incarcerated for murder in the infamous Folsom Prison. Most painfully, I was also given strict orders not to mention anything about the fact that I was gay.

She had gone into complete denial about her entire past; she had totally reinvented herself for Mickey. By the time he died, the mother I knew, with her honesty and her insatiable spiritual curiosity, was buried so deeply within her own invention that she was nowhere to be found. My guess was that Mom had weighed her options and figured that having fun with a boyfriend in her last years was more important than exploring her spirituality. Add to the scales the fact that, given this boyfriend's attitudes, he might turn her away if she admitted to her sordid and troubled past. She made her choices accordingly.

About a week after Mickey died, I received a call from a social worker at the Home, asking me to make a trip to DC immediately.

"Mr. English," he addressed me formally, "I have been working with your mother for awhile and she has not responded to me or anyone else for over a week. She won't get out of bed and, as you know, this is very unlike her."

"You're right, that's not like her," I acknowledged. "And I'm sorry, I didn't get your name?"

"Jake Ashby. And I want you to know I've grown very fond of Mrs. English ... of Elizabeth."

"Is she eating?" I queried, more concerned about my mother's health than this new person's fondness.

"Not as much as we would like her to. You know, I can't remember when we've ever had such an elegant lady here at the Home."

"She does take a lot of pride in herself," I agreed, while wondering, *Where is this going?*

"I don't know if you know this, Mr. English—"

I broke in. "Please, call me Don."

"Certainly, Don. Your mother's nickname here is 'Barbie,'" he chuckled. "The men gave her that name because she's always dressed to the nines. But she hasn't gotten out of bed to get dressed all week."

"I see," I murmured, pacing nervously around the table.

"So that's why I'm very concerned about her, Don," Jake paused, waiting for a reply.

I kept quiet, contemplating the urgency. Maybe she just needed some time to grieve.

"I usually don't like to alarm the family, but in this case, I would recommend you get a flight as soon as possible. Your mother needs you here."

I was moved by this compassionate-sounding man's genuine concern. "OK, I'll get a flight first thing tomorrow morning, so I should be there about 4 p.m., your time. Please tell my mom I'm coming."

"I will do that, Mister ... uh, Don. And please prepare yourself. Your mother has really gone downhill since her boyfriend died. She always speaks so highly of you, so I know when she hears you're coming, it will really lift her spirits. I look forward to meeting you tomorrow."

The five-hour flight from San Francisco to Washington DC gave me time to steel myself for what I was to find. As soon as I walked into my mother's room, I understood what Jake was trying to tell me. "Barbie" was no longer there. My mother looked just like the rest of the old sick women that occupied the rooms lining the corridors. Her platinum hair was dull and matted to her head, and she lay listless on her back, staring up at the ceiling. Her lips were naked of her usual coordinated shade of lipstick that complemented whatever she wore. Today, her colorless lips matched the pale, hopeless expression on her face.

She had just had her 87th birthday. But even in the state she was in, she still looked 15 years younger. Her cosmetic surgery 20 years before and her undaunted research on ways to maintain her youth had definitely paid off. I had long realized that her consistent streaming of such information to me was part of her simple strategy—if I looked younger than my real age, people would assume Mom was younger, too.

I stood at the side of her bed and looked around her room, surprised it was in such disarray. She'd always taken such pride wherever she lived, so to see all her things strewn all over was a contrast with who she was. I had started straightening up the mess when a nurse came in behind me and introduced herself in a very strong Jamaican accent. I turned, and before I could say anything, she stepped in front of me. She gently placed her dark copper-toned hand across my mother's forehead while liltingly singing out her name.

"Mrs. English, you have a visitor. There's someone here to see you."

Mom's face suddenly lit up as if life had been pumped back into her. "He's here?" She reached up to style her hair with her fingers.

"Mickey's here to see me?"

"No, Mrs. English. It's not Mickey. It's your son, Don."

"My son? No, no, no. My son's in California," she insisted. She was looking up sideways from the bed.

"Mom! It's me!" I exclaimed, placing myself fully in front of her, and praying this was a momentary lapse, that she just wasn't fully awake.

Her eyes flickered; she squinched them tightly together, still peering at me with suspicion.

I tried again: "I'm here now, Mom. When I found out Mickey died, I got here as soon as I could."

"Mickey died?" Mom sounded solemnly surprised. She directed her question to the nurse, still not acknowledging me as her son.

The nurse nodded in a way that made me certain she'd had this conversation several times before.

"Here, I want you to drink this," the nurse directed, pouring water from a pitcher into a paper cup she had taken from the nightstand.

Mother made a face, and like a child being forced to take medicine, took just a small sip.

"I'm going to go and get your dinner," the nurse announced. "Since you won't eat for me, Mrs. English, maybe your son *Don here*, can get you to eat a little something." Giving me a wink as she turned to leave, she added, "You go on now and have a nice visit with your son, and I'll be back in a bit."

Her eyes followed the nurse out of the room. When she was sure the woman was gone, she sat up and, in a childish manner, whispered to me, "She's one of the good nurses; the others don't give a damn."

"Mother, they are all just trying to help you get better," I assured her, feeling a rush of appreciation for them all.

I sat down on the edge of her mattress and tenderly grasped her frail hand. I noticed she was staring intently, examining my face. My identity must have clicked into place because Mom suddenly questioned me.

"What is it about you, Donnie? You look so different."

I was surprised she noticed the change, but was glad that she was acknowledging how much better I looked since I'd embraced my homosexuality. Thinking the inner joy I felt must have been physically radiating from me, I smiled.

"Mom, I want you to know something." I paused, reached for her other hand, and held them both together. "For the first time in my life, I am so happy with who I am. I am truly, truly happy, Mother."

"Bullshit!" she whooped. "You've had a Goddamn facelift, haven't you?"

I released her hands and rose from the bed. The air had been sucked out of me. Her hateful comment hurt deeply; it felt a little like her drunken explosions of old. I stepped away from the bed and, with my back to her, started straightening the top of her dresser. Tears rushed over my cheeks and landed on her set of purple crystal perfume bottles.

But then I was able to recognize that my mother wasn't in her right mind. Realizing I couldn't be sure she knew what she was saying, I struggled to gather my wits about me and to ignore her hurtful challenge.

"No, Mom, I didn't have a facelift," I slowly answered, my back still turned towards her. I wiped my tears and bent down to pick up her bathrobe off the floor.

I managed to calmly state, "You know, I'm tired from my flight this morning, so I think I'm going to go now. I'm staying right here at the guest quarters, about a block away, so I'll be back in the morning to take you downstairs for breakfast."

I leaned over to kiss her forehead.

"You're going? When are you coming back?" she demanded.

"Tomorrow, Mom. I'll tell the nurses so they can help you get dressed, and we can have breakfast together. You get some rest now ... and I'll see you in the morning."

I walked towards the door and glanced back at her bed. She'd fallen back into her trance. I hoped she was reliving all the good times she'd had with Mickey.

"I love you, Mom," I whispered. Feeling the heaviness in my step, I walked out the door.

Three hundred acres of mature grounds surround the Armed Forces Retirement Home, which is well known for its remarkable landscape. Mother told me shortly after she first arrived that she saw President Clinton through her window, playing golf on the sprawling course that weaves gracefully around and through the lush trees.

The building where family guests could stay is nestled amidst grassy hills. From my window, I could see the spectacular rose gardens. When I awoke the next morning, I pulled the heavy tapestry drapes open and drank in the sunrise along the emerald green horizon. The ancient air conditioner clanged loudly, probably revving itself up for what the forecasters predicted would be a sweltering first day of August. I sat down on the unmade bed and meditated awhile about how I was going to handle the seriousness of my mother's decline. Unfortunately, my time with Mom was very limited because, with such short notice, it was impossible to reschedule more than a couple of days of clients. My flight was leaving that afternoon.

After I finished packing my bags, I set them by the door and rushed out into the cool air that lingered from the night before. The brisk walk over to LaGarde helped clear my mind before I entered her room.

"Mother," I called out, as I opened her door. I was glad to see the night nurses had passed on the word to the next shift to get her up and have her dressed. They were early in fact; it was only 7:15, and I had said I would be there around 7:30. Mom was sitting comfortably in the leather chair beside her bed, but still looking forlorn. Her Louis Vuitton purse, a birthday gift in some year past, was sitting upright across her lap.

"How long have you been waiting, Mom?" I asked.

"Not long, son," she said firmly.

I could tell right away that my mother was more coherent and aware. I could see her hair had been washed and her fuchsia pink lipstick matched the print of the chiffon blouse that was tucked neatly into her alabaster white slacks.

"Can you hand me my wallet, Don?" she asked, pointing to her nightstand. "I want to show you a picture of Mickey and me."

I handed it to her, uncertain whether she remembered he was dead.

"Mom, it's beautiful outside," I enthused, looking out the window and attempting to change the subject. "So what do you think, want to take a stroll around the grounds before we go to breakfast?"

She considered my suggestion while she unzipped her purse to drop in her wallet. She had seemed to forget about the photo. "I'm not really hungry, so it doesn't matter to me," she indifferently replied.

I stepped around to the side of the bed and stood behind the wheelchair, motioning to her that we were ready to go. She was a bit cautious in standing up, but she then took two very strong steps. During my more or less semiannual visits over these years, I was very grateful that my mother was so youthfully vibrant for a woman in her eighties. I never imagined she would ever need this kind of assistance. Just as she was about to sit down on the black vinyl seat, I suddenly realized I had never pushed anyone in a wheelchair.

"So Mom, you're going to have to bear with me. I'm not too sure how to operate this chair."

She just stared down at her white patent leather shoes. In my moment of panic, a flush of perspiration flowed over my body. I didn't know how to release the brake. I was glad she was patiently waiting and not paying any attention to how freaked out I was. *Do I dare go and ask the nurse? Nope, too embarrassing* ... I fooled some more with the brake handle.

"Oh, thank God!" I muttered aloud when I finally got it to release. In that moment of victory, I confidently backed her up and directed the chair out of the room.

Maneuvering Mom in the wheelchair into the elevator was a lot harder than I had expected. When we reached the lobby, I was happy to see how spacious it was, something I hadn't noticed when I had come through earlier. A few of her friends walked by and nodded or greeted her, but she didn't respond. I tried not to be disheartened, and focused on our journey. The more I pushed the wheelchair around, the more confident I became, so much so, that when I saw the automatic glass doors that led to the outside slide open, I decided to make a mad dash and rush through them. I was shocked as the chair hit the raised metal threshold, causing the wheels to stop rotating, and *almost* sending my frail mother flying headfirst to the ground.

"Donald!" Mom shouted, holding onto her purse for dear life.

"Whoooa!" I yelled, gripping the handles as if they were attached to a runaway horse. "It's OK, Mom! I got it, I got it!"

After both wheels made contact with the ground, I dug my feet into the concrete. I managed to bring her to a stop just short of one of the four brick columns that flanked the building's entrance. I looked behind me to see if anyone had seen this little fiasco and then scanned the grounds for someplace to sit. I spotted a granite stone bench in a small courtyard and carefully pushed the wheelchair to the side of bench.

"Is this OK, Mom?" I stopped, conscientiously setting the brake.

She didn't answer. She only slouched further down into her chair.

"Mother, do you smell the honeysuckle?" I tried to engage her as I inhaled the aroma from the vine-covered wall alive with the low hum of bees. A row of garden sprinklers turned on, causing a few bees to swarm over toward her head. I couldn't believe it—one of the bees burrowed itself into her platinum curls. I had to give it a swift swat with my hand.

"What are you doing?" Mom gasped, ducking her head away from me.

"It was a bee, Mom," I replied, feeling the cool overspray from the sprinklers. "Not to worry, he's gone now."

We sat quietly for awhile, listening to the melodic sounds of water drenching the tall foliage that filtered the morning sun. Streams of light revealed the sallow color of Mom's complexion, despite her haphazardly applied makeup.

Interrupting the awkward silence, I breezily asked, "So, Mom, when's the last time you talked to your doctor?"

"I don't remember. I don't listen to the doctors anymore. They are all full of shit."

"Mom, don't say that."

"Well, they are," she retorted. "They didn't help Mickey. They just let him die."

I saw the pain in my mother's eyes; I heard the distress in her voice. I tried to remember how long she and Mickey had been together. It had been a year, I concluded, and remained quiet, as she relived the worst.

"It feels like a dream. I went to his room that morning and I knew something was wrong.... He didn't answer me. I went to his bed and shook him.... Wake up! Wake up!"

"I'm sorry you had to find him, Mom," I tried to console her, but realized that she could not hear me.

"He left me!" she agonized, clenching her fists. "He called me a whore and accused me of sleeping with other men."

"Mother, calm down," I soothed, taking hold of her tiny wrists. "He wasn't in his right mind, Mom. You know that."

"He died! He died!" My grasp did not stop her; she repeatedly pounded her fists on the top of her purse. "I told him there was no one else.... I *told* him."

I tenderly set her trembling hands down on the top of her purse and petted them, feeling the thin paper-like skin, now stained with purple spots from the IV drips that had been keeping her alive. I racked my brain for something helpful to say and remembered how in the past, she had always turned to her spirituality.

The thought came to me so quickly that I just blurted it out. "What about your spiritual practice, Mom? You know how much that has helped you before."

She looked at me, startled. "I don't believe in it anymore!" she blasted back, pulling her hands away, her eyes boring into her lap. "Mickey didn't believe it. So I gave it up. It's all crap."

"Mom, I cannot believe you're saying this." My voice quivered in disbelief. "Mother, look at me," I said, lightly lifting her chin with my forefinger, desperate to be able to look into her eyes. I knew I had to pull her back from the abyss of this dismal attitude, but she still couldn't look at me.

I persisted. "Don't you remember, Mom, that we used to talk about how hard we needed to work to do good in this life, so we could come back and be together again? Don't you remember?" I repeated, moving closer to her.

"I can't believe it anymore, son ... I can't."

"Yes, Mom, you can. I know you can," I pleaded, expelling a long frustrated sigh. I was determined to dredge up the most compassionate means of encouraging my mother.

"You know we're all going to die … right, Mom? Since we don't know where we go or what happens after we die, let's assume we're going to come back."

Her eyes lit up with a brief spark of interest. She repositioned herself, scooting back in her chair, thus making her back straighter and her head lift up slightly.

"So Mom, what do you think you want to be in your next life?"

The stillness of the thickening air wrapped around us while I watched her intently ponder this question.

If it is possible for time to stand still, it did then.

When her tear-filled eyes finally rose up to meet mine, our entire past whisked by in the words she fervently spoke. "In my next life, Don, I just want to come back as a *good person.*"

CHAPTER FORTY

Goodbye

2004, Palo Alto, California

"I'm very sorry, Mr. English. Your mother passed away at 10:30 this morning," the doctor from LaGarde said. "I'm sorry ... I guess she couldn't wait."

No matter how much you try to prepare for a loved one's death, you never are *truly* prepared. I was in the Chicago airport sitting on the floor, after a mad search for an available electrical outlet to plug in my dying cell phone.

That was the message I listened to, sinking forward in despair.

Late the night before, her doctor told me to get a flight back there as soon as possible. I had seen my mother a month ago and had spoken with her the previous week. I was pleased with how she seemed on both those occasions, but I did not hesitate to follow the doctor's suggestion. I booked the earliest flight of the day, a 7 a.m. departure from San Jose International with a three-hour layover in Chicago. There I now sat, leaning against the wall and staring at the hot dog concession stand across from me. The sound of the metallic voice in the message rang in my ears: *"I guess she couldn't wait." My mom couldn't wait ...*

I looked up at the high ceiling and stared at the array of crisscross metal beams. I wanted tears to pour from my eyes, but they wouldn't. Everything within me froze. *"Mom is dead."* Like an etching, the phrase was carved into my sullen mind. I thought about Michael. It had been months since I had written him, and at least five years since I'd seen him. Since he had moved to the prison in Bakersfield, he knew better than to request a visit from me. I had let him know that my life was much too busy to travel so far; at least that was my excuse. A flood of family memories began to seep through the shock and sadness of our mother's death. My mind could only focus on one notion: *We are family ... and now he and I are all that is left.*

I wasn't sure I wanted to try to contact him right then to tell him she had died, but deep inside, I knew I had to do it. Finally, the delayed flood of tears began pouring down my face. I bent forward, resting my head on my knees, and let them fall into the stiff fabric of my jeans.

I'm not sure how long I was huddled there, but when my tears finally ceased, I picked up my phone. Still shaky, I managed to get in touch with some staff person at the prison who said the best she could do was to deliver a message to Michael. No matter how adamantly I insisted the appropriate thing to do was to let me personally tell my brother our mother had passed away, she insisted even more firmly that it was against prison policy. She made it just as clear that I was not going to get to any higher-up either.

"Now," the woman asked bluntly, "what do you want me to write?" I drew a blank. After a long pause, I finally dictated a brief and hopefully gentle message: *"Our mom passed away at 10:30 this morning. She went peacefully. Your brother, Don."* I asked her to read it back; she refused. "I got it, I got it," I heard as she hung up.

I found out later he never received my message.

Jim had wanted to make the trip to Washington with me, but I wanted to go alone. His offer was particularly generous; he hates to fly. I was fortunate in that I had remained very close with my friend Rose, the lawyer who helped Michael with his divorce. Years earlier, she had relocated from Monterey to DC to work for a national advocacy group. She was always part of my visits to my mom and was there waiting for me when I got off the plane. When she saw my face, Rose knew Mom had passed away. Her warm embrace was exactly what I needed.

Our drive to the Armed Forces Retirement Home took less than 30 minutes. I was quiet for most of the way, but did call Jake, the social worker who had encouraged me to come see my mother the last time, after Mickey had died. He gently told me that my mother, her body that is, was already being taken to the mortuary, but that I was free to go to her room, think about what I wanted to do with her possessions, and meet with him about the next steps.

When we arrived at the Home, we parked in the guest parking area, as usual, and Rose started to get out of the car. When she noticed that I wasn't moving, she stopped herself and looked over at me and apologized. "I am so sorry, Don, I should have asked if you want me to …" she paused. "You know I'll do whatever you need."

I couldn't articulate why, but I wanted to go in on my own.

Rose gave my shoulder a squeeze as I loosened my seat belt. "I'll be right here, a cell phone call away," she smiled warmly.

When I walked into my mother's room, the aroma of White Shoulders perfume lingered in the air. A light knock at the half-opened door startled me. A man introduced himself; it was Jake, whom I had only met over the phone. He was checking to see if it was alright to come in.

I nodded and he approached me, extending his hand. "Hello, Don. I am so sorry about your mother. We are going to miss Elizabeth here at the Home."

I shook his hand. Feeling a lump rising in my throat, I still managed to choke out "Thank you." I was hoping I wouldn't break down.

Jake walked over to Mom's dresser and picked up one of her nightgowns, which was strewn over her collection of bottled perfumes. "I'm sorry her room is such a mess. I was trying to get someone to clean it before you got here."

"Oh that's OK," I said glancing over at her unmade bed. "The doctor said she passed away at 10:30 this morning. Is that right?"

"Yes, that's right," Jake whispered, turning towards me. He gave my shoulder a soft pat and then asked, "Do you have time to sign some papers, Don? Also, I made an appointment at the mortuary just in case you want to view her body. They said they would have her ready anytime after 6 p.m."

I checked my watch; it was four o'clock now. I could see her in two hours. I thanked him and replied that I did have time then to go over the papers.

I followed Jake to his office, feeling sorry for him, having to deal with grumpy old veterans day in and day out. He revealed his kindheartedness by the way he defended his clients when I mentioned what a difficult job I thought he had. I couldn't help but be thankful that such a genuinely nice person had been looking out for my mother in her last years.

"I know my mom gave you a hard time there for awhile. She could get pretty ornery at times." We had just sat down when I brought up Mom's little episode with Mickey a short time ago.

"You know, Don," Jake instantly replied, "I think she was having a rough time. After you left the last time, she asked me to call Alcoholics Anonymous and have someone come and talk with her. I did and they must have brought

351

her some books, because until she died, about all she did was read those books."

I was relieved to hear she found her way back to her spiritual path. Jake's manner put me at ease; I decided to share more about her.

"Yes, my mom is … *was* a recovering alcoholic and she was having a hard time at the end."

"Well," Jake commented, rubbing his forefinger gingerly over his chin a few times, "you would never know your mother had a problem with anything. She was the classiest woman we've ever had here, and I've been here a long time."

When I told him about my mother's terrible history with alcohol, my father's early death, and her son being in prison for murder, he could not believe it. He said he would have lost money if anyone had asked him to wager on what Elizabeth's background was. He assumed she was born with a silver spoon in her mouth. "Just the epitome of elegance and grace," were his exact words.

The more I talked about Mom's life and mine, the more questions Jake had. When I mentioned my work with interior design, he said that he too had been through a whole redesign project of his home. And somewhere along the line, I must have mentioned meditation or chanting because a little while later, he commented, "For all you and your mom have been through, I'm impressed by the way you're handling all of this. Does that practice of meditation you mentioned have anything to do with it?"

I told him I was a practicing Buddhist and did a form of active meditation called chanting, and that our mantra was *Nam-myoho-renge-kyo*.

"That's a coincidence!" he said with surprise. "I have been checking out different meditation groups. And just the other day a friend of mine suggested that meditation with a mantra might help me with all the stress I have here at the Home."

I was debating about what I should say next and glanced down at my watch, concerned about how long it had been since I had left Rose. Reaching in my shirt pocket for my cell phone, I told Jake, "I have a friend waiting for me outside," and began punching in her number.

"Don," he said putting his hand up, "wait. This may sound a little unusual, but since you have to wait awhile before going to the mortuary, perhaps you and your friend would like to come to my house for a glass of wine? I live not too far from here."

I was about to answer when a loud rumble shook the windows.

"Whooh!" I gasped, almost jumping out of my chair.

"Thunder—isn't it amazing! That must be the start of the summer storm we've been expecting. I guess you're not used to this dramatic weather, living in California and all."

Feeling a bit embarrassed, I tried to smile and went on to thank him for the invitation. "Thank goodness for cell phones," I murmured, dialing Rose's number. I explained about having to wait until six and about Jake's offer of hospitality.

Rose said she would love to meet Jake and a glass of wine sounded good.

"It's pouring outside!" she alerted me and then suggested I go see if my mother had an umbrella in her room.

Jake said he would wait in the lobby until I came down.

Finding Mom's umbrella was a lot harder than I thought it would be. When I moved her things around, I found the AA books Jake had spoken about. I was so happy my mother did not die in the same frame of mind she was in the last time I saw her. Now I knew she had been able to rediscover her strongest self. I knew that she went in peace.

"Here it is!" I cried out, almost stepping on the purple handle that was half under the bed.

I picked up the vivid lavender umbrella and communed for a moment with my mother: *I'll always remember, Mom, purple is your favorite color.*

It was good that Jake's house was only a couple of miles away. The rain was cascading down, forcing me to sit with my face up to the windshield the entire time we were following behind his car. It was a challenge to see anything.

"Look, Rose, I think he's turning into that driveway up ahead."

"That's a parking space, isn't it?" she implored, trying to gauge the space through the car window on my side. I looked and told her it was.

Jake had not exaggerated in his description of the work he had done on his home. Even through the sheets of rain, I could tell the classic Craftsman's style house was by far the beauty of the neighborhood. Jake suddenly appeared through the striking burnt orange front door. From the large covered porch, he waved for us to come in. Huddled arm in arm under Mom's small, but much needed umbrella, Rose and I dashed down the path and climbed the mahogany-stained porch stairs.

The house was just as sensational on the inside as it was on the outside.

Jake immediately offered us a glass of wine then began the house tour carrying with him an album of before and after pictures. They had done an amazing job, especially refinishing the original oak built-in cabinets that were in almost every room. Our conversation went from interior design to Jake having questions about the Buddhist practice. Rose told him his house was about a mile from the SGI-USA Buddhist community center and she would be glad to follow up with him; getting him some reading material and a schedule for when there would be an introductory meeting. Some months later, I received the news that Jake joined the SGI and became a Buddhist.

Having that conversation with Jake and the glass of wine helped take the edge off the anxiety of my recurring thought: *In less than an hour I will see my mother's dead body.*

I was surprised by how calm I was by the time we reached the mortuary. When I mentioned how lucky we were to find a parking space right in front, Rose muttered under her breath, "Well it's not like it's a popular place ... especially at night."

We laughed.

"Look Rose," I said pointing to what was written in gold leaf on the window by the door.

Established In 1917

"That was the year my mother was born! How creepy is that?"

"Don, knock it off.... We don't need anything else to add to how creepy it is to be visiting a mortuary during a raging thunderstorm at night."

The lady who showed us to the room where mom was to be viewed was a petite black woman with a smile that lit up the room. She spoke softly and was warm and charming, not creepy at all.

"Since your mother is to be cremated she won't be embalmed, so be prepared."

When she warned me I thought *It couldn't be any worse than when I saw my dad and he was embalmed!* The lady asked us to wait for a minute, leaving us standing in front of a room with a pair of closed, heavy carved wooden doors. Rose excused herself and said she needed to find a restroom. I was left by myself with my mind racing, not having a clue to what to expect. I stared at the doors.

"Sorry to keep you waiting," the lady said, apologizing. She stepped in front of me and opened the doors. I looked over my shoulder to see if Rose might be there ... but she wasn't.

"Just let me know when you're through," she said, directing me into the room.

My feet felt heavy. My eyes went directly to Mom's body that lay across the shiny metal table. The white sheet covered most of her body.

We were alone.

I stared at what resembled my mom, but I could tell that the essence of Elizabeth English had left her body. The words my father spoke, when he came back to me in the dream after he died, played through my mind. Gazing at my mother's body, I remembered how Dad described our bodies as shells we use to live out our lives. It made sense. *Mom isn't in there—this really is only the shell she used for so many years.*

A glow of well-being infused and surrounded me. Although the spirit of my mother was gone, I stroked her chilled face and combed her hair with my fingers. Feeling relieved, I pressed the sheet snug over her shoulders and then turned to leave. I stopped to take one last glance. *"Goodbye,"* I whispered, and silently thanked the 87-year-old shell that had served her so well.

CHAPTER FORTY ONE

She's Home

2004, Palo Alto, California

As Rose and I left the mortuary, the director called my name and asked me to please step back inside.

"I forgot to tell you, Mr. English, a chaplain from Arlington National Cemetery will be contacting you about scheduling the service for your mother."

I immediately looked at Rose and was glad she was there to hear this incredible news: Mom would be laid to rest in the same place as John F. Kennedy. I remembered watching his funeral procession on TV with our parents. Mom mentioned that we used to live near there. "Your father and I visited Arlington cemetery," she said, through her tears. "You and your brother were just little then."

Still absorbed in my memory, I acknowledged the director with a smile, and asked, "Do you have my contact information? I have a card." I began to reach for my wallet when she nodded and said that she did.

Rose then stepped to my side, threading her arm through mine, and asked, "Do you happen to know about how long it might take for the service to be scheduled?"

"It usually takes about a month once all the paper work is done."

We smiled and thanked her, then walked briskly back to the car.

Her estimate turned out to be accurate. A month later, I arrived in DC; the service would be the next day. I had booked a mini-suite at the Willard Hotel, where I usually stayed. When I walked into my room, there was a grand flower arrangement of red, white and blue flowers on the round marble table in the room's foyer.

I opened the card and read the kind words of condolences from the hotel staff. With tear-filled eyes, I declared, "These are for you, Mom, just for you."

A timely flash of lightening lit up the room, followed with a predictable clap of thunder. "OK, Mom … I'm glad you heard me," I smiled. Rain started to pound against the room's large picture window.

I unpacked my bag quickly, wanting to take the hot shower I had been looking forward to since I stepped off the plane. I turned the shower knob to the steam setting, and stepped onto the cold white marble as my mind wandered back to that stormy night, just a month ago, when I visited my mother's dead body at the mortuary. I recalled how I had expected a feeling of suffering to envelope me when I saw her, but it never came. Thunderclaps echoed outside now, just as they had then.

The steam from the shower engulfed any loss or sadness that I tried to call upon. Now as I stood showering and breathing in the steam, I felt at peace. After stepping out from the shower, I reached for the towel. Again my thoughts were about Mom: *Tomorrow I will be with her ashes; her physical body no longer exists.* Once again, a deep sense of appreciation for my mother's physical body swept over me. That body was the vehicle that carried me into this life.

When I awoke the next morning, a humid drizzle filled the air. On our way to Arlington National Cemetery, Rose constantly fiddled with the windshield wipers. I noticed she was wearing a pair of my mother's earrings. Mom had mentioned she wanted Rose to have her jewelry, and in fact, had insisted on giving her some pieces during their last visit together.

I reached out to touch them, a cluster of tiny lapis, pearls and rubies. They were red, white and blue, just right for the occasion. "You know these were my mother's favorite?"

Rose nodded, "She told me that when she gave them to me."

The wipers clicked back and forth.

I thought about when Dad gave Mom those earrings. It was that Christmas in Moss Landing when Dad fell into the silver Christmas tree. Around the same time, Michael was arrested for the first time, for knocking down old ladies, stealing their purses and almost causing one of them to die from a heart attack. It's funny how a piece of jewelry can encapsulate and inspire such vivid memories. Mom wore those earrings more than any others she had. After Dad's death, she hardly ever took them off. I was just twelve years old then. Michael was only twelve years old when he stole Dad's car and drove to San Francisco. How had we been so different from each other? Why Mom didn't just leave us and run away during that time still puzzles me.

But instead, she eventually took the high road, choosing to join AA and face those mountains that had seemed impossible to scale. She climbed every one of them *sober*.

"Don," Rose asked delicately, recognizing I was deep in thought, "What time was your appointment? Eleven?"

"Yes," I answered, looking at the car's clock, and then at the traffic in front of us. "Do you think we'll make it?"

"I hope so," Rose sighed, "I think the weather is what's causing the backup."

The clock read 10:59 as we approached the tall gothic iron gates. The grandeur of the architecture here was beyond anything I had imagined. The lush landscaping that flanked the entrance was daintily laden with a cape of mist. A line of cars waited ahead of us.

"Damn!" Rose muttered apologetically, "I forgot all about the extra security since 9/11."

It was 11:05 a.m., and we were still three cars back from the entrance. Panic engulfed me. The mist had turned into a light shower that gusted by, just as the cars ahead of us began to move through the gate. After we passed through, I was relieved that the main office building didn't take long to find. I turned and looked for the lavender umbrella Rose now carried in the back seat. Noticing the sky had suddenly begun to clear, I decided not to use it.

"Are you sure you don't want the umbrella?" Rose asked, reaching into the backseat.

"No. Thanks, though."

Looking down as I stepped out of the car, I observed that the curb was painted yellow. "I don't think you can wait here, Rose."

"Go on then. I'll find a place," she hurriedly said. "Call me when you find out what is happening and I'll bring the car back around here."

I shut the door and scaled a mountain of cement stairs, worried I was going to be too late for my mother's own memorial ceremony. At the top, a group of people, all wearing dark clothes, stepped out one at a time from the tall revolving door of the entrance to the registration building. I waited until the last person came through, and then pushed on the brass-plated handle of the next glass panel until I found myself standing in front of an elevated curved reception desk. I surveyed the large circular room and then glanced at the dome ceiling. I stared in awe at the sea of ornate wood-carved moldings that framed the skylights.

A woman's voice came from behind the curved desk, startling me out of my reverie. "Can I help you?"

"Yes, thank you." I brought my eyes down from the ceiling to meet hers. "I am here for my mother's service—"

"Just a moment," she interrupted, holding the palm of one hand up towards me and reaching for her buzzing phone with the other. I nodded and took a deep breath, sweeping my hand across my sweaty forehead. I was still recovering from the workout the barrage of stairs provided me.

"Mr. English?" A deep voice called out. I turned and, from his garb, I knew this was the chaplain. Two other men were with him.

"Yes."

"Oh, good, you made it," the second man, dressed in civilian clothes, chimed in. Then the third man, in military uniform, asked in unison with the other two: "So you must be Elizabeth English's son?"

Surprised by the simultaneous greeting, I stepped back and almost took a bow. A rush of gratitude came over me, relieved I wasn't too late.

"A couple of more minutes," one of the trio said, "and we would have put you down as a no-show." At that moment, it dawned on me that I didn't know exactly what was going to happen. What would I have been too late for? It was never made clear to me what they planned to do with my mother's ashes. Was there a small church we would be going to, or a prayer service? Since there was a chaplain, I assumed there would be some type of ceremony.

The man in civilian clothes introduced himself, saying that he represented the business side of Arlington Cemetery. The man in uniform said he represented the military side. The chaplain stepped forward and said with an authoritarian tone: "Well, last but not least, I am the chaplain and I represent *God!*"

Chortles filled the room.

The man in the suit asked, "Where is your car parked?"

"My friend is waiting outside. I told her I would call once I knew the plan."

"Good." He continued, "You know where you came in, at the front of the building?" I signaled that I did. "Please have your friend park in the yellow zone at the bottom of the stairs. We'll be around in a couple of minutes."

"Thanks," I replied, shaking his hand. "What kind of car should I look for?"

"A black sedan. We'll pull up behind you and then you can follow us," the chaplain said, answering my next question. He then motioned for the other men to follow him.

For a few minutes, we followed the black sedan around the maze of small winding streets that snaked through short blocks of manicured lawn graveyards. When we came to a stop, my mouth flew open. Soldiers in dress uniforms were lined along the walkway, their backs facing a hillside of uncountable tombstones. Layers of mist danced amongst gravestones lined up in perfect rows for as far as I could see.

"Rose," I gasped, "do you see what I see?"

"Omigosh, Don, did they tell you your mother was having a full military ceremony?"

I shook my head and watched the sedan's two front doors ominously swing open simultaneously. It was haunting … everything had become so quiet and orchestrated. I struggled to take it all in.

"Look, Don, the chaplain is trying to get your attention. I think he wants you to come join him."

"Aren't you going to come with me?"

"Oh, in the rush I forgot to ask—I have my video camera in the back. I thought maybe you would want me to film everything for you?"

"Yes, yes, that would be perfect!" I leaned over and kissed her on the cheek. "Thanks, you're the best."

The chaplain was coming around the back of the sedan and looking at me through the car window. He gestured in the direction of three rows of five brilliant emerald velvet chairs, which were placed under a large white canopy. The chairs were empty. I nodded, then opened the car door, and stepped out onto the lush green of an expansive lawn. A bit hesitantly, I made my way over to the empty chairs. The chaplain stood in front and motioned for me to take a seat. I stared at the empty seats for a moment, wishing the people who loved Mom could be there with me. Especially Edna and George, the AA sponsors who never left her side during her early battles with those inner demons that she fought so hard to overcome. Visualizing that time, it almost seemed Mom and I were two characters in a movie.

We were a mother and son on the road to hell, and darkness was all we knew. But when Mom came to that fork in the road, when the police were about to take me away from her, she chose to give up those bottles of liquid courage, and found true courage within the love she had for me. I will be forever grateful to AA and to the band of AA angels who patiently waited for the forlorn mother and her twelve-year-old son.

Maybe these seats aren't really empty after all, I contemplated, still staring at the folding chairs of emerald velvet. *Maybe they only look vacant to those who have not yet passed over. My dad could be sitting next to me, and next to him all of my mother's poodles.* I smiled with the thought of her "Cindys," each miraculously sitting still on a chair, dressed with those irritating bows tied in their topknots. I sat down in the front row and looked back to view the audience—the audience I imagined might be there to greet her in the next world.

The rain had stopped. I breathed deeply, inhaling the sweet scent each blade of grass was giving forth. It was the perfume *green.*

I watched the speakers find their places. The chaplain placed the container of Mom's ashes on a small oak wood podium directly in front of me. I watched a uniformed officer appear with an American flag folded tight into a triangle. He positioned himself at the far end of the podium; six officers flanked him on each side.

The ceremonial unfolding of the flag commenced. Once it was fully displayed, Mom's flag was held tight above the urn. There was total silence. I felt one with the still air. The cloak of mist gracefully lifted from the never-ending marked graves dotting the expanse across the way. Each marker represented a brave and dedicated hero. I hoped that, somehow, they were all gathered, ready to welcome my mother home.

I looked up and saw clouds parting, exposing a patch of blue sky. Everything was motionless. To my right, one of the uniformed officers stood alone, statue-like, gripping a trumpet by his side. On some silent cue, his arm began to move and he brought the trumpet to his lips. The first reverential note hung in the air, then drifted past me. It swept me up in the melody of farewell. In that moment, it felt like we were the only ones for miles; not a sound could be heard over the clear high trill that ended the song. When he finished, a sequence of orders was called to the seven soldiers who stood at attention with rifles across their chests.

BOOM! BOOM! BOOM! Twenty-one times the rifles sounded, crashing into the sky, vibrating through my body. I stared at the American flag held taut across my mother's remains. I fell into a trance, remembering my last conversation with her, when I asked her what she wanted to come back as in her next life. "I just want to come back as a good person," she had answered, with such solemnity that I nearly cried.

My mother and I had had so many talks about karma, about how our past life choices might show up and affect our present lives. I spent years afraid, trying to imagine what terrible things I must have done in a past life to deserve the "Karma of Michael." But, as a Nichiren Buddhist, I have come to understand that it is not about consciously knowing which past life cause produced which current effect. I wished, as I listened to the rifles again, that I'd had a chance to tell my mother what I had learned. What Buddhism truly teaches is that—since we cannot scientifically prove we have lived before and therefore we cannot fathom just what we may have done in those previous existences—the key to creating absolute happiness is to fearlessly face our present reality and to work to transform our lives, to "change poison into medicine."

My mother did learn to turn the poisons in her life, internal and external, into the medicine of courage and compassion. *Mom, you were so courageous to make it through the way you did*, I declared to her in my heart. *I know I couldn't have done what you did. You were truly an enlightened hero to us all.*

The re-folding of the flag, what I thought of as her final attire, began. I know it might have been my imagination, but just as the soldier made the final fold, a breeze carrying a whiff of White Shoulders perfume wafted by. Then a woman in an Army uniform stepped forward and began to speak.

"We are grateful and honored for the amazing courage and dedication with which your mother served her country. The role of women in the

American military is what it is today because of the pioneers, like your mother, who fought at the beginning to overcome the many challenges of entering into a man's organization."

As she spoke, the chaplain knelt down and presented me with my mother's flag. The faint sound of birds chirping filled the silence that seemed even more profound after the trumpet and blasting of the rifles. Tears streamed down my cheeks as I listened to the Army representative speak of my mother going down in history as a hero. When she concluded, she handed me an ivory envelope with a card offering the Army's appreciation. It closed with words I would remember forever: "Elizabeth English was one of the heroes behind the scenes."

My mother, who, in the end, was my hero behind the scenes.

Another scented breeze engulfed me. I drew it in with a deep breath, closing my eyes and imagining her *there*. I saw the multitude of heroic souls, arms wide, calling out to her, and then, when I opened my eyes, I felt her ethereal presence begin to stroll by me, first stopping to tenderly kiss the top of my head.

She had said her last goodbye and was finally going home.

Illumination   2004, Palo Alto, California

Feeling elated that everything had gone so well, I splurged on a first class ticket for the flight home from my mother's stunning service. I settled into my seat and reached for the magazine in the seat pocket. It was an issue of *People* magazine with a cover story about Scott Peterson, a man sitting on California's death row for murdering his pregnant wife and unborn child. Halfway through the flight, I discovered that I was seated next to a psychiatrist. We began talking about the Peterson case.

She said, "In my opinion, Scott Peterson is a psychopath."

"This may be a stupid question," I looked down at the magazine's full page picture of the handsome Peterson, "but what's the difference between someone who suffers from a chemical imbalance, like bipolar disorder, and someone like Scott here?" I pointed to his picture.

She explained that although she used the term "psychopath," there was (and there still is) an ongoing controversy about the term as an actual diagnosis, so she suggested a website containing the criteria for Antisocial Personality Disorder. She told me I would find a list of seven typical impairments that people with this disorder have. The next day I looked it up. My brother had every single one. The one that said "lack of remorse, as indicated by being indifferent to or rationalizing having hurt, mistreated, or stolen from another," was the one I thought most strongly described Michael. What I had thought were his "special powers" boiled down to seven traits which were part of a very serious mental illness. I began to study this illness with a vengeance.

During that week, I received a package from Rose with the photos and the video she had taken at the Arlington Cemetery. She so perfectly caught the light and shadow of that overcast day. I looked at myself and at the expression on my face, sitting alone, experiencing one of the monumental moments of my life. I gasped when I came to the picture of the flag after it had been completely unfolded. The brilliant red, white and blue colors filled the picture with my mother's "final attire."

The memories spurred on the idea of having a memorial for my mom. I would invite my friends to celebrate her extraordinary life with me. A bit overwhelmed with all the information I had amassed about Michael's illness, I decided to put my research aside and focus on something much more positive—planning a party, because that was what I wanted this memorial to be.

The two hundred clients whose hair I colored and styled had followed the saga of my mother's torrid love affair with her very handsome boyfriend. I told them I thought Mickey looked like what Clark Gable might have, if he had lived to 85.

Relationships are always a popular topic while styling hair, and I still remembered the relief I felt when I began sharing my joy in finding Jim, and discovered that my clients embraced my happy homosexual relationship with the same enthusiasm they would a heterosexual one. They enjoyed hearing about my mother's past-middle-age romance as well. Sometimes when I would think about Mom and Mickey, I would smile, remembering what my mother said to me before introducing us, "Wait until you meet him, Donnie. He has a full head of hair and he still has all of his teeth—it doesn't get better than *that*!" He was truly her Prince Charming.

I was so happy to now share with them my profoundly moving experience with the surprise 21-gun military service at Arlington and the Army's recognition of Mom as one of our country's heroes. Their many positive responses encouraged me to invite everyone, friends and clients, and to hold a memorial service at the Silicon Valley Buddhist community center. The invitations contained both the suggestion to wear their mothers' favorite colors and a copy of my first written piece, a poem honoring all mothers who had passed away:

What I know now
Of that day or that night
When our own mother's life
Returned to the light

If moments could tear
Then that's what I felt
Or was it the seam
That tore in my heart

With what I know now
Is only for mom
But I share this with you
Because of our bond

Yes this bond that we share
Takes on its own life
And will help us prepare
Our own steps toward the light

So let's march hand-in-hand
As we follow our vow
And give one last salute
To what we know now

Amazingly, almost 200 people, including 100 of my clients, attended. I caught my partner Jim's eye at one point. He smiled broadly, winked at me, and with a sweeping motion, reminded me to take in everything.

Since most of my friends had never had a chance to meet my mother, the first few speakers offered words of appreciation to me for putting together such a great event. They also seemed to enjoy elaborating, with loving detail, on what a caring person I was. I could not keep my eyes on them; my head naturally dropped down from the embarrassment at all the nice things that were being said.

More importantly, I learned from the presenters that this celebration of all our mothers was meaningful and healing for them, including for those who mothers were still alive. A good friend of mine spoke last and asked everyone to give me a hand for all I had done. I started to feel like I had been the one that had died; perhaps I was a ghost attending my own funeral. At one point, I pinched myself, literally to make sure I still had a body.

When it was my turn to take the podium, I took a moment and beheld the audience, taking in the sea of festive-colored clothing. Wearing our mother's favorite color allowed each of us to bring a part of our mothers with us to the celebration. I wore a vivid lavender shirt with my black suit and felt it: *Mom was with me.* I took a deep breath and scanned the faces of my friends and clients before once again catching Jim's eye and receiving another supportive grin. At that moment, I was filled with an overwhelming sense of gratitude for all the people looking back at me.

"I want to thank each and every one of you, not only for your attendance, but for what you mean to me. When I was thinking about what I wanted to say today, what kept coming to mind was how I might describe all of you to my mother, if she were here."

Something struck me, and I slightly changed my tone. "Knowing my mother, who was filled with compassion, I bet she has gathered all of your mothers and grandmothers and brought them here today, and they're celebrating right beside us." Chuckles filled the room as people looked from side to side.

"So, in trying to describe you all to Mom, an image entered my mind. My friends, you are what I like to think of as my "Village of Angels." Yes, each of you has been an angel to me, at one time or another. From the depths of my heart, thank you. Thank you so much, Angels, and please … keep up the good work!"

I then turned slightly so that I could point to the enlarged pictures on the easels behind me. One was of my mother and me, and the other one was of the uniformed soldiers holding Mom's flag taut across the urn filled with her ashes. I turned back towards my friends.

"I would like to share with you how Elizabeth English not only played her part as a hero for our country, but how she also was a hero to so many tortured souls during the 36 years of her sobriety. Whenever she went to an AA meeting, which was almost every week, she would listen to people's struggles and look about the room. Then she would select a pertinent story from her vast catalogue of experiences, especially if there were any newcomers that night. She would recount with them how time and time again, even when she stumbled through seemingly hopeless situations, she never once succumbed to taking a drink. She was determined to demonstrate that it could be done, to show the actual proof of her own life. One night, she was surprised by a first-timer's response. As she had been doing for some years, my mother introduced herself by saying she had been a widow for twenty years, had one son who was in prison for murder and had another son who was gay. After the meeting, this newcomer, who was about her age, approached her. He was astounded that my mother did not get drunk when she found out her son was gay. He said nothing about her other son, the murderer. When she told me this story, it stung for a moment, but then I realized that some people from her generation would actually prefer their sons to be murderers than to be homosexuals. Yet she encouraged that person with grace. We were able laugh together at the man's insane ignorance. It is unimaginable how many people from all walks of life she inspired week after week."

I turned back around from the podium and stared at the picture for a moment.

I finally felt I could stand in front of my friends and clients as myself, my true self.

Many of my clients, over time, had learned of the struggles I'd had with my sexual orientation. Many had said they were proud of me when I reported that I had started the Gay Lesbian Bisexual Transgender Buddhist group in Silicon Valley. I had truly burst out of the closet. Their expressions of acceptance and enthusiasm about my deepening relationship with Jim were, in large part, what I had needed to feel free to be myself.

At this moment, though, I was finding it difficult to speak without breaking down, so I inhaled deeply again and said that I wanted to close by reading my poem. When I got to the stanza, *"So let's march hand-in-hand, as we follow our vow, and give one last salute,"* I brought two fingers up to my forehead and saluted *"to what we know now."*

The ceremony ended with the Buddhist chorus singing a song titled "Mother." After a big group photo was taken, we all adjourned to the Community Center's café, where Jim had put together an elaborate buffet. Everything was decorated with shades of purple; even the sterling silver fountain flowed with raspberry punch. The only thing missing was a "Cindy" decked out with purple bows. I weaved through aisles of people, eavesdropping on the myriad of conversations filled with love and joy. It was a perfect end to such a celebration.

For months after, people still mentioned what a wonderful experience it had been to collectively celebrate Mother's Day while participating in the memorial service for my mother. I hired a scrapbook designer to display the various thank you cards and photos, so I would never forget how I felt in those moments. The pictures of all the food Jim prepared and the flowing fountain could have easily have been displayed in the magazine *Gourmet*.

A week after the memorial service, I went back to my research on Michael's mental illness, learning that psychopathy is a subtype of Antisocial Personality Disorder. Eventually, I became convinced that Michael is a psychopath. And from the research I had done, everything pointed to one critical fact: my brother is incapable of ever feeling true compassion; he is not wired that way. This upsetting discovery led me to more exploration and contemplation of good and evil, cause and effect, and creating value versus creating harm.

I took myself through an inner spiritual ceremony, chanting and meditating. This final act allowed me to accept that there was no chance Michael could change without some major medical discovery.

Ever since the last visit, when Michael tried to destroy the loving image of our father, in my heart I had given up on him. And now, after all that I had learned about a psychopath's inability to care about anyone but himself, I realized that I had to take care of myself, by breaking out of that destructive codependent relationship.

Shortly after our mother died, Michael drew the final straw that convinced me that I had to take a different tack. He had not responded to the message I had left with the prison, so after returning from DC, I wrote to him. He quickly replied that my letter brought the first news of Mom's death and that he was very upset that the prison staff had not told him. Then a week later, he wrote again, telling me that someone in the Probate Department of the DC courts had written him regarding some inheritance he was supposed to receive from our mother.

What Michael did not know was that our mother had disinherited him in her will and that she thought she had made sure all her accounts would pass directly to me. However, she had failed to do so on one $3500 DC bank account, and, therefore, it did have to go through probate. Michael's misguided assumption was that Mom had *intended* for him to have one-half of this money.

His letter proved to me that he lived in a psychopathic non-reality state. It was filled with bundles of fantasies about how he knew our mother always loved him, and that now he could go to *his* grave knowing she had not given up on him since the money was *the* sign of her forgiveness.

"She was such a good mother to us, Donnie," he wrote. "Now that she is gone, maybe we can get closer, since we are all the family that is left."

I believe Michael made himself out to be the fallen angel—now redeemed by his loving mother from beyond the grave—because the Parole Board could potentially see this communication as part of his upcoming annual parole review.

Michael, true to form, continued his efforts at manipulation. The letter went on:

There is a good chance I will receive a parole date and was hoping you'd vouch for me and be there for me when I get out. I haven't told you, but Josephine has left me, and I haven't heard from her for over a year. I'm sure I'll get on my feet right away, and I promise I won't be a bother to you. You don't have to worry about me breaking the law— having been incarcerated as long as I have— I've really learned my lesson.

I can't tell you what it means to me to find out Mom never really gave up on me. I've known in my heart she always loved me even though I didn't deserve it at times. Now I will only remember the good times we had and what a happy family we once were.

That's how I exist in here, Donnie: I relive all of those special memories of how happy we all used to be. I'm not sure ... but I bet wherever Mom is ... she's looking down on us, happy to see that her sons will finally be together.

(Wiping away my tears)

Hope to see you soon! Can't wait to give you a hug ...

Love your bro,
Michael

The only thing I could feel after reading his letter was disbelief. How could he write such lies? Then I remembered my research. One neuroscientist mentioned that psychopaths' emotional capabilities are shallow; that is, in terms of complex emotions, such as devotion, guilt or joy, they are only capable of a textbook understanding. They may be able to get a sense of such emotions, and to mimic them from observing others, but cannot actually experience them. It has been said that they "know the words, but not the music."

Michael sure had a good set of words, I contemplated. *But, now I am sure, he has never heard a single "note" of music in his life.*

Who is the real person behind my brother's mask of sanity? I wondered. From what I had read, he never had a conscience, but instead, filled that void with a barrage of superficial needs. He is alive—but lives without even having the compassion of an animal.

Sorrowfully, his is a deadened heart.

After reading his letter, the shock of my brother's insatiable desire to mold the truth, especially after our mother's death, allowed me to redefine the hope I had held in my heart for him. He had become a master of sucking me in.

I had offered him all the love I could. But now I knew if I continued in any relationship with him, it would only fuel and exacerbate his psychopathic compulsions. I needed to cut the myriad threads I had used in my futile efforts to find some healthy way to weave our lives back together.

It was time.

I wrote him a letter containing a money order for his share of the cash from Mom's checking account. The letter was critical for two reasons. Most importantly, it was time for me to no longer "go along with the hopes of getting along." I had to give my brother an honest dose of reality. Additionally, I assumed the Parole Board would likely read my letter, since it included such a large sum of money.

I chose my words carefully:

Dear Michael,

I have enclosed monies left over after I paid for our mother's cremation and a few other incidentals. Also, here is a copy of a page from her Last Will and Testament. You will see, where I have highlighted, that she had disinherited you. You see, the only reason her checking account was going to have to go through probate was because she had simply forgotten to put me down as her beneficiary on that account, although she had done so on her others.

She wanted you to have nothing.

Do you remember the last time she came to visit you? It was many years ago, when you were still at Folsom. It was on Christmas Day. Mom was so excited and happy we would be spending Christmas with you. I remember her enthusiasm when she said, "The three of us might as well spend Christmas together as a family. After all, we are all that is left."

Do you remember how excited you were when I told you about our plan for Christmas? "I can't wait! I'm so happy!" was what you said.

And do you remember what happened that day, after we arrived at the prison?

Of course you do. You had been caught that morning trafficking marijuana and were sent to the "Hole." You took that kind of stupid chance on the day you knew we were coming to visit, and on Christmas day no less.

Mom was absolutely devastated. You hurt her in the worst way. I'll never forget what she said when I tried to defend you on the drive home. Through her tears, she sobbed, "Donnie, I can't do this anymore. I just can't!" She wiped her tears and took a deep breath, and said, "I've decided. I love Michael as my son … but I hate him as a person. I never want to see him again."

And of course, you know she stayed true to her word ...

How I ended the letter I don't remember, or I have chosen to forget. I have not communicated with him since sending it. Still, for some reason, even after all I know and after all that I experienced with Michael, he still holds a small place in my heart.

How crazy is that? I sometimes ask myself. But I will always continue to hope and pray for some kind of a miracle that might heal my brother's evil state of mind. I have already seen in my own life that some of what seemed impossible, I have made possible. Prayers have become the lifeblood of my existence.

With all that I have learned ... and with all that I have been through, I have decided to only focus on what is in front of me right now. I love the freedom of understanding that what is important is that I strengthen my ability *to accept the things I cannot change, the courage to change the things I can ... and the wisdom to know the difference.*

Enlightenment is really about transforming poison into medicine, about dealing with the evils in life by summoning up the courage to bring light into the darkness. Building an absolutely happy life is truly about manifesting my own inherent enlightenment right *in* the process of transforming evil effects, no matter whether they are from what I have done or what someone has done to me.

This has been the most amazing journey ... and I cannot wait to see what comes next!